A Legacy of Hatred:
Why Christians Must Not Forget the Holocaust

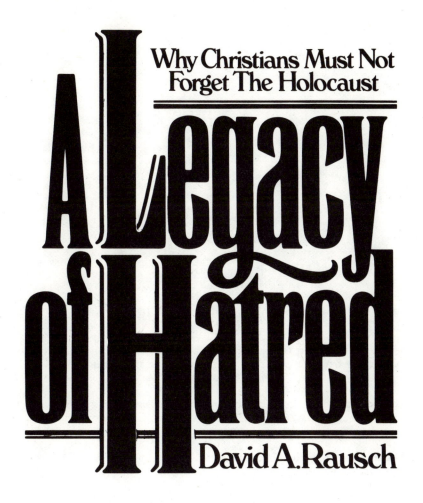

Why Christians Must Not
Forget The Holocaust

A Legacy of Hatred

David A. Rausch

MOODY PRESS

CHICAGO

Library of Congress Cataloging in Publication Data

Rausch, David A.
  A legacy of hatred.

  Includes bibliographical references.
  1. Holocaust, Jewish (1939–1945)   2. Christianity
and antisemitism.   I. Title.
D810.J4R37   1984   940.53'15'03924   84–6743
ISBN 0-8024-0341-7

1 2 3 4 5 6 7 Printing/AF/Year 88 87 86 85 84

Printed in the United States of America

Contents

To My Students
and the Survivors Who Have Shared

Preface

Hundreds of scholars have deemed the Holocaust a subject worthy of careful study. My footnotes are designed to enable the student of the Holocaust to penetrate as deeply as he wishes in any aspect of further study. Sources cited are in English, so that the majority of readers may comfortably refer to them. For those competent in foreign languages, several of the works listed in the footnotes give ample reference to foreign language sources amidst detailed bibliographies. I include accessible collections containing primary documents (for example, John Mendelsohn's recent eighteen-volume edited work, *The Holocaust*, 1982, which contains reproductions of documents from the National Archives), rather than force the reader to travel to archives. It is my hope that this will contribute to future research.

I am indebted to universities and research facilities across the United States and overseas. Chief among them are the National Archives (Washington, D.C.), YIVO Institute (New York City) and Yad Vashem (Jerusalem, Israel). Special thanks go out to Mrs. Chana Abells, head of the Photo and Film Archives at Yad Vashem. Our own librarian, Brad Weidenhamer, has provided gracious assistance (as has the library staff of Ashland College). The administration and faculty of the Ashland College and Theological Seminary, Ashland, Ohio, have also been a great encouragement to me.

I want to thank personally the editorial committee of Moody Press for its foresight in understanding the significance of this project and for its trust in me. Textbook editor Philip Rawley has been a significant help, as have editors Steve

Cory and Garry Knussman. My graduate assistant, James R. Burns, helped proofread this manuscript and offered many helpful suggestions. Miss Sheli Glasser is a fine, helpful, and much appreciated typist. Both of these members of my staff have gone beyond the call of duty.

A number of individuals from diverse walks of life have read portions of this manuscript for clarity. From teachers to housewives, ministers to students, electricians to senior citizens, I want to thank them for their enthusiastic response. My wife, Lynne, and sons (David Joshua, Jonathan, and Benjamin) have lent a smile and a hug. As I look at my own children, my heart agonizes for the million or more Jewish children—a whole generation—murdered by the Nazis.

Finally, this book is dedicated to my students and the survivors who have shared. My students and I on a number of campuses have experienced growth and love together, sharing tears and joys as our lives and ideas have been molded through interaction and friendship. Of the survivors of the Holocaust who deserve a medal of merit for assisting us in this endeavor, Mrs. Esther Shudmak and Mrs. Hinda Kibort deserve a special thanks. All of these individuals—students and survivors—will always be special to me.

DAVID A. RAUSCH
Ashland Theological Seminary
Ashland College Graduate Division
Ashland, Ohio

1

The Meaning of the Holocaust for Today

Jesus Christ had a flawless attitude toward those of other religious or racial backgrounds. The Samaritans in John 4 were both religious and racial outcasts, and yet Jesus treated them with a sensitivity and balance that was truly remarkable within the confines of the society in which He lived. As we trace the encounters Jesus had throughout His life and ministry, we are constantly amazed by His unblemished demeanor toward women, children, and the outcasts of society—the unloved and unlovely. Jesus saw the potential of the individual; He had divine perspective; He knew the *total* picture. His love and compassion have drawn people of all races, religions, and walks of life ever since.

Ironically, His followers have faced and continue to face some of their greatest challenges in the area of prejudice and racism. In striving to imitate the life of Christ, the Christian often encounters his most difficult struggle in trying to match Christ's balance, compassion, understanding, and love toward all others.

Prejudice infests us all; the most dangerous attitude we can have is to think that we have no prejudice. The next danger is to believe that it cannot make us cold and indifferent—that it does not harm our society and that it takes no toll on our spiritual life.

For history teaches us differently. Caricatures and stereotypes can have awesome consequences. The Polish people hated the Nazis; but Nazi propaganda nourished such a hatred of Jews, even in Poland, that after the detested Nazis were defeated, some Poles pulled emaciated Jews who had barely survived the work camps off trains headed for safety and killed them. For years the hatred of both nations had been transferred to the "international culprit," the Jew; and

1

the citizens learned to vent their frustrations in an "appropriate" manner. Even after Adolf Hitler's death, Jewish children had to be smuggled through Poland disguised as Gentiles.[1] Prejudice has no age of accountability: young and old are subject to the venting of irrational hatred, and the results are often disastrous.

History broadens our perspectives unlike any other subject; and we can use the Holocaust period as an object lesson, a *case study*, to unlock truth. Knowledge of the Holocaust is important not only for the factual material concerning the rise of Nazism, but also for what it tells us about the structure of evil, the dangers of civil religion, and moral responsibility in an immoral environment. Hitler drew upon centuries of anti-Semitism, and his slogans existed long before he was born. Threads of politics, economics, and religion, seemingly harmless by themselves, were woven together to produce the horrid "Final Solution," the attempt to exterminate all of European Jewry. The student of the Holocaust experience becomes more sensitive, alert and informed about the world around him. With an understanding of the Holocaust, he sees the consequences of even latent racial and religious prejudice.

HARD QUESTIONS ASKED BY THE HOLOCAUST

CAN IT HAPPEN HERE?

Such an object lesson is needed during the current economic difficulties of our nation, as religious and racial hate groups, many claiming to be Christian, are spreading even to the doors of our unsuspecting churches and college and seminary campuses. Their materials are published and distributed with fervent evangelistic effort, with the intent to rewrite and falsify the history about which most Christians know so little. Increasingly, pastors and educators are becoming alarmed at their success. With Bibles in their hands, they enter church meetings, Bible studies, and classes and try to prove that Jesus was not a Jew, that God commands racial segregation and that blacks, Orientals, and Indians are inferior beings. Such groups have existed throughout the history of our nation—as the history of immigration will show.[2] We need to be alert to these current perpetrators of hate.

Although the Jewish Holocaust experience must of necessity remain a focal point of this case study,[3] there are general implications that underscore the im-

---

1. Even in the summer of 1946 (a year after Hitler's death), pogroms against Jewish survivors occurred. On July 4, 1946, forty-two Jews were murdered by Poles in Kielce. Note Earl Vinecour and Chuck Fishman, *Polish Jews: The Final Chapter* (New York: McGraw-Hill, 1977), p. 6. Compare Yehuda Bauer, *A History of the Holocaust* (New York: Franklin Watts, 1982), pp. 340–42 on the *Brichah* ("flight") underground Jewish organization, which helped survivors flee Poland.
2. Note Leonard Dinnerstein and David M. Reimers, *Ethnic Americans: A History of Immigration and Assimilation* (New York: Dodd, Mead, 1975) for a history of this phenomenon.
3. Although millions of others died during World War II, the Jewish dimension of the Holocaust is unique. The Nazis were determined to kill all Jews, and they searched out every hovel, thwart-

portance of Holocaust study. Without an understanding of the Holocaust, we cannot fully comprehend the ability of human beings to be inhumane to other human beings—even in a civilized society. The retort, "It can't happen here in the United States!" must be evaluated in light of the Holocaust. Germany was thought to be an oasis of culture and civilization in the Western world before and during the rise of Hitler. German Jews thought that the last place that would succumb to pogrom was their beloved country—a country in which many Jewish families had lived for centuries.

Nevertheless, in the land of the Reformation, religious institutions were powerless to protect Jewish citizens. As we shall see in Chapter 15, the plight of the German church under the Nazis shows us the immense hardships and difficult decisions Christian leaders have to make under impossible conditions—decisions the American church may likely face someday.

For those of us who put our faith in law and order, it comes as a shock to learn that Hitler and his officials were elected legally and that they used the law to institute anti-Jewish policy. In fact, legal persecution of Jews made it easier for the Nazis to secure the cooperation of German citizens and to justify their actions to the world. The horrors of the Holocaust could take place only when acts of discrimination were made lawful. The Führer thus gained the cooperation of the masses, who would have had no part of an illegal action. As we shall see in Chapter 16, the most common defense used by those accused during the Nuremberg Trials was that they were "only following orders."

A study of the history of members of the black community in the United States and their "legal enslavement," or the violation of the rights of Japanese Americans on the West Coast during World War II are perfect examples that our own legal system is not immune to the same threat of legalized racism.[4] Indeed, neo-Nazi groups in the United States today claim they will use legal process to turn our nation into a fascist state.

WHO IS MAN?

The inhumanity exhibited during the Holocaust boggles the mind and has led a number of theologians and philosophers to reevaluate their former view of the essential goodness and upward progress of man.[5] How can we believe in

---

ing their own war effort to do so. Conversion was no longer a refuge. See Henry L. Feingold, "Determining the Uniqueness of the Holocaust: The Factor of Historical Valence," *Shoah* 2 (Spring 1981), pp. 3–11.

4. Even after the legal slave trade was abolished and the Civil War had brought emancipation, the newly acquired privileges of the black community were legally nullified. Books such as Peter I. Rose et al., eds., *Through Different Eyes: Black and White Perspectives on American Race Relations* (New York: Oxford U., 1973) give helpful insight into the black community's view of this history. See the end of chapter 10 on the Japanese.

5. In the face of these horrors, some Christians have discarded their faith—an act that does not help the Jewish community or themselves. Note A. Roy Eckardt and Alice L. Eckardt, *Long Night's Journey into Day: Life and Faith After The Holocaust* (Detroit: Wayne State U., 1982) for a saddening example of this theological reconstruction.

ned, progressive world in the light of Nazi murder squads, composed
dinate number of Ph.D.'s and lawyers, whose belt buckles declared
s with us"; or murder squads that would use children for target practice   mash an infant's head against the wall to hear it pop? How does anyone
justify belief in the goodness of man in light of German soldiers so hardened
that they could kick old men in the streets, slice off beards and flesh from Orthodox Jews with knives, stuff hoses down throats to fill stomachs with water
until they burst, burn screaming human beings alive—and then go home to
celebrate Christmas with their families while on leave?

How do we explain the apathy of the general population of Europe (not just
the German citizenry) and the ready compliance of a select number eager to
help the Nazi regime in any way possible? Ukrainians, Lithuanians, Poles and
Hungarians all helped. Even in France, Nazi leaders were astounded by the
eagerness Frenchmen displayed in trying to please their conquerors.

In addition, we find the strange world of both the extermination camps and
the labor camps: some as small as fifty persons; others with standing populations of small cities. Camps where inmates starved while guard dogs ate like
royalty; where rats as large as cats chewed fingers off corpses and attacked the
dying and those who dared to fall asleep, oblivious of other humans, crouched
in corners. Camps in which medical experiments were performed by doctors
and scientists using human beings for guinea pigs, and that provided for a German university (at its request) a skeletal collection of male and female Jewish
corpses for anatomical research.

European ghettoes astound us with their daily atrocities. A ghetto where a
Jewish physician's daughter could be blinded by drunken soldiers who plucked
out her "beautiful black eyes" and where subsequently a law would mandate
deportation to extermination camps of those who were crippled *and blind*. Survivors of the Holocaust have viewed pictures of the starving people of Cambodia in the late 1970s and marveled, "Why it's just like the ghetto!" Such is
the stark reminder of the ability of human beings to be inhumane to other
human beings. I will never forget the student who told me that were it not for
her class on the Holocaust she would have "missed" the plight of the Cambodian refugees.

WHAT WOULD *WE* HAVE DONE?

Without an understanding of the Holocaust, we would not question what
our reactions might be while watching others being persecuted. How much of
your life would you risk for another racial or religious group? The study of the
Holocaust cautions us against a quick answer. We see that often the jeopardizing
of a career, a wife, children, or community set up circumstances that made a
clear-cut decision difficult. Good, decent citizens were conditioned or coerced
to turn their backs on the plight of others; indeed, to promote the Nazi plan.

The historian is overwhelmed with the question, *What made the difference?* What made the difference between the few who helped the Jewish people during their dreadful persecution and the multitude who turned their backs on them? Why did a few put themselves, their families, their possessions, and their careers on the line for a persecuted people, while most did not? What is that moral kernel within our psychological, mental, or religious makeup that makes some react differently from the multitude in the face of prejudice, scapegoating, caricature, oppression, and outright physical violence to a race or religious group different from their own?

That is a difficult question in light of the Holocaust, as its study reveals that only a few evangelicals, a few Protestants, a few Catholics, a few Orthodox, a few agnostics, and a few atheists (*and* not necessarily in that order) helped the Jewish people during their persecution. Varian Fry, a bespectacled, frail, moody intellectual; a man who would seem to be a most unlikely candidate to stand against the Gestapo, succeeded in organizing the escape of approximately fifteen hundred men and women from Nazi occupied France in 1940–1941. A man who appeared to have no religious motivation, Fry explained to his mother that he stayed because it took courage and "courage is a quality I hadn't previously been sure I possessed." To his wife he wrote: "Now I think I can say that I possess an *ordinary* amount of courage."[6]

Are Christians really different from the rest of society? Some Christians throughout Europe not only opposed the Nazis but also helped and defended the Jewish people. They met the challenge that was suddenly thrust upon them. However, they were relatively few in number—a fact that perplexed Richard Gutteridge as he studied German evangelical response to Nazi racist propaganda. Gutteridge concluded: "Most tragically of all, what was missing was a spontaneous outburst at any point by ordinary decent Christian folk, who certainly existed in considerable numbers."[7] Even after the war, when the call for a national Christian repentance for such neglect was made in the Stuttgart declaration, Catholic and Protestant German church leaders developed what John Conway has termed "collective amnesia" about their role in the Nazi era. They explained that the majority of the German people did not know about the Nazi excesses or that their cries had been quickly silenced by the all-powerful German police state. Hitler and his minions, they said, were to take full blame for that dark period in German church history.[8] The church, in another failure to meet the challenge, shirked her responsibility by seeking to lay the blame on others.

Modern psychology has much to say about the capacity within man to com-

---

6. Donald Carroll, "Escape from Vichy," *American Heritage* 34 (June/July 1983), p. 91. Italics added.
7. Richard Gutteridge, *Open Thy Mouth for the Dumb!: The German Evangelical Church and the Jews, 1879–1950* (Oxford: Basil Blackwell, 1976), p. 304.
8. John S. Conway, "The German Church Struggle and Its Aftermath," in Abraham J. Peck, ed., *Jews and Christians After the Holocaust* (Philadelphia: Fortress, 1983), p. 40.

mit atrocities. Stanley Milgram has spent decades studying this phenomenon, and in his book *Obedience to Authority* he stresses that we all have something to worry about when hate, distrust, or dislike of other racial or religious groups permeates our society. He emphasizes:

> This is, perhaps, the most fundamental lesson of our study: ordinary people, simply doing their jobs, and without any particular hostility on their part, can become agents in a terrible destructive process. Moreover, even when the destructive effects of their work become patently clear, and they are asked to carry out actions incompatible with fundamental standards of morality, relatively few people have the resources needed to resist authority. A variety of inhibitions against disobeying authority come into play and successfully keep the person in his place.[9]

To understand such societal pressures one has only to recall how difficult it is to speak out when a member of one's family, a boss, or a friend tells a joke about an ethnic or religious group. Even those who dislike such jokes are hard pressed to overcome peer pressure, and they give in with a half-hearted laugh. An awareness of the Holocaust experience makes such jokes ring hollow, because the student is suddenly aware that even "innocent" caricatures and stereotypes shape attitudes and behavior.

Self-examination is certainly an important result of Holocaust study. We learn that those who believe that such collaboration with the forces of evil is beyond their potential are sometimes the first to succumb to genocide; and we see that we might do the same.

Hard Lessons Taught by the Holocaust

Turning Against Their Own

Without an understanding of the Holocaust, we would fail to understand that racists will devour their own people. Once unleashed, racial theory begins its own pecking order even among the "white races." Hitler had plans to weed out the human race in favor of the purest of the pure Aryan. Slavs, Ukrainians, and Poles who helped him had no idea he planned either to enslave or exterminate them. In discussing the "mastering" of the plague of racial impurity, Hitler noted in *Mein Kampf*: "This also is only a touchstone for the value of a race, and that race which does not pass the test will die and make room for races healthier or at least tougher and of greater resistance."[10] As the German people found, this could extend to individuals even among their own people—individuals who were *not* Jews, blacks, or Gypsies.

9. Stanley Milgram, *Obedience to Authority* (New York: Harper & Row, 1974), p. 6.
10. Adolf Hitler, *Mein Kampf* (Boston: Houghton Mifflin, 1939), p. 339.

A few months after Hitler became Chancellor in 1933, the Law for the Prevention of Progeny with Hereditary Disease was instituted. That law decreed mandatory sterilization for mentally retarded, deaf, blind, epileptic, or physically deformed persons. Soon afterward, the director of the Racial-Policy Office declared that those who would have compassion on people suffering from hereditary disease were false humanitarians and were committing a "sin against the Creator's own laws of life." On the eve of World War II in 1939, the top-secret Euthanasia Program was decreed by Hitler. He and his staff had decided on the "mercy-killing" of the mentally ill, deformed, and "incurables" throughout the Reich. Between 1940 and 1941 an estimated fifty to one hundred thousand German citizens were transferred and subsequently killed by doctors in special institutions under fictitious authorities such as the "National Coordinating Agency for Therapeutic and Medical Establishments," "Charitable Foundation for the Transportation of the Sick," and "Charitable Foundation for Institutional Care." The victims' families were told that the state could better care for their children and that the Reich had their best interests at heart. Upon arriving at one of the half-dozen "institutes," the victim would be shot, injected, or gassed to death. In an interesting parallel to the later gassing of Jews, gas chambers were camouflaged as shower rooms, hermetically sealed, and connected to engines that piped in carbon monoxide. The centers also had crematoria, and families were notified on preprinted forms that their beloved had died suddenly from heart failure or pneumonia and, for sanitary reasons, had been cremated.[11]

Rumors soon abounded that the Nazi regime was killing German citizens. Even allegations that badly wounded soldiers were "mercy killed" were circulated. The public was outraged. Conscientious citizens cried out, and both Catholic and Protestant clergymen preached against the abuse. In a sermon in August 1941, Catholic bishop Galen protested the "mercy-killings"; his protest sermon has been called by Richard Grunberger "the most successful single act of resistance ever undertaken in the Third Reich."[12] The well-known prelate did not suffer any punishment from the Nazis for his sermon, but three parish priests who had distributed his sermon as a tract were beheaded by the Gestapo. Hitler backed down and officially suspended the euthanasia program, but the institutions continued to function sporadically until the end of the war, killing by some estimates as many as 275,000 by injection, starvation, and gas. Chronically and mentally ill patients, senile persons, Gypsies, foreign forced laborers, children from mixed marriages, and Russian prisoners of war suffered death at the hands of a "healthier" member of the race.[13] Nevertheless, the massive outcry of irate citizens stemmed a large scale annihilation, and we can only speculate how much

11. Gerald Reitlinger, *The Final Solution: The Attempt to Exterminate the Jews of Europe, 1939–1945*, 2d ed. (New York: Thomas Yoseloff, 1968), pp. 130–38. Compare Leo Alexander, "Medical Science Under Dictatorship," *The New England Journal of Medicine* 241 (14 July 1949):39–41.
12. Richard Grunberger, *Hitler's SS* (London: Weidenfeld and Nicolson, 1970), p. 55.
13. Yehuda Bauer, *A History of the Holocaust* (New York: Franklin Watts, 1982), p. 208.

more could have been done if public opinion had wished to help the Jewish community in the same manner.

THE FALSE APPEAL TO FAITH

The church would soon learn after Hitler's rise to power that Hitler was not a Christian. However, Hitler used religious language to fool church leaders at the outset. *Mein Kampf* appeals to God, contains passages that sound biblical, and purports to defend Christianity. In chapter 2, "Years of Study and Suffering in Vienna," Hitler concluded a diatribe against the Jews by declaring: "Therefore, I believe today that I am acting in the sense of the Almighty Creator: *By warding off the Jews I am fighting for the Lord's work.*"[14] As he compiled *Hitler's Letters and Notes*, Werner Maser was amazed to find that Hitler's draft for a monumental history of mankind dealt with the Bible. "What is remarkable about these notes," Maser asserted, "is that they contain so many references to the Bible, a book to which Hitler paid scant attention in *Mein Kampf*."[15] Indeed, Hitler's first point in his introduction is *1. The Bible*. The Bible is mentioned in at least four more points throughout his draft. As a master propagandist, Hitler would lead people down the path of destruction with words and phrases they wanted to hear.

Hitler in fact stated that if war came he "would take up and resolve this question of euthanasia because it was easier to do so in wartime, when the church would not be able to put up the expected resistance."[16] Hitler may have underestimated the outcry of Christians when their own families and parishoners were subjected to "mercy-killing," but Christians certainly underestimated the ravaging effect that racial slurs and racial hatred have on a nation, a community, and an individual. The lessons of the Holocaust are a stern warning to all of us. The Nazis had enough gas left to kill 20 million more people. Who was next?

THE DANGER TODAY

Organized racism presents a challenge facing each American today. As our country has gone through a period of economic instability, a resurgence of prejudice and hatred is erupting in an alarming number of racial incidents and forming insidious hate groups. Daily it becomes less possible to ignore blatant racism as it knocks at the doors of our cities, our schools, and our churches. Ironically, just as during the Holocaust, the fast pace of American life and our preoccupation with personal problems relegates such incidents to the fringes of our con-

14. Hitler, *Mein Kampf*, p. 84.
15. Werner Maser, *Hitler's Letters and Notes* (New York: Harper & Row, 1974), p. 283. Note pages 278–83 for the notations.
16. Reitlinger, *The Final Solution*, pp. 132–33.

sciousness. And, just as during the Holocaust, this "new" surge of racism deserves more than a passing glance or a shake of the head. Consider, for example, the following occurrences in the past few years.

In Minnesota in 1981 two women with Jewish backgrounds were attacked during the school year on *Christian* college campuses in the Twin Cities. One was a Jewish Christian in her first year of teaching in the biblical studies department at a Baptist college; the other was a Jewish nursing student at a Lutheran college. The biblical studies teacher suffered verbal harassment and written threats that shocked administration, faculty, and student body. The last note slipped under her door—apparently from an insider—read: "Christ-killers get killed or get out." She resigned after months of such notes and telephone calls. The nursing student suffered verbal threats and several physical assaults on the Lutheran campus by assailants who emphasized that her "kind" was not welcome on the Lutheran campus.

In Pennsylvania the same year, a young minister took a position in a Free Methodist church only to find that three of his board members were active in the Ku Klux Klan; and in West Virginia the Klan forced a United Methodist minister to resign his pastorate after he refused to allow them to promote the Klan during a Sunday service. The Methodist minister then found a butcher knife stuck through the upholstered back rest of his chair, and both he and his wife were threatened.[17] Neither of those ministers was an activist, but they, their friends, and their families were made painfully aware of the horror of being surrounded by the terrorist tentacles of small but growing hate groups.

Black Christians are also suffering abuse. A black Baptist minister from a prominent urban church spoke to a radio audience in September 1982 on the topic of "Black Theology Today." This pastor has been very active in helping to educate and retrain blacks in computer technology, and his church is known for its charity and social concern. He received in the mail a carefully drawn gross caricature of a black man hanging from a Ku Klux Klan gallows with the caption, "The Best Kind." The note, filled with profanity, read: "You [vulgarity] Stinkin' [vulgarity] colored African Monkies [*sic*] belong in Zoos with other Animals—Not among an [*sic*] White Human Society." A swastika was drawn below, with three K's in spaces between its prongs. The same swastikas have appeared on synagogues recently, a grim reminder of a not-too-distant past.

Pastors are increasingly finding both mild and fanatic adherents to these groups within their own congregations. A pastor in the Christian Church, for example, is constantly receiving material from two wealthy parishoners in his congregation. In fact, there appears to be a concentrated effort to "convert" denominational officials, and propaganda is received monthly, such as this letter to a dis-

17. "Klan Terrorizes UM Pastor, Forces Him to Flee Church," *The United Methodist Reporter*, 16 January 1981.

trict superintendent in the Methodist church from a New York Baptist pastor, which stated in part:

> There are many advantages to living in upstate New York. Due to the low minority population we have a lower crime rate. The one draw back [*sic*] is not being personaly [*sic*] involved with others who share my opinions. I do not accept the 6 million hoax; I believe Adolf Hitler was the greatest leader of the 20th century; I believe the modern jews are Khazars; I believe whole-heartidly [*sic*] in the Zionist conspiracy; and do not believe in race mixing.

Anti-Semitic literature was enclosed in an attempt to bolster this minister's racist creed. He also enclosed a *Christian Vanguard* newspaper and an article from *The Spotlight*, "The Paper You Can Trust."

CHRISTIAN RACISTS

These developments are frightening for a number of reasons. First of all, most of the hate groups call themselves "Christian." A classic example is the *Christian Vanguard*, the official publication of the New Christian Crusade Church. It claims to be "A Publication Compiled for the Elect" and to declare the "Gospel of the Kingdom." In one issue, the reader finds the cover article by the Reverend Oren F. Potito, "Jesus Was Not a Jew," in which Potito declares: "Anyone who would say . . . that Jesus Christ was a Jew racially is guilty of nothing less than blasphemy." He emphasizes that Christians who teach this are trying "to satisfy the Jews and escape persecution [by the Jews!]."[18] Subsequent articles—all in the same issue—include "Bible—Not a Jewish Book," "Can Anything Be 'Judaeo-Christian'?" "God Commands Racial Segregation," and "7th Comm. Forbids Race Mixing." This last article announces that "Thou shalt not commit adultery" means that one must not *adulterate* the races or, in the words of the author, "mongrelize with a non-White." It includes ten pictures of "non-white" racial groups, including American Indians, blacks, Jews, and Asians. Editor Thomas E. O'Brien concludes:

> No scientist, no Jew psychiatrist, no liberal professor, no minister, no priest, no politician, not even our senile Supreme Court can improve a child genetically; only your Creator could do that, and I am sure He has no intention of doing so.
> To the non-whites who may have read this article, it pains me ever so deeply to point out your inadequacies, but I must tell the truth, there is no alternative. You see we Whites have to prepare ourselves for an after-life with our Father, YOU DO NOT.[19]

This racist "Christian" newspaper is replete with Bible verses taken out of context. Yet it declares that Christians who disagree with its conclusions on race

18. Oren F. Potito, "Jesus Was Not a Jew," *Christian Vanguard* 69 (1977), p. 1.
19. Thomas E. O'Brien, "7th Comm. Forbids Race Mixing," ibid., p. 19.

are omitting certain sections and statements in the Bible. (The particular issue in which these quotes appear is number 69, first published in 1977 but distributed throughout the United States in the past few years because it is a favorite for recruitment.)

It is significant that such hate sheets keep declaring that the United States is a "Christian Nation." One soon realizes that their brand of Christianity is not only heretical but dangerous. Ku Klux Klan publications emphasize that KKK members are fine, upstanding *White Christians*, and that they are dedicated to preserving our *Christian Nation.* Sixty years ago Adolf Hitler claimed to be a good Christian and a loyal German patriot under the platform of his fledgling Nazi Party. It is frightening how similar this modern racial propaganda is to Nazi literature of a half century ago. It is alarming to see the same tactics utilized. For example, in Missouri a man who had worked a number of years for a company was notified that he had been layed off with little chance of being rehired. Immediately on his work bench appeared a card from the Knights of the Ku Klux Klan with the message "Racial Purity Is America's Security" and the address and phone number of the Klan in Metairie, Louisiana. On the back was this venomous message:

> There are thousands of organizations working for the interests of Blacks. But, how many groups stand up for the cultural values and ideals of the White Majority? Not many? As a result we are faced with reverse discrimination in jobs, promotions, and scholarships—busing for forced integration—high taxes for minority welfare— a high rate of brutal crime—gun-control—anti-White movies and TV programs— in short, a society oriented to the wishes of minorities. We of the Ku Klux Klan are unapologetically committed to the interests, ideas, and cultural values of the White Majority. We are determined to maintain and enrich our cultural and racial heritage.

The card concludes: "We are growing fast and strong because we have never compromised the truth."[20]

This card is an indication of the slick soft-sell of the modern Klan. It is subtle propaganda of which Joseph Goebbels, Hitler's Minister of Propaganda, would have been proud. Goebbels believed that if one told a lie long enough, people would believe it. He also believed that mixing in a little truth as bait on the hook would reel in many an unsuspecting sojourner.

A GROWING NETWORK

The incident mentioned above leads to the second reason such modern groups are frightening. These organizations are building a network to foster racism and to capitalize on racial fears and tensions. For example, in September 1979 a Christian woman was murdered in Akron, Ohio. The murderer happened to be

20. The card, which is now in my possession, suggests: "Interested in finding out more? We'll send you a free copy of the CRUSADER newspaper and 10 free copies of this card."

a black man. Within one month after the murder, her husband, daughter, and four sons each received *The Thunderbolt* newspaper mailed from Marietta, Georgia to their respective addresses.

Published for over twenty years, this sixteen-page hate sheet claims to present "The White Mans' Viewpoint." The issue (October 1979) sent to the grieving Akron family carried the article "White Families Suffer from Negro Murders." Under the caption "Negro Murder and Rape Rampant" it prefaced five murder stories by declaring:

> Government figures show that for the year 1977 negroes committed 87% of all murders in our major cities. They murdered 9,751 people and raped 89,425 women. For years most of the victims of negro crime were other blacks but now things are changing and an ever growing percentage are Whites. More and more frequently they murder their rape victims. Psychologists say that this is because they hate the entire White Race and are taking their mass hatred out on a single victim—most often a defenseless White woman. Here are but a few vicious crimes which have been committed in recent months and when all are lumped together demonstrate how deadly allowing negroes to live within our midst has become.[21]

The murders of an eleven-year-old Georgia boy, a twenty-two-year-old New Jersey female night desk clerk, a twenty-five-year-old New Jersey nurse, a sixty-eight-year-old woman, and an eleven-year-old Michigan girl were all then recounted in heartrending detail to arouse pity and desire for revenge. Pictures of some of the victims, along with two of their black "killers" were included in this article, which was designed to instill rage and prejudice toward the black community.

The cover story for this particular issue was "Refugees Cause Murder—Disease—Welfare." The racist article was against Boat People. The caption under a picture of crowds of little refugee children asked: "Is America to be taken over by Asiatic hordes? There are at least 20 million who want to come to America." Other articles include "Jews Say They Are 'Master Race,'" "Degenerate Race-Mixers Organize" and a large piece on Africa entitled "Africa Reverts to Jungle Savagery as Whites Driven Out." One of the most pathetic aspects of the paper was the pictures of indoctrinated little children involved in a demonstration by the National States Rights Party (the party supported by *The Thunderbolt*) against the Asian refugees.

Men promoting this racism are showing up unannounced in congregational services and Bible studies. Laden with prooftexts that they interpret "from the Greek," they seek to befuddle Bible study teachers and to turn the study toward their particular interest. In St. Paul, Minnesota, they attended a Central Baptist Church Bible study only to find a professor, well acquainted with New Testament Greek, teaching the lesson. Needless to say, he exposed their ignorance,

---

21. "White Families Suffer from Negro Murders," *The Thunderbolt* 246 (October 1979), p. 13.

yet they caused a great deal of disruption before being asked to leave. In Ashland, Ohio, in a Pentecostal church service, one of these individuals stood up during the testimony time and made quite an impression on some of the congregation by eloquently claiming to have all the gifts of the Holy Spirit. He would not stay for the entire service, but put photocopied racist hate sheets on all the car windows. The congregation soon learned from the sheets that this "noble Christian" was against all churches as well!

It is a pathetic fact, however, that most proponents are not as visible as these intruders. Church members within a large part of Protestantism and Catholicism are distributing similar material to their fellow church members and friends. Colleges and seminaries are also receiving such literature and sporadic "evangelists" of this cause. The reference librarian at the Moody Bible Institute, Chicago, was amazed at the racist literature an elderly, gray-haired lady donated to the Institute. That little lady, who looks like anybody's grandmother and has the zeal of a missionary, is Gerda Koch, the leader of a "Christian" research institute—an organization that spreads materials claiming that the Holocaust never happened and that there is a Jewish Zionist plot to take over the world. "Pray for me and Christian Research," she wrote, "that we may meet our Great Responsibilities toward our Nation and the World today!"[22]

AN UGLY CIVIL RELIGION

It is perplexing how anyone could fall for such propaganda—that is, until we study the Holocaust. The Holocaust experience teaches us how easy it is to get caught up in such absurdity—to have lies possess your spirit and totally absorb your being. But the lies are often the most easily marketed products of these hate groups. They promote simplistic solutions to complex problems, emphasizing that their solutions are the *only* solutions. This is the third reason these modern hate groups are frightening. A good example is the issue of *The Thunderbolt* sent to the Akron family. It states the following at the end of its article on black murderers and their victims:

> THE ONLY SOLUTION: The National States Rights Party calls for the eventual deportation of every black in America to their native homeland in the jungles of Africa. They have failed their golden opportunity to adjust to civilization. If we are to survive as a Race and Nation there is but one solution left and that is Abraham Lincoln's back-to-Africa plan. "The American Colonization Society" sent over 20,000 negroes back to Liberia in Africa. A national enlightenment will help us to complete this great task and save civilization.[23]

22. This statement appeared on one of her "Christian Book Lists" for Christian Research, Eureka Springs, Arkansas. She also added, "As God provides we give out thousands of pieces of literature during the year." See Morton Ryweck's assessment of her booth at the Minnesota State Fair in Peter Ackerberg, "Anti-Semitism in Minneapolis," *Minneapolis Star*, 10 October 1978, p. 9a.
23. "White Families Suffer," p. 13.

A study of the Holocaust will bring a chill to the reader of these words. National "enlightenment" is their goal. As Hitler "enlightened" with propaganda and force, so these organizations have their simplistic solutions. As German citizens, because of race, were divested of centuries of family heritage and citizenship under the Nazi regime, so in the name of "civilization" these groups would propose to violate the rights of American citizens.

In such a distorted gospel, a view of the world develops that disdains the rights and privileges of human beings and seeks to dehumanize any but the approved group. When one looks beyond the religious facade, an ugly civil religion appears. This religion equates *Christianity* with *American* and *God's Chosen People* with the *pure white races*.

The warning is clear. Week after week a CB operator drove up and down Interstate 71 in Ohio calling:

> Detroit, Michigan . . . Detroit, Michigan. . . . If you don't want another little Atlanta coming up there in Detroit and destroying all of those little pickaninnys [a slang term for Negro children] out there on the street . . . you all better straighten up because the Ku Klux Klan . . . the Southern Louisiana Ku Klux Klan is going to take care of you. . . . If you don't start working and get off the welfare rolls, so the other people in the United States don't have to pay for your living and your propagation . . . we are going to kill those little niggers out there so that the big niggers don't grow up. If we have to kill those big niggers out there, we will do that too![24]

He called them "black animals." He called himself "The Nigger Eradicator." His solution is extermination, and yet he talked of "spiritual values."

They all do. The masthead of the *Christian Vanguard* reads: "HE WHO KNOWS THE TRUTH AND DOES NOT SPEAK OUT, IS A MISERABLE CREATURE"—a caption that rises above Potito's article, "Jesus Was Not A Jew." Even the American Nazi *White Power* paper promotes a civil religion and declares: "Only a spiritual rebirth can rescue our young people from the inner emptiness which has overtaken them. . . . Unless we can turn our young people away from leading lives guided by empty materialism and inspire them with a new set of spiritual values, the outlook for our Race is very, very dark."[25] One should not be surprised to hear a modern American Nazi say such a thing. The twenty-fourth point of Hitler's Nazi party platform in 1920 stated in part: "The Party, as such, stands for positive Christianity." The same point denounces the Jewish people.

In Montgomery County, Maryland, outside of Washington, D.C., thirteen hate-violence incidents, two-thirds of which were anti-Semitic, were reported in 1980. In 1981 the number exploded to 101, and in just the first nine months

---

24. This particular broadcast was taped by the Reverend Joseph Heilman on March 4, 1981. Mr. Heilman is presently a Methodist pastor in West Virginia.
25. Martin Kerr, "What's Happening to Our Kids?" *White Power* 89 (January-February 1979), p. 7.

of 1982 was at 143. The first half of November 1982 had at least eight reported incidents, including one at the Georgetown home of author Herman Wouk (the author of *The Winds of War*). A young Jewish girl who had viewed the display of swastikas, slogans of hate toward Jews, and the eight-foot Nazi eagle defacing the Shaare Tefila Synagogue in Silver Spring that month later viewed a similar defacement of her elementary school in Rockville. This time the perpetrators of hate drew gas chambers and painted slogans such as "Hitler was right," "Death to Jews and Gooks," and (next to the gas chamber) "Silent but deadly genocide." The little Jewish girl turned to her mother with questioning eyes and said, "I thought they caught those guys." Her mother responded saying that this was done by "other guys" and that "there are *more* of them."[26]

Because of these facets of racist ideology in our modern era, Christian response is no longer an option—it is a mandate. We cannot allow the "Christian" attitude to be interpreted through the words and actions of these hate groups. We must be prepared. We must know the consequences; we must be able to sift the wheat from the chaff. Our study of the Holocaust will help us do this. Our remembrance of the love of Jesus, a love that directed Him to declare that even *enemies* are to be loved, should strengthen the Christian on this journey. If we are to love our enemies, should we not also love our fellow neighbor of a different race, ethnic origin, or religious faith?

We begin our journey into the Holocaust experience long before the rise of Nazism; in fact, long before Hitler's birth. We begin our history less than a century after Jesus' death. Before we begin our voyage, let us listen to the pleas of two victims who in their agony tried to preserve a record for us: one from the ghetto; one from the camp. The twenty-year-old leader of the Warsaw Ghetto uprising, Mordechai Anielewicz, wrote the first; Zalman Gradowski in Auschwitz wrote the second:

Aware that our days are numbered we urge you: remember how we have been betrayed.[27]

I know you will not believe me. I know, but you must.[28]

26. Michael Kernan, "The Specter of Anti-Semitism, The Unending Web of Fear," *Washington Post*, 1 December 1982.
27. "Last Letter of Mordekhai Anielewicz," in Ber Mark, *Uprising in the Warsaw Ghetto*, trans. Gershon Freidlin (New York: Schocken Books, 1975), p. 54.
28. Elie Wiesel, "The Holocaust as Literary Inspiration," in *Dimensions of the Holocaust* (Evanston, Ill.: Northwestern U., 1977), p. 11.

2

Between Church and Synagogue: Two Millennia of Christian Anti-Semitism

A third-generation minister in the Hungarian Reformed church, Janos was a reserved man, almost withdrawn and shy at first meeting. One would hardly associate him with foaming-at-the-mouth Hitler brownshirts. And yet by his second month in seminary, some students were calling him "the campus Nazi"; others were deeply troubled by his theological views. Quiet Janos became very vocal at the mention of the Jewish people, whether in class or in church, and he would immediately launch into an exposition of how "Jews control the world" or how "Jews were *trying* to control the world." To Janos, the Jewish Holocaust never occurred; and Jews, whom he believed to be in control of the press and media round the world, were exploiting this "lie" to further extend their sinister reach. Janos refused to preach from the Old Testament (the "Jewish" Bible), and he claimed that competent historians had found that Jesus was not really a Jew. Conspiracy and hate literature was a part of Janos's life; he did not realize how much it consumed him. He would talk incessantly against the Jews, unaware that this topic dominated his conversations. At times he claimed that two-thirds of the ministers in the Hungarian Reformed church agreed with this message, and that the congregants "knew all about it." His superior promoted anti-Semitism in special "ministry" classes that completely separated Jesus from Judaism.

Janos is a victim, and it will take a powerful miracle to cleanse him completely from the spiritual cancer that has infested his being.

THE WORLD CONQUERORS: A DISTILLATION OF CENTURIES OF HATE

Men and women who call themselves Christians in Hungary, Vienna, and New York City have encouraged and bolstered Janos's views. His favorite book is popular in these circles in New York City and has been circulated by some of the racist groups already mentioned. It is Louis Marschalko's *The World Conquerors: The Real War Criminals*, translated from the Hungarian by A. Suranyi. In this book, the real criminals of World War II are the Jews. German Nazis are portrayed as those who "tried most earnestly to establish co-operation and partnership among the European *élite*."[1] The German Nazis were looking for "those considered good patriots in their own country," and they "recognised that the individual has social rights." Although the "National Socialist revolution" had a peaceful and cooperating Europe "in the making," Marschalko insists that the Jews began a propaganda campaign to discredit Hitler's altruistic motives. According to *The World Conquerors*, Hitler was slandered by the Jews as a power-monger who had a low opinion of other European nations—whereas in fact the Führer was only a peaceful visionary for unity. Marschalko continues: "Meanwhile, in 1938, Roosevelt, who can only be regarded as a puppet of the Jewish brains trust, sent the following gaily worded wire to Churchill for the promotion of war preparation: 'You and I can rule the world.'"[2]

As the student of World War II can plainly see, Marschalko not only rewrites the history of the Holocaust (Chapter 11 is entitled, "What Has Become of Six Million Jews?"), but also rewrites the whole history of the war! His concluding statement in the book is that the "new slogan" for those who are an "awakening people" has to be: "Anti-Jewish people of the world unite before it is too late."[3]

An important element in *The World Conquerors* is the author's attempt to separate Christianity from its Jewish roots and Jesus from Judaism. This is typical of today's racist literature. Marschalko seeks to drive a wedge between the Old and New Testaments by portraying the Old Testament as "Jewish holy books" filled with Jewish violence, criminal activity, and fanatical tribal nationalism that killed neighbors and sought to conquer the world under the "national laws of the God-Führership." According to Marschalko, the Jewish prophets and kings deserved total condemnation, "but the so-called Christian churches condemn nothing, yet continue teaching Gentile children that most pornographic and bloodthirsty book—the Old Testament."[4] After denouncing the Old Testament, he attempts to show that Jesus condemned both it and the Jewish people. Using Houston Stewart Chamberlain's *The Foundations of the Nineteenth Century* (see next chapter), Marschalko explains that Chamberlain "deduces clearly the fatal

1. Louis Marschalko, *The World Conquerors: The Real War Criminals*, trans. A. Suranyi (1958; United States: Christian Book Club, reprint, 1978), p. 75.
2. Ibid., p. 78.
3. Ibid., p. 295.
4. Ibid., p. 14.

consequences attending Jewry's entry into world history and is the earliest author to discover that Christ, insofar as racial descent is concerned, was not a Jew."[5] He then proceeds to portray the Jewish people as "Christ-killers," incapable of being good citizens, deceptive manipulators of both capitalism and Communism in their venture as "world conquerors." Marschalko in his first chapter constantly speaks of "we Christians"; and by the time he reaches the rewriting of World War II and the quote cited above concerning Roosevelt and Churchill, he boldly adds, "World Jewry declared war on Europe *and on Christianity* at the very moment Hitler came to power, or perhaps even before."[6] By separating Christianity from Judaism, Jesus from Jews, Christians from Jews, and ultimately, Jews from God, Marschalko is in a position to declare anything he wishes against the Jewish people. Thus he supplies a rationale for his readers who are swept along on his perilous journey of hate.

Although traditional Christianity would disdain Marschalko's eradication of the Old Testament, the concept of separation is unfortunately not new. It originated in the early conflict between the church and the synagogue—a conflict that would plague historic Jewish-Christian relationships.

THE BIBLICAL ERA

Jesus was a Jew. Those who first followed him were Jews. He chose only Jews as his disciples. Christianity was the child of Judaism, and Jerusalem was the center of Christianity in the early decades of the church. That early Christian believers were Jewish is evident in Acts 15, which records that at a Jerusalem council around A.D. 50 (a couple of decades after Jesus' death) Jewish Christians debated whether or not Gentile converts should be under the Mosaic law. In other words, they were asking: "Should the Gentiles become Jewish *before* they become Christians?" Only after great debate and a spirited speech by Peter (who had debated on the other side a few years earlier), did James the Just, the presiding elder of their congregation, express his judgment, that they "not trouble those who are turning to God from among the Gentiles [i.e., not trouble them to become Jewish first], but that we write to them that they abstain from things contaminated by idols and from fornication and from what is strangled and from blood" (Acts 15:19–20). The suggestions were very Jewish-oriented, and historical records reveal very *Jewish* followers of Jesus. Recent scholarship has convincingly maintained what some scholars of the past had asserted, that is, that the apostles continued their own Jewish identity and practices and probably encouraged other Jewish believers to do so as well. Paul himself appears to have remained an observant Jew his whole life, and it has been pointed out that salvation by grace is a very Jewish concept. A vibrant Jewish Christianity devel-

5. Ibid., p. 18.
6. Ibid., p. 78.

oped in Judea during the apostolic period, being considered by the Romans a sect of Judaism.[7]

EARLY TRIUMPHALISM

The Roman intrusion into Judea and the widespread acceptance of Christianity by the Gentiles complicated the history of Jewish Christianity. The Roman wars against the Jews not only destroyed the Temple and Jerusalem, but also resulted in Jerusalem's relinquishing her position as a center of Christian faith in the Roman world. In addition, the rapid acceptance of Christianity among the Gentiles led to an early conflict between the church and the synagogue. The Gentile Christians interpreted the destruction of the Temple and Jerusalem as a sign that God had *abandoned* Judaism, that He had provided the Gentiles freedom to develop their own Christian theology in a setting free from Jerusalem's influence. Theological and political power moved from Jewish Christian leaders in Jerusalem to centers of Gentile Christian leadership such as Alexandria, Rome, and Antioch. It is important to understand this change, because it influenced the early church Fathers to make anti-Jewish statements.[8]

This historical background also underscores the problem that the Gentile Christian church faced. Unlike Marschalko in *The World Conquerors*, and even though the Gentile Christian church disdained Judaism and Jewish nationalism, the church believed that the Jewish Scriptures were *her* Scriptures—the Scriptures used by Jesus, Paul and the disciples! Early church Fathers quoted from the Jewish Scriptures and even defended themselves to the Romans from the Jewish Scriptures.

And yet, the use of the Jewish Scriptures by the Gentile church required some reinterpretation because, according to those Scriptures, the Jewish people are the chosen people of God, the people of the Covenant and the people of the Book, with an immense responsibility to the world. The Gentile church attempted to reconcile this difficulty by reinterpreting those Scriptures to state that the Christian church is the true Israel, the "new" Israel—not just grafted in as Paul declared in Romans 11:17, but totally *replacing* the Jewish people. This triumphalism, the attitude of celebrating a victory over an "enemy," has fanned

---

7. Note E. P. Sanders, *Paul and Palestinian Judaism* (Philadelphia: Fortress, 1977). Compare W. D. Davies, *Paul and Rabbinic Judaism* (London: S.P.C.K., 1958); and W. D. Davies, *Christian Origins and Judaism* (London: Darton, Longman & Dott, 1962). Recent Jewish scholarship, which is most interesting, includes David Flusser, *Jesus* (New York: Herder and Herder, 1969) and Richard L. Rubenstein, *My Brother Paul* (New York: Harper & Row, 1972). Journal articles abound. See, for example, Leonard Swindler, "The Jewishness of Jesus: Some Religious Implications for Christians," *Journal of Ecumenical Studies* 18 (Winter 1981):104–13. On salvation by grace in Judaism, note David H. Stern, "Non-Messianic Judaism Teaches God's Grace" (unpublished essay), as quoted and discussed in David A. Rausch, *Messianic Judaism: Its History, Theology and Polity* (New York: Edwin Mellen, 1982), pp. 122–23.
8. For an extended treatment of this topic refer to my book *Messianic Judaism: Its History, Theology and Polity* (New York: Edwin Mellen, 1982), pp. 1–20.

the flames of religious anti-Semitism ever since. Let us analyze the rhetoric of the ante-Nicene church Fathers (those before the Council of Nicea in A.D. 325).

THE ANTE-NICENE FATHERS

On his way to martyrdom by the Romans, Ignatius, the Bishop of Antioch, claimed in his *Epistle to the Philippians* at the beginning of the second century that Satan "fights along with the Jews to a denial of the cross"[9] and that "if any one celebrates the passover along with the Jews, or receives emblems of their feast, he is a partaker with those that killed the Lord and His apostles."[10] This is ironic, because Jesus and the apostles always observed the Passover. Ignatius upheld the prophets and declared, "And the 'Prophets,' let us love them too, because they anticipated the gospel in their preaching."[11] Nevertheless, a few lines later he wrote, "Now, if anyone preaches Judaism to you, pay no attention to him."[12]

"NOT YOURS, BUT OURS"

The Epistle of Barnabas, which circulated about the same period, explained that the Jewish sacrifices were abolished, their fasts not acceptable to God; and that Christians, not Jews, were actually the heirs of God's Covenant with Abraham. To those who believed the Jewish people still had a future through the Covenant, the epistle harshly stated: "Take heed now to yourselves, and not to be like some adding largely to your sins, and saying, 'The covenant is both theirs and ours.' But they [the Jews] thus finally lost it."[13] This epistle was highly regarded in the church and was even included in some of the early canon lists. Reading between the lines, one notes the existence of Christians who believed that the Jewish people definitely had a future through the Abrahamic Covenant and were quite vocal about it.

Alas, many in the church were not content with claiming an interest in the Jewish Scriptures, but proceeded to try to make the Old Testament the exclusive domain of the church. Justin Martyr, one of the greatest Christian defenders of the faith, took up this theme. In his *Dialogue with Trypho* (c. A.D. 140), Justin quoted fluidly from the Jewish Scriptures and then proclaimed to Trypho, the Jewish escapee from the Second Jewish Revolt:

> For these words have neither been prepared by me, nor embellished by the art of
> man; but David sung them, Isaiah preached them, Zechariah proclaimed them, and

9. Ignatius *The Epistle to the Philippians* 4. All references from the early church Fathers can be found in Alexander Roberts and James Donaldson, eds., *The Ante-Nicene Fathers: Translations of the Writings of the Fathers down to A.D. 325*, 10 vols. (Edinburgh: The Ante-Nicene Christian Library, 1885–1896).
10. Ignatius *Philippians*, 14.
11. Ignatius *Philippians*, 5.
12. Ignatius *Philippians*, 6.
13. *Epistle of Barnabas* 4. Compare 2, 3, 5, and 13.

Moses wrote them. Are you aquainted with them, Trypho? They are *contained* in your Scriptures, or *rather not yours, but ours*. For we believe them; but you, though you read them, do not catch the spirit that is in them.[14]

Later Justin remarked to Trypho: "For the prophetical gifts remain with us, even to the present time. And hense you ought to understand that [the gifts] formerly among your nation have been *transferred to us*."[15]

"CHRIST-KILLERS"

Justin was a Gentile, born in Samaria around A.D. 110 and very possibly of Roman descent. Other church Fathers based their Gentile-biased arguments on his First Apology to Antoninus Pius written around A.D. 155. Early in his First Apology he wrote that Jesus was "crucified under Pontius Pilate."[16] Later, however, he declared: "The Jews who are in possession of the books of the prophets did not recognize Christ even when he came, and they hate us who declare that he has come and show that he was crucified by them [the Jews] as predicted."[17] Although Justin is milder than other early Fathers, the "Christ-killer" theme permeated church history—wreaking havoc on the Jewish community.

Another historic justification for persecuting Jewish people was Jewish persecution of Christians. Justin emphasized: "[Jews] consider us their enemies and opponents, putting us to death or punishing us, as you [Romans] do, whenever they can, as you can realize—for in the Jewish War recently past, Bar Cochba, the leader of the revolt of the Jews, ordered Christians only to be subjected to terrible punishments unless they would deny Jesus the Christ and blaspheme [Him]."[18] Decades earlier, Justin remarked to Trypho the Jew:

> For the circumcision according to the flesh, which is from Abraham, was given for a sign; that you may be separated from other nations, and from us; and that you alone may suffer that which you *justly* suffer; and that you may be desolate, and your cities burned with fire; and that strangers may eat your fruit in your presence and not one of you may go up to Jerusalem. . . . Accordingly, these things have happened to you *in fairness and justice*, for you have slain the Just One [Jesus], and His prophets before Him; and now you reject those who hope in Him, and in Him who sent Him—God the Almighty and Maker of all things—cursing in your synagogues those that believe on Christ. For you have *not* the power to lay hands upon us, on account of those [the Romans] who now have mastery. But as often as you could, you did so.[19]

14. Justin Martyr *Dialogue with Trypho, A Jew* 29. Italics added. There is some debate among scholars as to whether Trypho actually existed or was a composite figure Justin drew from conversations with a number of Jews.
15. Justin Martyr *Trypho* 82.
16. Justin Martyr *First Apology* 13.
17. Justin Martyr *First Apology* 36.
18. Justin Martyr *First Apology* 31.
19. Justin Martyr *Trypho* 16. Italics added.

Justin admitted that the Jews were not responsible for most of the persecution against Christians. Jews, in fact, had a very difficult time maintaining their own religious rights in the Roman Empire after the revolts in Palestine. Nevertheless, according to official church interpretation the curses of the Scriptures were applied to the Jewish people whereas the blessings of the Scriptures were applied to the church. The Jews were supposed to "justly suffer" as the "Christ-killers," an emphasis that has continued to be used to the present day.

These themes permeate the writings of the early Fathers of the Christian church. Irenaeus, Bishop of Lyon after A.D. 177, declared that the Jews were "disinherited from the grace of God" and "would never have hesitated to burn their own Jewish Scriptures."[20] Hippolytus of Rome wrote around A.D. 200: "Hear my words, and give heed thou Jew. Many a time dost thou boast thyself that thou didst condemn Jesus of Nazareth to death . . . Of what retribution does Jesus speak? Manifestly of the misery which has now got hold of thee."[21] Origen of Alexandria and Cyprian, Bishop of Carthage, both blamed Jews for the persecution of Christians that occurred about A.D. 250. Cyprian demanded that all Jews be forced to leave his diocese or die.[22] Tertullian of Carthage pounded another nail in the Jews' coffin when he wrote around A.D. 200:

> In former times the Jews enjoyed much of God's favor, when the fathers of their race were noted for their righteousness and faith. So it was that as a people they flourished greatly, and their kingdom attained to a lofty eminence. . . . But how deeply they [the Jews] have sinned, puffed up to their fall with a false trust in their noble ancestors, turning from God's way into a way of sheer impiety, though they themselves should refuse to admit it, their present national ruin would afford sufficient proof.[23]

The foundation had been laid and the message was clear. The Jews were no longer God's chosen people. They had persecuted and killed Jesus Christ and Christians. The Jews deserved persecution and the loss of their land. The Christian church had inherited the covenant promises of God—the church was God's chosen people. The curses of the Bible were ascribed to the Jews; the blessings of the Bible to the Christians. This was religious anti-Semitism, and even Hitler would draw on this foundation.

THE CHURCH WITH WORLDLY POWER

When church and state were linked in the fourth century, due initially to Emperor Constantine, Christian persecution of the Jewish people became a regular practice. By the end of the fourth century, Christianity was the official and

20. Irenaeus *Against Heresies* 3. 21.
21. Hippolytus *Against Jews* 1. 5.
22. See Dagobert Runes, *The Jew and the Cross* (New York: Philosophical Library, 1966), p. 41.
23. Tertullian *Apology* 21.

exclusive religion of the Roman state. It would seem the church would have no more reason to fear Judaism. Ironically, the church's paranoia got worse; attacks against the Jewish community became more bitter. In A.D. 325, Constantine as a "Christian" emperor forbade Jews to live in Jerusalem. They were not allowed to engage in any proselytizing. At the Council of Nicea it was decided that Easter should not be determined by the Jewish Passover calendar, and that Christians should "have nothing in common with this odius people," the Jews. Emperor Constantius in A.D. 357 confiscated the property of a Christian who dared to convert to Judaism, and Hilary of Poitiers wrote that the Jews were a perverse people accursed by God *forever*. Ambrose of Milan was so upset with Emperor Theodosius I for ordering the synagogue in Milan to be rebuilt that he wrote: "I hereby declare, that it was I who set fire to the synagogue; indeed, I gave the orders for it to be done so that there should no longer be any place where Christ is denied."[24]

"I WISH TO DRAW MY BATTLE LINE"—JOHN CHRYSOSTOM

The Fathers were men of piety, noted for moral excellence in other areas of the Christian life. When it came to the Jewish people, however, they were found wanting. A classic example of this phenomenon is the most famous preacher of the fourth century, John Chrysostom, known as the "Golden Tongue." A man admired by the common people and a fearless advocate of modest Christian living to the most pompous of royalty, Chrysostom showed complete lack of restraint toward the Jewish people in a series of eight long sermons delivered in Antioch in A.D. 387.

The only reason Chrysostom was so upset was because some Christians were fellowshipping with Jews. That the Christian church had separated herself from the Jewish parent and severed all ties in an irrational paranoia is amply evident in Chrysostom's raging denunciations. The church, firmly in control of Roman society, presented a bold contrast to the Jewish community, which was choked by rules and restrictions. Yet Chrysostom deemed it necessary to strike out against the Jewish people. In these sermons one clearly sees where the rhetoric of the early church Fathers led—and even more frightening, where it can go.

Chrysostom began by discussing an "illness" that had infected the church. He declared:

> What is this disease? The festivals of the pitiful and miserable Jews . . . There are many in our ranks who say they think as we do. Yet some of these are going to watch the festivals and others will join the Jews in keeping their feasts and observing their fasts. I wish to drive this perverse custom from the church right now . . . if I should fail to cure those who are sick with the Judaizing disease, I am afraid that, because of their ill-suited association and deep ignorance, some Christians may par-

---

24. Note Paul E. Grosser and Edwin G. Halperin, *The Causes and Effects of Anti-Semitism: The Dimensions of a Prejudice* (New York: Philosophical Library, 1978), pp. 77–79.

take in the Jews' transgressions . . . For if they hear no word from me today, they will then join the Jews in their fasts; once they have committed this sin, it will be useless for me to apply the remedy.[25]

"But do not be surprised that I call the Jews pitiable," he explained. "They really are pitiable and miserable."[26]

According to Chrysostom, the Jews were murderers, and worse than wild beasts. Their synagogue "is not only a brothel and a theater; it is also a den of robbers and a lodging for wild beasts." "No Jew adores God!" he exclaimed. His proof for this statement: "The Son of God says so."[27] Chrysostom held the whole Jewish people culpable for the killing of Christ, using statements that would be reaffirmed by anti-Semites for the next sixteen centuries: "So the godlessness of the Jews and the pagans is on a par. But the Jews practice a deceit which is more dangerous. In their synagogue stands an invisible altar of deceit on which they sacrifice not sheep and calves but the souls of men."[28] "Finally, if the ceremonies of the Jews move you to admiration, what do you have in common with us?" Chrysostom asked his audience.

One can easily see that a Jewish Christian who wanted to hold on to his heritage or a Gentile Christian who wanted to learn more about the parent of Christianity would have found it extremely difficult under this pressure. Furthermore, Chrysostom sought to separate Christianity totally from Judaism. For example, in the fourth sermon he cajoled:

> Let me, too, now say this against these Judaizing Christians. If you judge that Judaism is the true religion, why are you causing trouble to the church? But if Christianity is the true faith, as it really is, stay in it and follow it. Tell me this. Do you share with us the mysteries, do you worship Christ as a Christian, do you ask him for blessing, and do you then celebrate the festival with his foes? With what purpose, then, do you come to the church?[29]

"I have said enough against those who say they are on our side but are eager to follow the Jewish rites . . . it is against the Jews that I wish to draw up my battle line."[30]

Four more sermons of vitriolic hatred ensued, bringing the number to eight in all; each contained diatribes against Jews, Judaism and the synagogue; each separated Jesus Christ from the Jewish people who gave him birth. Chrysostom in the seventh sermon began: "Have you had enough of the fight against the

---

25. John Chrysostom, *Discourses Against Judaizing Christians* 1. 1. 5. This discourse as well as others from the period can be found in Philip Schaff, ed., *A Select Library of the Nicene and Post–Nicene Fathers of the Christian Church*, 14 vols. (Buffalo, N.Y.: Christian Literature Company, 1886–1890).
26. Chrysostom *Discourses* 1. 2. 1.
27. Chrysostom *Discourses* 1. 3. 1–2.
28. Chrysostom *Discourses* 1. 4. 4.
29. Chrysostom *Discourses* 4. 4. 1.
30. Chrysostom *Discourses* 4. 4. 2.

Jews? Or do you wish me to take up the same topic today? Even if I have already had much to say on it, I still think you want to hear the same thing again. The man who does not have enough of loving Christ will never have enough of fighting those who hate Christ."[31] The message is clear, according to Patristic reasoning. Those who love Jesus hate Jews—and fight Jews.

Chrysostom ended his eighth sermon by asking his congregation to pay him interest on the "money" (message) he deposited with them, demanding imperative "action on your own part."[32] Tragically, centuries of anti-Semitic incidents resulted. In spite of her high position in the Roman Empire, the Christian church remained paranoid about Judaism.

"I RENOUNCE ALL"—PROFESSIONS OF FAITH FOR JEWISH CONVERTS

The professions of faith required by Jewish converts to Christianity in the ancient and medieval periods indicate the total separation from Judaism required by the church. "I do here and now renounce every rite and observance of the Jewish religion, detesting all its most solemn ceremonies and tenets that in former days I kept and held," the convert had to affirm in one creed. "I altogether deny and reject the error of the Jewish religion," he proceeded. "[I] shun all intercourse with other Jews and have the circle of my friends only among honest Christians." The convert had to admit that "because of our pertinacious lack of faith and the ancient errors of our fathers" he had been held back from the Christian faith, and therefore, he would not "become involved in any Jewish rites or customs nor associate with the accursed Jews who remain unbaptized." He was not to shun "swines' flesh," and for him and his family he must swear, "We will not on any pretext, either ourselves, our children or our descendants, choose wives from our own race; but in the case of both sexes we will always link ourselves in matrimony with Christians."[33]

Others were forced to declare that they would never return "to the vomit of my former error, or associating with the wicked Jews. In every respect will I lead the Christian life and associate with Christians." Denunciation of their Jewish families and Jewish heritage was always required. Such denunciation was sometimes very thorough. For example, the church of Constantinople required in part:

> I renounce all customs, rites, legalisms, unleavened breads and sacrifices of lambs of the Hebrews, and all the other feasts of the Hebrews, sacrifices, prayers, aspersions, purifications, sanctifications and propitiations, and fasts, and new moons, and Sabbaths, and superstitions, and hymns and chants and observances and synagogues,

---

31. Chrysostom *Discourses* 7. 1. 1.
32. Chrysostom *Discourses* 8. 9. 9.
33. Such professions are plentiful and follow the same basic patterns. For a selection, note James Parkes, *The Conflict of the Church and the Synagogue: A Study in the Origins of Antisemitism* (New York: World, 1934), pp. 394–400.

and the food and drink of the Hebrews; in one word, I renounce absolutely everything Jewish, every law, rite and custom, and above all I renounce Antichrist, whom all the Jews await in the figure and form of Christ; and I join myself to the true Christ and God.[34]

The penalty for eating and feasting with one's Jewish family, or for going astray from the oath in any way, also had to be declared by the Jewish convert to Christianity. In this case he declared that if he lapsed from his oath, "then let the trembling of Cain and the leprosy of Gehazi cleave to me, as well as the legal punishments to which I acknowledge myself liable. And may I be anathema in the world to come, and may my soul be set down with Satan and the devils."

Such declarations are even sadder because a large number of Jews were forced to convert to Christianity under the penalty of death! For example, Byzantine emperors such as Heraclius, Leo III, and Basil I promoted forced conversions during the medieval period. After outlawing Judaism, Leo III commanded that all Jews in the empire undergo baptism. Some died rather than convert, but a large number underwent baptism—and later "unbaptized" themselves.

INFERIOR CITIZENS

Those Byzantines then had to satisfy themselves by disrupting synagogue worship and enacting laws prohibiting Jews from holding government posts, evangelizing, or owning Christian slaves. Jews were clearly considered inferior citizens.[35] In the West, kings such as Chilperic, a Frank of the sixth century,[36] ordered the baptism of a large number of Jews, setting a precedent that culminated in massive forced conversions of thousands of Jews (and death and expulsion of others) during the Spanish Inquisition in the latter fifteenth century. The medieval Roman church progressively stripped the Jewish people of legal rights, rights that had taken centuries to procure under the pagan Roman Empire. The decrees of the Fourth Lateran Council of 1215 during the papacy of Innocent III ordered Jews to wear distinctive garments, ostensibly to curtail intimate relationships between Jews and Christians. The distinguishing badge took many forms: in Italy a disk was sewn on the clothing; in German areas a distinctive hat was worn; and in England two strips of white linen or parchment were sewn on a prominent part of the clothing. Ironically, during this time English princes needed Jews to get around the usury laws of the church, and therefore ignored anti-Jewish legislation put forward by the council—and turned the badges into forms of protection.[37]

---

34. Ibid., 397.
35. Note Andrew Sharf, *Byzantine Jewry: From Justinian to the Fourth Crusade* (New York: Schocken, 1971), especially chapters 4 and 5.
36. Parkes, *Conflict of Church and Synagogue*, pp. 334–35. Compare Peter Lasko, *The Kingdom of the Franks: North-West Europe Before Charlemagne* (New York: McGraw-Hill, 1971), pp. 64–65.
37. Marion Gibbs and Jane Lang, *Bishops and Reform, 1215–1272: With Special Reference to the Lateran Council of 1215* (1934; reprint, New York: Oxford U., 1962), pp. 134–35.

TWO WHO STOOD FOR WHAT WAS RIGHT

Most Christians were products of their culture, imbued with the anti-Jewish propaganda passed down from the early church Fathers. Some, when it was in their best interest, (as with the princes above) were compelled to help the Jewish people. A few, however, stepped out because they believed that persecution of Jewish people was wrong, or had gone too far.

A good example is found in Bernard of Clairvaux, a distinguished figure of the twelfth century who was asked to preach a sermon to get the Second Holy Crusade off the ground. The Christian Crusaders to the Holy Land during the First Crusade (1096–1099) had viciously plundered and killed the Jews of Europe to finance their trip. Once in Jerusalem, they rushed through the streets killing every human being in sight—man, woman, and child. These knights were savages, and the streets were running with blood. They burned the Jews alive in the chief synagogue, circling the screaming, flame-tortured humanity singing "Christ We Adore Thee!" with their Crusader crosses held high. Bernard was aghast at such conduct, and in his sermon he emphasized that on this Crusade the knights must not persecute Jews. There were fewer Jewish victims because of his convictions, although incidents occurred. One Jewish man was stabbed five times by a group of Crusaders "in memory of the wounds suffered by Jesus."[38]

During the Reformation period, Johann Reuchlin was also forced to make a decision and felt compelled to take a stand for what was right. A famed Hebraist and Christian humanist, Reuchlin was a product of his age and had considered Jews to be blasphemous and barbaric. And yet, when a Hebrew Christian, Joseph Pfefferkorn, and the Dominicans obtained permission to seize copies of the Talmud and burn it, Reuchlin tried to convince educators, church leaders, and princes to save the Jewish literature. For his courageous act, he suffered abusive accusations that he was a "Judaizer" and was receiving money from Jews. He was forced to appear before the Inquisitors. In his tract *Spectacles* he asserted that a Christian should have conversations with Jewish people, learning from them and buying from them. "A Christian should love a Jew as his neighbor," Reuchlin maintained, "all this is founded on the law." Reuchlin finally appealed to Pope Leo X and was acquitted. The Talmud books were spared.[39]

MARTIN LUTHER AND THE REFORMATION—AN UNFULFILLED PROMISE

Unfortunately the Jewish people could not count on another famous Christian humanist of the period, Desiderius Erasmus. "When an overly zealous Jewish convert to Christianity wished to destroy the Jewish books, Erasmus said that so long as the New Testament was secure he would prefer to let him have

38. Hans Eberhard Mayer, *The Crusades*, trans. John Gillingham (New York: Oxford U., 1972), pp. 99–100.
39. Edward H. Flannery, *The Anguish of the Jews: Twenty-Three Centuries of Anti-Semitism* (New York: Macmillan, 1965), pp. 150–51.

the Old rather than disturb the peace of Christendom."[40] Thus, one of the most gifted and brilliant men of the period was willing to tolerate a bad situation. In contrast, Erasmus' future opponent and the great Reformer of the period, Martin Luther, defended Reuchlin when replying to scholars who had written to him concerning the affair.[41]

Luther appeared to be a breath of fresh air in the midst of a dismal situation. Initially, he had high regard for the Jewish people because he expected them to convert en masse once they were presented with a Christian message free from "papal paganism." In his treatise *That Jesus Christ Was Born a Jew* (1523) the German Reformer demonstrated that Jesus Christ was a Jew, born of the seed of Abraham, and provided a sad commentary on the medieval church's treatment of the Jewish people. He wrote: "If I had been a Jew and had seen such dolts and blockheads govern and teach the Christian faith, I would sooner have become a hog than a Christian." At this time he took a firm stand against the mistreatment of Jews, and advocated a new relationship with them. He concluded:

> Therefore, I would request and advise that one deal gently with them [the Jews] and instruct them from Scripture; then some of them may come along. Instead of this we are trying only to drive them by force, slandering them, accusing them of having Christian blood if they don't stink, and I know not what other foolishness. So long as we thus treat them like dogs, how can we expect to work any good among them? Again, when we forbid them to labor and do business and have any human fellowship with us, thereby forcing them into usury, how is that supposed to do them any good? If we really want to help them, we must be guided in our dealings with them not by papal law but by the law of Christian love. We must receive them cordially, and permit them to trade and work with us, hear our Christian teaching, and witness our Christian life. If some of them should prove stiff-necked, what of it? After all, we ourselves are not all good Christians either.[42]

It is no wonder that Jewish people viewed the Reformation as an opportunity for religious freedom, an opportunity to be treated as human beings.

Alas, Luther became irritated when the Jewish people continued to resist conversion. In 1526 he complained of the Jews' stubbornness, and by the 1530s he was presenting the common medieval stereotypes accorded to Jews. In conversations in *Table Talks* he caricatured Jews as "stiffnecked," "ironhearted," "stubborn as the Devil," and "usurers." In 1543, at the end of his life, he wrote three derogatory treatises against Jews, which anti-Semites would quote for the next four hundred years. So horrible were his statements that Julius Streicher, Hit-

---

40. Roland H. Bainton, *Erasmus of Christendom* (New York: Scribner's, 1969), p. 143.
41. Note Martin Luther to George Spalatin, Wittenberg, January or February 1514, in Preserved Smith, ed. and trans., *Luther's Correspondence and Other Contemporary Letters* (Philadelphia: Lutheran Publication Society, 1913), pp. 28–29.
42. Martin Luther, *That Jesus Christ Was Born a Jew*, 1523, trans. Walther I. Brandt, in *Luther's Works* (Philadelphia: Muhlenberg, 1962), 45:229. See p. 200 for earlier quote.

ler's hate-sheet editor and propagandist in *Der Stürmer*, cited Luther at his Nuremberg trial to justify his actions.

One of these treatises is *On The Jews And Their Lies*. In it Luther called the Jews "venomous," "bitter worms," and "disgusting vermin"; he asserted that they were all thieves and should be deported to Palestine. He made numerous suggestions concerning treatment of the Jewish people throughout the treatise, including these:

> What shall we Christians do with this rejected and condemned people, the Jews? . . . I shall give you my sincere advice. First, to set fire to their synagogues or schools and to bury and cover with dirt whatever will not burn, so that no man will ever again see a stone or cinder of them. This is to be done in honor of our Lord and of Christendom. . . . Second, I advise that their houses also be razed and destroyed. . . . Third, I advise that all their prayer books and Talmudic writings, in which such idolatry, lies, cursing, and blasphemy are taught, be taken from them. Fourth, I advise that their rabbis be forbidden to teach henceforth on pain of loss of life and limb. . . . Fifth, I advise that safe-conduct on the highways be abolished completely for the Jews. For they have no business in the country-side, since they are not lords, officials, tradesmen, or the like. Let them stay at home. . . . Sixth, I advise that usury be prohibited to them, and that all cash and treasure of silver and gold be taken from them and put aside for safekeeping. . . . Seventh, I recommend putting a flail, an ax, a hoe, a spade, a distaff, or a spindle into the hands of young, strong Jews and Jewesses and letting them earn their bread in the sweat of their brow.[43]

Luther's about-face caused extreme bitterness among the Jewish people, some of whom had hailed him as the forerunner of the Messiah and a new age. Jews were forced out of Saxony the same year.[44]

A LEGACY OF HATRED

As shall be seen in these pages, synagogues would be burned and homes demolished; Jewish books would be destroyed and rabbis killed. There would be no safe place in Germany (or in most of Europe) for Jews; rich and poor, all would have their money confiscated by the Third Reich. Work gangs of young and old men would provide twelve- to fourteen-hour days of slave labor. Even Martin Luther could not have foreseen the horrible way in which his words would be used.

The religious animosity we have been looking at was to continue for the next two centuries among both Protestants and Catholics. During the Catholic Reformation, in the latter half of the sixteenth century, the popes in their attempt

43. Martin Luther, *On the Jews and Their Lies*, 1543, trans. Martin H. Bertram, in *Luther's Works*, 47:268–72. The total treatise is found on pages 137–306.
44. Note the discussion of Luther in Leon Poliakov, *The History of Anti-Semitism*, trans. Richard Howard (London: Elek, 1965), pp. 216–26.

to bolster the church began segregating the Jewish people into ghettoes. This act would have significance for the twentieth century as well.[45]

Even the eighteenth-century Enlightenment—the age that had supposedly emancipated the Jew—nourished a continued stream of religious anti-Semitism. Joseph Samuel Levi, a German Jew, found to his chagrin that in the "enlightened" year of 1795 no Jew was permitted to remain in Rostock, Germany overnight without special permission from the magistrate. Although he was seeking a Christian to explain to him the gospel message, the local minister and magistrate met him with suspicion. They finally sent him to three neighboring towns on the condition that if he was *not* accepted he could return to Rostock. A minister in the neighboring town of Wismar befriended him and led him in studies in the New Testament. He was baptized later in another town by a Lutheran minister who had him take on additional names and drop his family name of Levi. He thus became Joseph Samuel Christian Frederick Frey. One would think that this would have been enough for the Christian European community, but when Frey entered a seminary to become a missionary and preach to Gentiles, he was informed that he could not take the examination for the Danish Missionary Society "on account of his having been a Jew." Later, however, he was "allowed" to become an assistant to a missionary in Africa. Delayed in London on his way to Africa, Frey became (in the words of famed Hebrew Christian, Louis Meyer) "The Father of Modern Jewish Missions" by establishing the London Society for Promoting Christianity Among the Jews in 1809.[46]

Such maltreatment toward this exceptional young man underscores the ever-present suspicion of Jews (and even of Jewish converts to Christianity) in many areas of Europe during the Enlightenment and afterward. One also notes in this incident the seeds of a racial anti-Semitism that will be coupled to religious anti-Semitism in the nineteenth century. As the history of the conflict between church and synagogue up to the nineteenth century is evaluated, one is struck by the candor of Erasmus when he avowed: "If it is Christian to hate the Jew, then we are all good Christians."[47]

45. Abram Leon Sachar, *A History of the Jews* (New York: Alfred A. Knopf, 1964), pp. 251–55.
46. See Louis Meyer, *Eminent Hebrew Christians of the Nineteenth Century: Brief Biographical Sketches*, ed. David A. Rausch (New York: Edwin Mellen, 1983), pp. 113–19.
47. Quoted in Flannery, *The Anguish of the Jews*, p. 151.

3

Nineteenth-Century
Germany

In June 1983 religious leaders representing a wide range of theological viewpoints were joined by scientists in a declaration urging Congress to ban experiments that might change human genetic characteristics. Jerry Falwell, Bishop James Armstrong (President of the National Council of Churches), as well as Roman Catholic and Jewish leaders were among those signing this remonstrance. They were concerned that humans not be treated like animals and that science not abuse its abilities. Disregard for the fine line between removing genetic defects ("good genetics") and tampering with the human race is cause for anxiety, especially because racist groups today are enthusiastically promoting eugenics programs.

The National Alliance in Washington, D.C., for example, bills itself as an educational organization, and it wants to expand eugenic operations. Its magazine, *National Vanguard*, has given considerable attention to new developments. Editor William L. Pierce has actually stated that "we ourselves are concerned only with race-based eugenics." In response to a reader's question about Robert Graham's eugenics-oriented sperm bank, the Repository for Germinal Choice, Pierce wrote:

> Every new birth of a genetically superior baby brought about through his program is to be commended, of course, but unless Graham's program is massively expanded, ultimately with full governmental backing, and coupled with a strong *negative eugenics program to weed out the accumulated genetic refuse of centuries* of dysgenic breeding, it will accomplish nothing in the long run. It is a step in the right direction—a

31

very important step—but many more steps must be taken before we can say that such programs have a chance of putting the race once again on the upward path.[1]

Pierce explained that the reason some people were afraid to take the "racist position" on eugenics was because of "Jewish control of the news and entertainment media." His objection to the position of most of those advocating eugenics was that "they would just as soon use sperm from an intelligent Negro or Eskimo or Jew as from an intelligent White man."

The National Alliance wants to eliminate the non-white "genetic refuse" from America. Its statement of faith, published on the back cover of the *National Vanguard*, emphasizes that "no multi-racial society can be a truly healthy society" and "no government which is not wholly responsible to a single racial entity can be a good government." It declares that "all young people of our race must have instilled in them a sense of quality instead of equality" and that the first step toward these goals "must be the gathering together of all those men and women of our race who share our beliefs and who are willing to participate in our effort to raise the consciousness of others." The Alliance's creed affirms:

> We believe that our people must be united by the common goal of building a better world and a better race. Today, without a common national-racial purpose, we are unable to focus our energies and achieve the great things which otherwise would be within our grasp. But once we are united on the basis of common blood, organized and disciplined within a progressive social order, and inspired by a common set of ideals, there will be no problem which we cannot overcome, no enemy whom we cannot vanquish, and no goal which we cannot attain.[2]

This sounds like a speech from Hitler, but its roots actually go back even further—to the nineteenth century. What happened in Nazi Germany grew out of the racial theory that permeated philosophy, science, and religion in that earlier era. Racial anti-Semitism was combined with religious anti-Semitism in a powerful delusion that infected the Christian church.

ANTI-SEMITISM—THE SHAME OF A HUMILIATED PEOPLE

At the beginning of the nineteenth century the armies of Napoleon were overpowering Europe, claiming to liberate citizens from dominating governments. The French National Assembly in 1789 had established the "Declaration of the Rights of Man and of the Citizen," an act that led to legal emancipation of the Jewish community in areas conquered by the French armies. Prussia, which had been at peace with France at the beginning of the century, decided to go to war when Napoleon's intention of controlling Germany became clear. The French crushed the famous Prussian army at the battles of Jena and Auer-

1. "Editor's Reply," *National Vanguard* 91 (December 1982), p. 3. Italics added.
2. "What We Believe" is on the back cover of the *National Vanguard*.

stadt in October 1806. Consequently, the Prussian king Frederick William III and his government fled east to be protected by the Russian czar. One year later, in 1807, the French and Russians joined forces by signing a treaty. Napoleon meanwhile continued to occupy Berlin with his troops, taking all Prussian territories west of the Elbe. This was a time of humiliation for the German people; and because Jews gained some freedom under French rule, the Germans accused them of plotting secretly with Napoleon.[3]

FICHTE—THE "MORAL DECADENCE" OF JEWS

This humiliation was intensified by the Germans' own emphasis on nationalism and the superiority of their race. Johann Gottlieb Fichte, professor of philosophy at the University of Berlin, delivered "Addresses to the German Nation" in 1807, which stirred the German people to realize their "exceptional heritage" and to believe that only under Germanic peoples could a new era of history blossom. In a period of anti-French feeling, Fichte's view that Latins (especially the French) and Jews were members of decadent, mongrel races while the Germanic race was the purest was particularly encouraging. Fichte maintained that world affairs were determined by man's moral purpose and that the German nation-state must be based on moral convictions—convictions best suited to the Germanic peoples. In spite of his deep respect for the Bible and for some individual Jews, Fichte wrote: "A mighty state stretches across almost all the countries of Europe, hostile in intent and engaged in constant strife with everyone else . . . This is Jewry."[4] He portrayed the Jews as in direct conflict with the national aspirations of the German people; in direct conflict with the "moral" German state.

HEGEL—THE STATE IS ALL

Georg Wilhelm Friedrich Hegel succeeded to the chair of philosophy in Berlin upon Fichte's death in 1814. William Shirer underscores his significance:

> [Hegel] is the subtle and penetrating mind whose dialectics inspired Marx and Lenin and thus contributed to the founding of Communism and whose ringing glorification of the State as supreme in human life paved the way for the Second and Third Reichs of Bismarck and Hitler. To Hegel the State is all, or almost all. Among other things, he says, it is the highest revelation of the "world spirit," it is "the actuality of the ethical idea . . . ethical mind . . . knowing and thinking itself"; the State "has the supreme right against the individual, whose supreme duty is to be a member of the State . . . for the right of the world spirit is above all special privileges" . . .

3. See R. R. Palmer and Joel Colton, *A History of the Modern World*, 5th ed. (New York: Alfred A. Knopf, 1978), pp. 382–96. Compare Marvin Lowenthal, *The Jews of Germany: A Story of Sixteen Centuries* (Philadelphia: Jewish Publication Society of America, 1936), pp. 217–31.
4. Jacob Katz, *From Prejudice to Destruction: Anti-Semitism, 1700–1933* (Cambridge, Mass.: Harvard U., 1980), p. 60.

Hegel foresees such a State for Germany when she has recovered her God-given genius. He predicts that "Germany's hour" will come and that its mission will be to regenerate the world. As one reads Hegel one realizes how much inspiration Hitler, like Marx, drew from him, even if it was at second hand.[5]

The Jewish people were to suffer just as much under Marxism as under fascism—and in racist literature would be unjustly accused of fostering both.

A CYCLICAL PATTERN

After Napoleon's defeat, the Germans took revenge on the Jews. 1816 was a year of severe famine and unemployment, and Jakob Friedrich Fries, an anti-Semitic philosopher who lectured at both Jena and Heidelberg universities, led demonstrations of ultra-nationalist students against Jews, urging that they be "destroyed root and branch." Christian Friedrich Ruehs, history professor at the University of Berlin, emphasized that Jews should not be citizens of the Christian German state, and that allowing Jews to prosper had brought decline and decay. During the same period, the Jewish community was claiming its right to freedoms provided by the Enlightenment, rights that were systematically being taken away from them. In 1819 riots against Jews broke out in Germany and spread to neighboring countries. Crying, "Hep! Hep! Hep! Death and destruction to all the Jews," mobs smashed windows and looted businesses and homes. Researcher Lucy Dawidowicz has suggested a cyclical pattern of German political relations with the Jews: "long periods of reaction, repression, conservatism, and anti-Semitism following brief spells of liberalism and the expansion of [Jewish] rights."[6]

SCIENTIFIC RACISM

In this environment, a scientific racism began to develop. It is ironic that one of the first contributors to this "science" of racism was a Frenchman who had no particular aversion to Jews. In his *Essay on the Inequality of the Human Races* (1853), Count Joseph Arthur de Gobineau used the word *Aryan* (a word linguistic scholars had used for a number of related languages, including German and Latin) to denote a supreme and original white race. Gobineau claimed that race was the determining factor in the rise and fall of civilizations, postulating a hierarchy of humanity ranging from the superior white race to the inferior black race. Racial mixing had brought decline to the Latin and Semitic peoples, whereas Aryan Germans—the western Germanic tribes—held the key to a successful hu-

5. William L. Shirer, *The Rise and Fall of the Third Reich: A History of Nazi Germany* (Greenwich, Conn.: Fawcett, 1959), pp. 143–44.
6. Lucy Dawidowicz, *The War Against the Jews, 1933–1945* (New York: Holt, Rinehart and Winston, 1975), p. 29. "Hep!" was a derogatory rallying cry against Jews common in Germany. There is debate about the origin, but some believe it was originally a cry for driving domestic goats.

man destiny. These powerful people, he said, could be brought down only by the degenerative effect of race mixing.[7]

Composer Richard Wagner, an anti-Semite who blamed all his problems on a fantasized Jewish control of the press and theater, and his son-in-law, Houston Stewart Chamberlain, were among those who broadened Gobineau's "Aryan" to include all Germanic peoples, that is, tall, blond, and long-headed peoples. Hitler noted in *Mein Kampf* of those to be admired: "Side by side with Frederick the Great stands a Martin Luther as well as a Richard Wagner."[8]

Scientific racism was influenced by a number of other pseudo-scientific theories promoted after 1850. The most important of these was Social Darwinism. In England, Herbert Spencer proposed that there was a constant struggle between humans in which the strongest would win. He suggested the existence of two kinds of knowledge: individual knowledge and racial knowledge. Spencer and his disciples believed natural law dictated that the weak and poor of society should *not* be protected. Social Darwinism was subsequently applied on the national level, implying that stronger nations were the best and had a right to rule others.

These ideas had grave consequences not only for the Jewish community but also for the Christian church. Thinkers like Karl Eugen Dühring, a Social Darwinist who taught at the University of Berlin, shared Wagner's thesis that Christianity was a product of "Hebraic orientalism" and that those who persisted in Christian tradition could not possibly fight Jews or defend the Aryan spirit.

Not only did anti-Semites berate Christianity; they supported a new paganism in its place. A movement to exalt pre-Christian German folk traditions bolstered nineteenth-century German nationalism—ironically, at the very same time that medieval Christian stereotypes of Jews and religious anti-Semitism were being brought into the modern age.

UNITED GERMANY

The Jew was between a rock and a hard place. Christians had been against him for centuries. Anti-Christian Nationalists also used him as a scapegoat. And even socialists blamed him for the problems of the world: Karl Marx accused Jews of initiating capitalism, and he used violent anti-Jewish language in his treatise *On the Jewish Question* (1844).

The Jewish response was to try to assimilate more to German society; to prove they were good Germans. Political developments worked in their favor. Under the leadership of Chancellor Otto von Bismarck, Prussia during the 1860s led the states of Germany toward unification. Among the political concessions

---

7. Michael D. Biddiss, *Father of Racist Ideology: The Social and Political Thought of Count Gobineau* (New York: Weybright and Talley, 1970), pp. 112–21.
8. Adolf Hitler, *Mein Kampf* (Boston: Houghton Mifflin, 1939), p. 287. Compare Robert W. Gutman, *Richard Wagner: The Man, His Mind, and His Music* (New York: Harcourt, Brace, Jovanovich, 1968), pp. 418–32.

to the National Liberal party was a final emancipation law in 1869, which granted Jews equal citizenship status. On January 18, 1871, the Second Reich (the second German empire) was established, and Germany was unified into one nation.[9]

The consolidation of Germany transformed the face of Europe, and the German empire became the greatest power on the European continent. King Wilhelm I of Prussia was proclaimed emperor, being maneuvered into place by the political genius of Bismarck and the might of the Prussian army. The founding of the Second Reich was such a remarkable success that it uplifted the whole nation, and many Christians felt that God was instrumental in founding this "Christian" state. Political parties, social and economic institutions, and even some scientific societies called themselves "Christians." A civil religion developed, equating "German" with "Christian." It was a religion that continued to romanticize the Germanic heritage; a heritage that was unique to the German *Volk* (common people) and *Volksgeist* (national character).

Both *religious* and *racial* anti-Semitism were to be found in the Second Reich. *Religious anti-Semitism* insisted that a Jew could not retain his Jewish identity, and it demanded that he convert and assimilate. Friedrich Paulsen, a prominent liberal humanist and outspoken critic of racial anti-Semitism, explained in his *System of Ethics* that "to remain a complete Jew and a complete German is impossible."[10] That a liberal would construct such an obstacle for Jewish identity underscores the enormity of the problem facing the Jewish community in the very conservative Second Reich.

Racial anti-Semitism treated the Jew as a parasite, a biological inferior that conversion and assimilation would not cure, a danger to the body politic. For example, Paul de Lagarde, an outspoken critic of Christianity and Christian theology, condemned those "who—out of humanity!—defend these Jews or who are too cowardly to trample this usurious vermin to death." "With trichinae and bacilli one does not negotiate," he explained, "nor are trichinae and bacilli to be educated; they are exterminated as quickly and thoroughly as possible."[11] Lagarde died in 1891, but his racial anti-Semitism continued to flourish.

Today one hears protests that the word *anti-Semitism* should not be used, because there are other Semites besides Jews. The term, however, was coined in 1879 by a racist named Wilhelm Marr. He was searching for a more scientific-sounding term than *Jew* when he founded the League of Anti-Semites. In the European context, the word *Semite* was used strictly for the Jews, and everyone knew that *anti-Semite* meant *anti-Jewish*. In his treatise *The Victory of Judaism over Germandom*, published in 1873, Marr applied the word *Semite* to Jews,

---

9. For primary materials from works by these individuals, note chapter 7, "Political and Racial Anti-Semitism," in Paul R. Mendes-Flohr and Jehuda Reinharz, eds., *The Jew in the Modern World: A Documentary History* (New York: Oxford U., 1980).

10. Uriel Tal, *Christians and Jews in Germany: Religion, Politics, and Ideology in the Second Reich, 1870–1914*, trans. Noah Jonathan Jacobs (Ithaca, N.Y.: Cornell U., 1975), p. 291.

11. Dawidowicz, *The War Against the Jews*, p. 32.

speaking of "destructive Semitism" and "Jewry" interchangeably. He also exhibited racist contempt for Christianity (after noting Jewish control of society, politics and thought) when he wrote:

> Further, we cannot count on the help of the "Christian" state. The Jews are the "best citizens" of this modern, Christian state, as it is in perfect harmony with their interests . . . German culture has proved itself ineffective and powerless against this foreign power [the Jews]. This is a fact; a brute inexorable fact. State, Church, Catholicism, Protestantism, Creed and Dogma, all are brought low before the Jewish tribunal, that is, the [irreverent] daily press [which the Jews control]. . . . Dear reader, while you are allowing the German to be skinned alive I bow my head in admiration and amazement before this Semitic people, which has us under heel. Resigned to subjugation to Jewry, I am marshalling my last remaining strength in order to die peacefully, as one who will not surrender and who will not ask forgiveness.[12]

Lest one believe that racism against Jews was only a European or German problem during this period, consider that in 1877 a Jewish lawyer was blackballed by the New York Bar Association, solely because of race; and that businessman Joseph Seligmann and his family were the same year refused lodging at the Grand Union Hotel in Saratoga Springs, New York because of their race. In America also, the Jew was seen by some as an alien.[13]

CHRISTIAN RESPONSES

ADOLF STOECKER AND CHRISTIAN ANTI-SEMITISM

In the midst of such venomous German racial anti-Semitism, the Reverend Adolf Stoecker stands as an enigma. A conservative Lutheran minister from the grass roots of German society, Stoecker rose in 1874 to the exalted position of Court and Cathedral Preacher in Berlin. He possessed a charismatic personality and was very energetic. Displaying a fervent devotion to the fatherland, he was concerned about the spiritual and material welfare of the lower classes. He endeavored to preach *only* the Word of God—"the pure Word of Scripture." He believed that politics did not belong in the pulpit on Sunday mornings, but he was deeply involved in the political arena during the week. He defended this by asserting that one's Christian convictions should be applied to public life; that religion belonged in the chambers of parliament just as much as it belonged in the believer's private life.[14]

---

12. Wilhelm Marr, *The Victory of Judaism over Germandom*, trans. Mendes-Flohr and Reinharz, in *The Jew in the Modern World*, pp. 271–72.
13. Paul E. Grosser and Edwin G. Halperin, *The Causes and Effects of Anti-Semitism: The Dimensions of a Prejudice* (New York: Philosophical Library, 1978), p. 221.
14. Paul W. Massing, *Rehearsal for Destruction: A Study of Political Anti-Semitism in Imperial Germany* (New York: Howard Fertig, 1967), pp. 22–31.

Stoecker, viewing the incumbent Social Democratic Party as liberal, atheistic, and materialistic, in 1878 launched his own "Christian" party—the Christian Social Workers' Party. In 1879 he began a vigorous campaign against the Jewish people, declaring that they were the most corrupting influence in society. In a speech delivered at a Christian Social Workers' Party rally on September 19, 1879, entitled "What We Demand of Modern Jewry," he told his audience that he intended to deal with the Jewish question "in the spirit of Christian love, but also with complete social truthfulness." He declared Jews to be "a great danger to German national life." He denigrated Judaism as an archaic religion in which the concepts of religious freedom and tolerance do not fit. "Hatred of the Jews is already flaring up here and there, and this is repugnant to the Gospels," he explained. But then, putting the blame on the Jewish people for anti-Semitic outbursts, he said, "If modern Jewry continues to use the power of capital and the power of the press to bring misfortune to the nation, a final catastrophe is unavoidable. Israel must renounce its ambition to become the master of Germany." Stoecker suggested that "Jewish social abuses" should be "eradicated by wise legislation." Jewish capital should be curbed, Jewish judges should be limited; and Jewish teachers should be removed from the grammar schools. He proposed that the "Christian-Germanic spirit" be strengthened, concluding:

> Either we succeed in this and Germany will rise again, or the cancer from which we suffer will spread further. In that event our whole future is threatened and the German spirit will become Judaized. The German economy will become impoverished. These are our slogans: A return to a Germanic rule in law and business, a return to the Christian faith. May every man do his duty, and God will help us.[15]

Stoecker reiterated that he was just a good Christian, *defending* his nation and its religion against attack by the Jews. Through this religious anti-Semitic stance, he gained wide publicity for himself and for his party.

In the fall of 1880 the "Anti-Semites' Petition" was circulated. When it was presented to Bismarck in 1881, it had garnered over 250,000 signatures. Among them was that of Adolf Stoecker, who had debated whether signing such a petition was the Christian thing to do. A number of pastors followed his lead.[16] Stoecker was elected to the Reichstag (parliament) the same year, a position he held from 1881–1892 and from 1898–1908. While in that post, he influenced the Conservative Party's *Tivoli Programme of 1892* (its political platform) to include a paragraph which read: "We oppose the many-sided thrustful and disintegrating Jewish influence upon our national life. We desire to have a Christian Government for our Christian people and Christian teachers for our pupils." Many Conservative delegates wanted to add the modifying clause, "We repu-

15. Adolf Stoecker, "What We Demand of Modern Jewry," trans. Massing, *Rehearsal for Destruction*, p. 287. Note pages 278–87 for a total text of the speech.
16. See Lucy Dawidowicz, ed., *A Holocaust Reader* (New York: Behrman House, 1976), pp. 28–30 for the text of the petition.

diate the excesses of anti-Semitism," but for some reason Stoecker successfully opposed it. The *Tivoli Programme* remained in effect until the outbreak of World War I.[17]

Amiable and energetic, Adolf Stoecker tried to make an alliance between his party and the more radical racial anti-Semites. He found this an impossible task, because the racial anti-Semites were highly critical of Christianity—especially of the evangelical, Reformation variety. Stoecker did not believe in racial anti-Semitism; he did not believe Jews were subhuman. He was, however, so imbued with the theories of "German Christian *Volk*-consciousness" and the international Jewish conspiracy that he was actually a great help to the cause of racial anti-Semitism within the religious community.

In the same fashion, another prestigious Protestant, Heinrich von Treitschke, professor of history at the University of Berlin, got caught up in the anti-Semitism of the 1870s. As editor of the prestigious *Prussian Annuals*, he added credibility to the racist position among intellectuals; and this even though his plea was for rapid assimilation of the Jewish people into German society. Treitschke coined the phrase "the Jews are our misfortune," a phrase later adopted by the Nazis.[18]

THOSE WHO SPOKE OUT

To their credit, a number of pastors, theologians, and Christian politicians spoke out against Stoecker and the upsurge of anti-Semitism. Some pastors wrote and preached that believers in Christ should not associate themselves with anti-Semites and anti-Semitic political parties. Others warned their congregations to beware of those who declared to be speaking "in the spirit of Christian love" against the Jews. They stated that the true enemies of the gospel and of Christ were the extreme nationalists. Moreover, they said, Christians who fanned the flames of hatred were threatening Christianity itself.

Michael Baumgarten, a professor of theology and a Reichstag deputy, warned the church that she was getting too close to a deceitful alliance with the anti-Semites. In the pamphlet *Stoecker's Falsified Christianity*, Baumgarten insisted that Stoecker's words and actions were anything but Christian. He called upon the German church to shed "tears of honest repentance" to wash the stains of anti-Semitic propaganda. In a second pamphlet, entitled *Christian Voice on the Jewish Question*, he declared that the church, not the Jews, needed to be reformed. He called for the church to organize an official day of repentance to eradicate Stoecker's "barbarous dishonour" to the Christian faith. The church, however, in the words of Richard Gutteridge, "was uneasy, but deemed it to be prudent to keep silent, though a motion put to the Berlin District Synod recommending that Stoecker should be given a brotherly admonition to refrain

17. Richard Gutteridge, *Open Thy Mouth for the Dumb!: The German Evangelical Church and the Jews, 1879–1950* (Oxford: Basil Blackwell, 1976), p. 7.
18. Note his speech, "A Word About Our Jewry, 1879," ed. Ellis Rivkin, trans. Helen Lederer, in *The Jew in the Modern World*, pp. 280–83.

from his anti-Jewish agitation, as unbefitting to his office as an evangelical clergyman, was only defeated by a narrow majority."[19] The leaders of the German
church had once again failed.

Across the Atlantic Ocean, in the United States, fundamentalist-evangelicals
seemed to sense the danger European anti-Jewish propaganda posed to the Jewish community. Ernst F. Stroeter, a German Methodist and professor at Denver
University, was one who was aware of some of the same hatred and bias toward
Jewish people in the United States. After joining Arno C. Gaebelein's Hope of
Israel Movement in New York in 1894, Stroeter was asked by a Christian clergyman if he had found any Jews *worth* saving. Stroeter was incensed at such a
question, for he was a staunch defender of the Jewish people. In the latter 1890s
he emigrated to Germany and traveled throughout Europe lecturing and writing on behalf of the Jewish people and defending biblical Christianity.[20]

In 1897 S. M. Vernon wrote an article published in *Our Hope* magazine entitled "The Hated Jew." Vernon summed up not only the situation of Jew-hatred
throughout the world at the end of the nineteenth century, but also provided a
commentary of its historical effect when he concluded: "Christendom has no
greater shame, no deeper sin, nor a better proof of low spiritual life and poverty
of thought, than its hatred of the Jews."[21] Such racial and religious hatred would
bear bitter fruit in a united "Christian" Germany.

19. Gutteridge, *Open Thy Mouth for the Dumb!*, pp. 5–6.
20. Refer to my book *Zionism Within Early American Fundamentalism 1878–1918: A Convergence of
    Two Traditions* (New York: Edwin Mellen, 1979), pp. 225–37 for information on Stroeter.
21. S. M. Vernon, "The Hated Jew," *Our Hope* 4 (August 1897), p. 59.

4

Chamberlain, the War, and Weimar

The United Nations Women's Conference was held in Copenhagen, Denmark in 1980. Jewish feminists in attendance were appalled to find that anti-Semitism was not only a product of right-wing lunatics, but that it also permeated their left-wing bastion of hope, the entire feminist movement. There they heard statements reminiscent of those by brutal female guards in Nazi concentration camps: "the only good Jew is a dead Jew"; "the only way to rid the world of Zionism is to kill all the Jews." These statements raged from the lips of those who hated right-wing groups; from lips that simultaneously cried out against racism and oppression around the world. A United Nations' staff person told Esther Broner, a Jewish professor of English at Wayne State University (Detroit), that the Germans "only did one thing right: they killed the Jews." Esther choked audibly, and the staff person asked: "Oh, did I hurt your feelings? Are you German?"[1]

Racism in general and anti-Semitism in particular have through the centuries infested the cultured parlors of Western civilization as well as the seedy barrooms of the illiterate. They have hidden behind a polished veneer of proper clichés and impeccable etiquette and, as these women found, are often cancerous lesions on movements and organizations that appear to offer the most hope for struggling humanity.

1. "Bitter Fruit: Anti-Semitism at the Copenhagen Women's Conference," *Ms.* magazine, June 1982, pp. 49–50. Compare Letty Cottin Pogrebin, "Anti-Semitism in the Women's Movement," pp. 45–46, 48, 62, 65–72 in the same issue.

H. S. Chamberlain—"Scholar" of Anti-Semitism

The nazification of German culture is a fascinating study. Respectable college professors, theologians, physicians, scientists, artists, and musicians marched to the beat of Hitler's drum. Composer Richard Wagner (noted earlier) was a harbinger of this bizarre tendency. He and his wife Cosima gathered their disciples together in societies, using the small Bavarian town of Bayreuth as a base of operations. After Wagner's death in 1883, the cult was carried on by Cosima, who lived to open the decade of the 1930s. Cosima, the daughter of Hungarian pianist and composer Franz Liszt, was a rabid anti-Semite who devoted her life to sponsoring literature and speakers for the Aryan cause. The Bayreuth Music Festivals brought pilgrims of class and culture into the Wagner circle. One such devotee was Houston Stewart Chamberlain, author of *Foundations of the Nineteenth Century* (1899), a popular two-volume set (twelve hundred pages) that has had significant impact on racist thinking in the twentieth century.[2]

Houston Stewart Chamberlain (not to be confused with Neville Chamberlain, later Prime Minister of England) was the son of an English naval officer. In 1870, at the age of fifteen, he was sent to Germany to be cured of an illness. There he completed his education through private tutors. Chamberlain was totally captivated by Wagner's works and the Germanic "race." A year before Wagner's death, Chamberlain attended the music festival at Bayreuth. As a result he became increasingly close to Cosima. Later, in 1895, he published a book on Richard Wagner, and with Cosima's encouragement wrote the *Foundations*. The *Foundations* gives a sense of the ideology of the Bayreuth circle, and Cosima was particularly delighted with passages dealing with Germans and Jews and their relation to religion. After leaving his first wife, Chamberlain in 1908 married Cosima's daughter Eva. They moved to Bayreuth in 1909. Claiming to be plagued by "demons" and visions that drove him on to new fields of study and compelled him to write, he was in ill health most of his life and was later partially paralyzed.[3]

In 1923 Hitler attended the music festival in Bayreuth and visited Chamberlain. They were quite impressed with each other. Hitler later criticized the political policy of the Second Reich in *Mein Kampf*: "the official authorities of the government passed by the observations of a Houston Stewart Chamberlain just as indifferently as this is still the case with us today." The "insightful" Chamberlain is contrasted by Hitler with politicians "too stupid to think for themselves, and too vain to learn which is necessary from others."[4]

2. Note Robert W. Gutman, *Richard Wagner: The Man, His Mind and His Music* (New York: Harcourt, Brace, Jovanovich, 1968). Compare Leon Stein, *The Racial Thinking of Richard Wagner* (New York: Philosophical Library, 1950), and Geoffrey Skelton, *Wagner at Bayreuth* (London: Barrie and Rockliff, 1965).
3. Houston Stewart Chamberlain, *Foundations of the Nineteenth Century*, trans. John Lees, with an intro. by George L. Mosse, 2 vols. (New York: Howard Fertig, 1968), pp. v–xix. On Cosima note Richard Du Moulin-Eckart, *Cosima Wagner*, trans. Catherine Alison Phillips, 2 vols. (New York: Alfred A. Knopf, 1931).
4. Adolf Hitler, *Mein Kampf* (Boston: Houghton Mifflin, 1939), p. 369.

Hitler was well aware of the *Foundations*. The work had catapulted Chamberlain to fame, and by 1942 had gone through twenty-eight printings of more than a quarter of a million two-volume sets. Chamberlain collected information from a vast array of history, philosophy, religion, and science to support his theories. He distorted findings to prove conclusions he had come by intuitively. German readers, as well as others, were swept away by his apparent command of facts that portrayed the Aryan race as superior, the savior race through all of human history. Using the words *Nordic*, *Teutonic*, *Aryan*, and *Germanic* interchangeably, Chamberlain carefully led his readers through the ancient world, the medieval age, and the modern era. He sought to prove that the Teuton or "moral" Aryan was responsible for all the important contributions to civilization. The "alien Jew" was portrayed as the disrupter of civilization—a corrupting influence. Even Jewish religion was pictured as a hybrid of polytheistic systems having nothing in common with monotheistic Christianity.

The confidence and authority Chamberlain projected in declaring and "proving" that he had mastered the theme of the history of mankind drew the commitment of a generation, ranging from the barely-educated to the highly-educated classes. His technique is like that used by racists today: voluminous facts are arranged, listed, and twisted into an astounding array of pseudoevidence. Accurate history is wrenched from its very foundation, and the uninformed are overwhelmed. Experts are cited, but are carefully edited and judiciously quoted if they are not in agreement with the overall thesis of the book. Arguments against the thesis are simplistically dismissed and obliterated with ridicule. And often, like Chamberlain, the modern racist "scholar" declares that he is not anti-Semitic, but only an honest student of history trying to get at the truth. Chamberlain in fact admitted admiring a number of individual Jews, but emphasized that their race was "mongrel" and must be eradicated from German culture.[5]

5. Many scholars underscore the fact that the *Foundations* "soon became the Bible of the racists and their anti-Semitic cohorts" [Joseph Tenenbaum, *Race and Reich: The Story of an Epoch* (New York: Twayne, 1956), p. 10], and yet Chamberlain stated in his introduction to the volume:

For I have become convinced that the usual treatment of the "Jewish question" is altogether and always superficial; the Jew is no enemy of Teutonic civilisation and culture; [Johann Gottfried] Herder may be right in his assertion that the Jew is always alien to us, and consequently we to him, and no one will deny that this is to the detriment of our work of culture; yet I think that we are inclined to underestimate our own powers in this respect and, on the other hand, to exaggerate the importance of the Jewish influence. Hand in hand with this goes the perfectly ridiculous and revolting tendency to make the Jew the general scapegoat for all the vices of our time. (p. xl)

In racial history and anthropology, the *Foundations* have been plagiarized more than cited by modern racists. Alfred Rosenberg, the Nazi theoretician who wrote *Myth of the Twentieth Century* (1930) was deeply influenced by Chamberlain. Even the modern Hungarian Marschalko, discussed in chapter 2, in *The World Conquerors* calls Chamberlain "that great thinker" (Louis Marschalko, *The World Conquerors: The Real War Criminals*, trans. A. Suranyi [1958; reprint, United States: Christian Book Club, 1978], p. 38). Marschalko quotes Chamberlain several times, giving the impression that Chamberlain's vast study totally supports his own conclusion. This is not so. For example, Marschalko twists a passage from the Old Testament to portray David as the master of a concentration camp and first gas chamber—an inhumane Jew. Then he

Chamberlain mustered "facts" to prove that Jesus was not a Jew, but an Aryan. He claimed Galilee was not a Jewish center, that Jesus taught the Aryan idea of grace as opposed to the Jewish idea of law. In his section "The Galileans," Chamberlain exclaimed:

> Whoever makes the assertion that Christ was a Jew is either ignorant or insincere: ignorant when he confuses religion and race, insincere when he knows the history of Galilee and partly conceals, partly distorts the very entangled facts in favour of his religious prejudices or, it may be, to curry favour with the Jews. The probability that Christ was no Jew, that He had not a drop of genuinely Jewish blood in his veins, is so great that it is almost equivalent to a certainty.[6]

By the same process, Alexander the Great, Julius Caesar, Dante, Leonardo da Vinci, Voltaire, Napoleon, and others were made Aryans and noble Teutons.

Martin Luther was appealed to on approximately eighty pages of the *Foundations*. In fact, the main body of the first volume begins: "'The world,' says Dr. Martin Luther, 'is ruled by God through a few heroes and pre-eminent persons.'"[7] To Chamberlain, Luther was one of those heroes, a noble Teuton. "Luther is above all a political hero," wrote Chamberlain, "we must recognise this in order to judge him fairly and to understand his pre-eminent position in the history of Europe." Luther, "the German patriot and politician," was devoted first and foremost to the nation and is quoted as stating, "For my Germans I was born, them I will serve!" Chamberlain reiterated Treitschke's emphasis, saying Luther believed that the "State is in itself a moral system," and concluded:

> That Luther was more of a politician than a theologian naturally does not preclude the fact that the living power which he revealed flowed from a deep inner source, namely, his religion, which we must not confuse with his Church. . . . Luther's fervent patriotism was a part of his religion.[8]

---

notes: "'The Jew shaped his own fate!' wrote Houston Stewart Chamberlain referring to these things." In fact, Chamberlain believed that David and other important early Jewish personalities were Aryans or at least had a good portion of Aryan blood as indicated by their great accomplishments. After noting David's "fascinating qualities," he said that David "treated the Philistines generously in war, but the Hebrew peoples with frightful cruelty, as though they were repugnant to him." Marschalko criticized Solomon as well, but Chamberlain viewed the David-Solomon era as "nothing else but an 'episode' brought about by the exultant strength of an entirely different [Aryan] blood. . . ." (*Foundations*, 1: 385–86; *The World Conquerors*, p. 16). Ironically, Chamberlain the racial "expert" was taken out of context by Marschalko in the same manner in which Chamberlain had taken others out of context. This example should underscore once again the deception that permeates contemporary racist material and its attraction for the unsuspecting reader.

6. Chamberlain, *Foundations*, 1:211–212.
7. Ibid., 1:3.
8. Ibid., 2:375. A section devoted to Martin Luther is found on pages 366–77 of volume 2. Chamberlain also stated on page 370: "Luther, however, while calling upon princes, nobles, citizens and people to prepare for the strife, does not remain satisfied with the merely negative work of revolt from Rome; he also gives the Germans a language common to all and uniting them all, and lays hold of the two points in the purely political organisation which determined the success of nationalism, namely the Church and the School."

Luther's "religion," according to the *Foundations*, saw the Jews for what they were. Throughout, Luther was used to defend racial slanders and anti-Semitic stereotypes. Chamberlain later declared that Luther was "genuinely Germanic, the child of a fortunate union,"[9] boldly proclaiming near the end of volume one: "And whoever says 'Anti-Luther' says Anti-Germanic—whether he is conscious of this or not."[10]

During Hitler's Third Reich, much was made of the "science" of physiognomy—the art of judging character by physical features. We have noted previously the modern utilization of pictures to point out "inadequacies of non-Whites" in such racist publications as the *Christian Vanguard*. Chamberlain entitled an entire section of the *Foundations* the "Science of Physiognomy," which he claimed is "at once spirit and body, mirror of the soul and anatomical 'factum.'" To him, the countenance of Dante Alighieri "is a characteristically Germanic countenance!" He continued:

> Not a feature in it reminds us of any Hellenic or Roman type, much less of any of the Asiatic or African physiognomies which the Pyramids have faithfully preserved. A new being has entered into the history of the world! Nature in the fulness of her power has produced a new soul: look at it, here she reflects herself in a countenance such as never was seen before![11]

Chamberlain provided the reader with a sketch of Dante followed by one of Martin Luther on the next page. It is quite apparent that these men, revered as noble Teutons, are quite dissimilar in physical appearance; but Chamberlain lamely explained: "Luther's countenance, like Dante's, belongs to all Germanic peoples. . . . Dante and Luther are the extremes [in the spectrum] of the rich physiognomical scale of great Germanic men."[12]

One of the most enthusiastic readers of the *Foundations* was the German Kaiser, Wilhelm II. They met soon after its publication and maintained a strong friendship until Chamberlain's death in 1927. "It was God who sent your book to the German people, and you personally to me," the Kaiser wrote. Chamberlain later responded that he had placed Wilhelm's picture in his study, opposite one of Jesus Christ, so that he could walk between his Savior and his sovereign. Chamberlain often supported Kaiser Wilhelm in written works and for his efforts received the Iron Cross from the grateful monarch. He became a naturalized citizen of Germany during World War I.[13]

9. Ibid., 1:522.
10. Ibid., 1:573.
11. Ibid., 1:538–39.
12. Ibid., 1:541. Immanuel Kant and his philosophy is also a particular favorite of Chamberlain, and near the end of volume 2 Kant is declared "a true follower of Luther; the work which the latter began Kant has continued" (p. 495).
13. William L. Shirer, *The Rise and Fall of the Third Reich: A History of Nazi Germany* (Greenwich, Conn.: Fawcett, 1959), pp. 156–58.

A DEVASTATING WAR

On August 3, 1914, the Germans launched seventy-eight infantry divisions against French, British, and Belgian divisions in what was intended to be a short war. Instead, it was the beginning of World War I, a war that would claim nearly 8.5 million servicemen and cost more than $337 billion. The assassination of the heir to the Austrian throne, Archduke Franz Ferdinand, by a Serbian nationalist on June 28, brought two huge power blocs into conflict. Supporting Serbia were the Russians, and obligated to Russia by alliance were France and England. On the other side, Germany was tied to Austria-Hungary by alliances. Both power blocs were convinced they could win decisively, and events moved rapidly. On July 28 Austria-Hungary declared war on Serbia. Two days later Russia ordered a general mobilization of her forces to the borders of Austria-Hungary and Germany. On August 1, Germany declared war on Russia; and on August 3, on France. After early German victories gave the false impression that the Germans had planned the conflict while the other nations were innocent, the war settled down to a stalemate on the land. In fact, all parties of both power blocs were responsible for the war in a number of ways, and were surprised and saddened by the outcrop of total war.[14]

Nevertheless, the rhetoric of the nineteenth century, culminating in the *Foundations*, did little to encourage the Kaiser to try to mediate the situation. Emphasis on the superior Germanic race and the responsibility of the Teuton to lead the world into new heights of grandeur was embedded in the psyche of the German population. The German church enthusiastically embraced the patriotism of the *Volk*. Ministers preached the sacredness of the fatherland's cause, and prayers for victory rose from congregations. Liberals and conservatives wholeheartedly participated in the national fervor. A Lutheran periodical proclaimed in the spring of 1918: "What God has begun He takes pains to fulfil. He does nothing by halves. If England still possessed clear-sighted Christians, they would be bound to arise and cry out in alarm to their Government: 'Enough! The Lord is on Germany's side!'"[15] On April 22, 1915, Germany introduced poison gas to the battlefield during the Second Battle of Ypres.

Jews of all nations enlisted in large percentages to prove their loyalty to their respective countries. In Germany, one hundred thousand Jews out of a population of six hundred thousand served in the German armed forces, twelve thousand dying for the fatherland—a high percentage for a small community. Sadly, their show of loyalty was for nought. The anti-Semitic atmosphere promoted caricature and scapegoating against the Jewish community and Jewish soldiers as misfortune and hardship enveloped Germany. Jews were accused of using the

---

14. Especially helpful in ascertaining joint responsibility for World War I is Joachim Remak, *The Origins of World War I, 1871–1914* (New York: Holt, Rinehart and Winston, 1967). Note especially chapter 5, "A Question of Responsibility," pp. 132–50.
15. Richard Gutteridge, *Open Thy Mouth for the Dumb!: The German Evangelical Church and the Jews, 1879–1950* (Oxford: Basil Blackwell, 1976), p. 27.

war to dominate the nation; their soldiers were accused of inhibiting the march of the mighty Teutons.[16]

Germany's problems, however, resulted from being blockaded by the British and French from the sea. International law distinguished between munitions or raw materials used for munitions (*contraband*), and food and clothing (*noncontraband*). Noncontraband was to be allowed free passage even in wartime. Ignoring the protests of the United States, Britain and France disregarded international law and totally blockaded Germany. Germany countered with the only effective weapon she had available, the submarine. Enumerating the flagrant violations of international law, Germany announced in February of 1915 that she would torpedo any enemy ship in the waters surrounding the British Isles, regardless of status. On May 7 the *Lusitania*, a British passenger liner carrying munitions, was torpedoed by a German submarine. Approximately twelve hundred persons drowned, including 118 Americans. Although the Germans had warned Americans (even publishing warnings in New York newspapers against traveling on the ship), citizens of the United States believed international law guaranteed that they could travel wherever they pleased and on whatever ship they pleased, as long as they were on peaceful errands. Such an uproar arose after the sinking of the *Lusitania* that Germany scaled down her use of the submarine. When Germany found it necessary to declare unrestricted submarine warfare once again on February 1, 1917, the United States responded two months later with a declaration of war on Germany.[17]

The German High Command rightly assumed that the United States would not be able to field a full-scale army for at least a year. They erred, however, in assuming they could crush the British in half that time. The entrance of the American army spelled the death knell for the German war effort. The German High Command, including General Erich von Ludendorff, informed the German government in September 1918 that they could not possibly win the war, asking that an armistice be arranged. Ludendorff would later claim (and the fledgling Nazi party would systematically spread the rumor) that Germany had not lost the war on the battlefield, but rather had been "stabbed in the back" by politicians and Jews at home. On November 9, Kaiser Wilhelm II abdicated and Germany was declared a Republic. On November 11 the armistice was signed by Germany. The German troops that remained deep in the Western front trudged home.[18]

A BITTER PEACE

Early in 1919 the representatives of the new republic met in the small town of Weimar to draft a new constitution. Woodrow Wilson, President of the United

16. Tenenbaum, *Race and Reich*, p. 11.
17. Note R. R. Palmer and Joel Colton, *A History of the Modern World*, 5th ed. (New York: Alfred A. Knopf, 1978), pp. 666–74.
18. On Ludendorff and the war effort, note D. J. Goodspeed, *Ludendorff: Genius of World War I* (Boston: Houghton Mifflin, 1966).

States, had insisted that the new government be democratic; and the German people, craving peace, hoped the victors would deal more kindly with the democratic Weimar Republic.

The Weimar Constitution was a progressive document that pledged to protect the civil rights of all citizens. Intending to pattern itself after the dominant political tradition of the West, it was drafted by a German Democratic Party constitutional law professor who viewed the British parliamentary system as relatively stable. It provided for a president, popularly elected, to take the place of the British monarch as a check and balance on the powerful and popularly elected German legislature, the Reichstag. The Reichstag was given most of the legislative power, and had authority to approve or disapprove the political executive or chancellor. The president served as a check and balance, in that he nominated the chancellor and, in case of an emergency, had the power to dissolve the Reichstag and rule alone (or appoint another to rule). Political parties were very important to the system; even the smallest one could gain parliamentary representation in the Reichstag. (It was through this system that Adolf Hitler was to rise to power legally.) German socialists in the Social Democratic Party committed themselves to moderation in their role as leaders of the Weimar Republic. They lashed out against radicals who suggested sweeping revision of the social and economic system. It appeared that the Weimar Constitution might serve as the basis for a stable, democratic Germany.[19]

Alas, to Wilson's chagrin the English, French, and Italians—who had entered the war in 1915—were bitter and greedy. They refused Germany a part in the peace discussions. They insisted on a ruthless and humiliating peace treaty, the Treaty of Versailles, which forced Germany to confess that she alone was responsible for World War I. They reduced her original territory by one-eighth, took away all of her colonies, and depleted both her farm land and her factories. In addition, Germany was to make reparations for the *total* war damages, civilian as well as military. The sums were so astronomical that the treaty provided for a future commission to determine the payment schedule. Immediately, the Germans were to make coal deliveries, surrender their merchant marine, and relinquish private property owned by their citizens abroad. All of this was leveled not upon a militarist emperorship, but rather on the newly formed democratic republic.

The Treaty of Versailles was a deep blow to the Weimar Republic and was to pave the way for the Nazi regime. When the Germans were first presented with the document in May of 1919, they refused to sign. They considered it an outrageous amalgam—a travesty of justice. The victors consequently threatened to attack Germany and devastate her land. On June 28, 1919, two shaken representatives of the Weimar Republic performed the hateful task of signing the treaty. The German nationalist newspaper, *Deutsche Zeitung*, carried the head-

---

19. Note the discussion in Arnold J. Heidenheimer, *The Governments of Germany*, 3d ed. (New York: Thomas Y. Crowell, 1971), pp. 15–19.

line, "Vengeance! German Nation," and continued: "Today in the Hall of Mirrors, the disgraceful Treaty is being signed. Do not forget it. The German people will with unceasing labour press forward to reconquer the place among nations to which it is entitled. Then will come vengeance for the shame of 1919."[20]

NEW OPPORTUNITIES FOR JEWS

The Weimar Republic spelled freedom for the Jewish community. According to the constitution, Jews could now participate freely in the political and social life of the nation. Willing to make democracy work, Jews were involved in the politics of the nation as never before. Several leaders within the German Democratic Party and the Social Democratic Party were Jews. Hugo Preuss, a Jew, had drafted the Weimar Constitution. The brilliant Walter Rathenau became Minister of Reconstruction, and later Foreign Minister of the republic (he was murdered in 1922 by right-wing extremists).

The Jewish community finally had the opportunity to advance both economically and socially. They were generally middle-class and felt quite well off. Education was now open to the Jewish community, and soon more than one-third of the doctors and lawyers in the large cities were Jews. According to the 1925 census, there were 564,379 Jews in the Weimar Republic, representing a little less than one percent of the population. Two-thirds had migrated to large cities, while another third lived in more than three thousand towns and villages.

Jews involved in radical movements such as the Communist Rosa Luxemburg disassociated themselves from their Jewish heritage. (In spite of this, the Jewish community was held responsible for their actions, as well as for the few Jewish financial scandals that occurred.) But on the whole, the German Jew became the most assimilated of all during this period. Mixed marriages and conversions to Christianity abounded. During the period 1921–1927, 44.8 percent of all Jewish marriages were to a Gentile, and Jewish Christians multiplied at the rate of five hundred a year. Jews were again trying desperately to be good Germans. They thought of themselves first and foremost as German citizens and regarded their German culture as the most enlightened in the world.[21]

CULTURAL STRIDES; ECONOMIC COLLAPSE

The culture and innovation in the new republic was incredible. Germans were a brilliant, talented, and fun-loving people. Creativeness in art, music, and theater gave rise to the expression "Weimar Renaissance." Novelists, playwrights, and historians excelled during the "Golden Twenties." German universities were intellectual centers, on the vanguard in science, philosophy, sociology, and psychology. Peter Gay has stated that "it was the cultural task of the Weimar Re-

20. This quote may be found translated into English in Tony Edwards, *History Broadsheets: Hitler and Germany 1919–1939* (Edison, N.J.: Heinemann Educational Books, Ltd., 1972), 3:11.
21. *Encyclopaedia Judaica*, s.v. "Germany: 1914–1933," 7:483–85.

public to capitalize on such noble sentiments [of healing, peace, and kindness], to restore the broken ties . . . the brilliance of the refugees from Hitler is a measure of that success."[22] Of those German refugees, the United States would receive Albert Einstein (physicist), Thomas Mann (author), Erwin Panofsky (art historian), Walter Gropius (architect), Paul Tillich (philosophic theologian), and many others.

But the economy was collapsing. The loss of industrial and farm areas; the occupation by the French of the Ruhr (the center of Germany's iron and coal production) in January of 1923; the massive reparation payments; all caused an inflationary spiral that was an unbearable burden on the German populace. In July 1914 four German marks equaled one United States' dollar. In January 1919 it had risen to nine marks per dollar; and by January 1922 to 192. From January 1923 to November 1923 it rose from an unbelievable 17,972 to 4.2 trillion marks per dollar. German citizens literally raced to the grocery stores with their bags of money to try to beat the hourly rise in prices.[23]

Inflation hurt the Jewish community as much as anyone else. The middle class was heavily hit by the social and economic crises. Nevertheless, anti-Semitic propaganda capitalized on the increased visibility of the Jewish people and their activity in the despised Weimar Republic. To divert the attention of the populace away from the actual beneficiaries of inflation—the giant financial and industrial complexes of "pure Aryan" barons of commerce—the Jew was once again scapegoated. The Jews were blamed for both capitalism and Marxism by the anti-Semitic press.

THE DNVP AND THE CHURCH'S RESPONSE

In the mid-twenties, most of the middle class voters deserted the German Democratic Party in favor of the moderate right-wing German Peoples' Party (DVP) and the more critical right-wing nationalist Protestant German National Peoples' Party (DNVP). It is estimated that seventy to eighty percent of the Protestant pastors allied themselves with this latter *Deutschnational Volkspartei*.[24]

The large majority of Protestant clergy in Germany viewed the Weimar democratic government as too liberal and non-Christian. They believed that the fatherland had incurred a monstrous stab in the back as they looked with nostalgia on the lost glory of "Christian" Imperial Germany. As one pastor declared: "From our Christian way of looking at life, we seek to act as breakwater against the democratic waves of the present time. All efforts to make the State democratic are basically designed to dechristianize the *Volk*. We Christians remain reactionaries by God's Grace."[25]

22. Peter Gay, *Weimar Culture: The Outsider as Insider* (New York: Harper & Row, 1968), p. 8.
23. Gustav Stolper, *The German Economy 1870 to the Present*, trans. Toni Stolper (New York: Harcourt, Brace & World, 1967), 73–124. A table of the inflation is on p. 83.
24. Gutteridge, *Open Thy Mouth for the Dumb!*, p. 35. Compare *Encyclopaedia Judaica*, s.v. "Germany: 1914–1933."
25. Ibid.

Anti-Semitism became an integral part of the DNVP program through the 1920s. This amalgam of conservatives, radical nationalists, and anti-Semites claimed to fight "against the Jewish predominance in government and public life." In the 1924 election campaign, DNVP posters called for resistance to Jewish influence on all fronts. One pastor defined "Christian anti-Semitism" as "Genuine Germans and convinced Christians—the best weapon against alien infection." A Bavarian pastor admitted, "When I make contact with a Jew, I have an instinctive repugnance, and feel myself to be uncomfortable. I say to myself involuntarily: he is one of the race that killed your Saviour." He prided himself on "not only being a Christian but an Aryan Christian." In addition, the principal church weekly publications in the 1920s consistently supported this "Christian" nationalism, preaching Jewish responsibility for the collapse of the "Christian and monarchial order."

This constant bombardment weakened the moral resistance of many church members to the initial anti-Semitic measures of the Nazis, blunting basic Christian humanity and outrage at sinful anti-Semitism. William Laible, editor of a Lutheran weekly with the largest circulation in the country, propagated anti-Semitic slanders, and in 1929 he editorialized that because of the Jews' responsibility for the religious, economic, and moral decline of the nation, readers should welcome "for the sake of the German people . . . every expression of justifiable anti-Semitism."[26]

Ernst Helmreich in *The German Churches Under Hitler* summarizes this period:

> There were few denunciations of anti-Semitism in German pulpits in the 1920s, or for that matter in most pulpits of the Christian world. There were far more condemnations of bolshevism, of increasing secularization, and of the decay of morality and old Christian virtues. These the Nazis also decried. Political allegiances ran strong, and denunciations of National Socialist activity by Protestant and Catholic leaders were more often in the nature of rallying support for other parties than repudiating Nazi ideology.[27]

Nevertheless, a few individual pastors, such as Eduard Lamparter in Stuttgart, courageously stood alone and without compromise against anti-Semitism. In a 1928 booklet entitled *Evangelical Church and the Jews*, Lamparter condemned the expanding anti-Semitism within the church. He wrote that the church ought "to feel it her duty to bear witness against the anti-Semitic violation of Right, Truth and Love." He denounced racial theories, saying they had no authentic scientific foundation. According to Lamparter, the church must right past wrongs and prevent future injustices; she must explode anti-Semitic stereotypes that

26. *Allgemeine Evangelisch-Lutherische Kirchenzeitung*, 1 February 1929, quoted by Gutteridge, *Open Thy Mouth for the Dumb!*, p. 2. See Gutteridge's chapter 2, "Anti-Jewish Sentiment in the Weimar Period," pp. 35–68 for many more quotes.
27. Ernst Christian Helmreich, *The German Church Under Hitler: Background, Struggle and Epilogue* (Detroit: Wayne State U., 1979), p. 125.

"worked like poison" within the Christian. In 1931 the Church of Wurttemberg, pastored by Lamparter, attempted to get the German Evangelical Church to pass an official motion condemning anti-Semitism. Their effort failed.[28]

In 1923, when Houston Stewart Chamberlain for the first time met Adolf Hitler at Bayreuth, Hitler had few followers. The magnetism of Hitler's personality, however, fascinated the aged racist scholar, for he wrote to Hitler the next day:

> You have mighty things to do . . . My faith in Germanism had not wavered an instant though my hope—I confess—was at a low ebb. With one stroke you have transformed the state of my soul. That in the hour of her deepest need Germany gives birth to a Hitler proves her vitality; as do influences that emanate from him . . . May God protect you![29]

28. Gutteridge, *Open Thy Mouth for the Dumb!*, p. 57.
29. Shirer, *The Rise and Fall of the Third Reich*, p. 158.

5

The Rise of Hitler and the Nazi Party

When speaking to members of Nazi organizations in the United States today, I have been amazed by their fervor, dedication, and sense of mission; I have been stunned by their cold, calculating spirit and overt racism. These modern-day followers of Adolf Hitler invariably claim that the Holocaust did not occur. They say of the well-documented extermination of millions of Jews, that it is a hoax fabricated by the "establishment press," which is controlled by Jews. Nevertheless, within the first fifteen minutes of any given conversation, they declare that, in fact, a few hundred thousand Jews may have been killed, adding that "if more were killed, it still wasn't enough . . . they should have gotten *all* of them." An anti-Jewish diatribe then ensues as the Nazi rants against the Jewish community that supposedly controls the world, fosters Communism, cultivates pornography, mixes the races in movies and on television, and mongrelizes the white world with Blacks and Asians.

As soon as they find out I am a Christian, they quickly inform me that the Jews killed Jesus. One Nazi said to me, "Jesus was a Christian, you know," implying that if I were a good Christian, I would hate Jews and work to eliminate the Jewish presence from the midst of our white society. As a letter from the National Socialist White People's Party (NSWPP), one of the many Nazi organizations in the United States today, explained while soliciting a contribution, "More importantly, you will have the satisfaction which comes from knowing that you are doing your part to assure a better world for your Race and your children in the years to come." The salutation began: "Fellow White American."[1]

Hitler would be proud of the longevity of his movement. More than sixty years after the German Workers' Party renamed itself the Nationalist Socialist German Workers' Party under the influence of Hitler's fiery speeches, these modern-day National Socialists display the swastika, stage marches, publish racist materials, propagandize for the cause, and distribute—in both paperback and hardback—*Mein Kampf*. Hitler photo albums are available from their publication enterprises, as well as a number of biographies of the Führer, advertised as containing "none of the anti-National Socialist bias" and relating "the exciting events and incidents culminating in the Leader's assumption of power on January 30, 1933." They even distribute Martin Luther's *The* [sic] *Jews and Their Lies* and have a large selection on "Aryan Culture and History." The NSWPP sells "business cards" with a swastika encircled by the member's name and the caption: "White Pride, White Unity, White Power." Swastika armbands and Hitler Youth armbands (for the younger generation of Aryans) are also advertised and stocked.[2]

Who was this man who could inspire such devotion and revisionism after a tragic loss of war and, more importantly, a betrayal of the whole German nation? Who was Adolf Hitler?

HITLER'S YOUTH

A CHILDHOOD OF FAILURE

Hitler was born in Austria in 1889, the product of his father's third marriage. His father had worked his way up to the highest grade in the Imperial and Royal Customs Authority (Austrian Revenue Office), so that by the time Adolf was born the family enjoyed a financially comfortable life. There has been speculation that the Hitler heritage was partly Jewish, but no evidence for this assertion exists. Adolf's father, Alois, was an illegitimate child, later legitimized in church records as the son of Johann Georg Hiedler (his probable father, who was not Jewish). In any case, Jewish tradition teaches that the mother determines the "jewishness" of the child. Alois' mother, Maria Anna Schicklgruber, was not Jewish. Alois changed his name from Hiedler to Hitler twelve years before Adolf was born.[3] The Hitler family appears to have been no more anti-Semitic than any other German Catholic family in Austria. Adolf's childhood records are

1. Letter from the National Socialist White People's Party (NSWPP), 2507 N. Franklin Road, Arlington, Virginia, no date.
2. These materials can be found in numerous Nazi periodicals and papers. In *White Power*, the NSWPP has been advertising them for years under their "NS Publications" department.
3. Note Alan Bullock, *Hitler: A Study in Tyranny*, rev. ed. (New York: Bantam, 1961), pp. 1–7 for the family history and ancestry chart.

meager, and his later attempt to put the best light on them in *Mein Kampf* is unreliable.

Adolf was a mediocre student, transferring from one school to another because of poor grades. His failures produced tensions between him and his father, as well as a phobia that would appear later in his writings and speeches concerning "educated gentlemen" with their doctorates, "a people of scholars" who are physically degenerate. Hitler maintained that "the folkish State has to start from the presumption that a man, though scientifically little educated but physically healthy, who was a sound, firm character, filled with joyful determination and will power, is of greater value to the national community than an ingenious weakling." He suggested that the folkish State direct its entire education to "the breeding of absolutely healthy bodies."[4]

Alois Hitler died in 1903, leaving a pension for his wife. Adolf refused to work a steady job ("bread and butter jobs" he called them in derision), preferring to laze around, sponging off his mother. With his young friend August Kubizek he attended the opera and developed a love for Wagner. He dreamed of being an artist, and set off for Vienna in 1907 to enroll in the Academy of Fine Arts. However, he failed the Academy's entrance examination because his test drawing was "unsatisfactory." This was a great disappointment for him, and he felt lost. A few months later his mother died and, joined by Kubizek, he lived off his orphan's pension and his mother's savings.

EARLY ANTI-SEMITISM

Vienna, where he lived, was (and still is) a hotbed of anti-Semitism. It seems the eighteen-year-old Hitler cultivated there a hatred for the Jewish people and an intense German nationalism, complete with the overworked clichés of the day. Running out of money and refusing work as a manual laborer, he became a derelict. He lived off the bread and soup distributed in poverty shelters and passionately talked about politics. Even when a Hungarian Jew, an old-clothes dealer in a hostel, felt sorry for him and gave him a black overcoat to keep him warm, Hitler had no qualms about ranting offensive anti-Semitic slogans in his presence.[5] He wrote later in *Mein Kampf* that he began reading anti-Semitic pamphlets in Vienna, noting, "Wherever I went I saw Jews, and the more I saw them, the sharper I began to distinguish them from other people. The inner city especially and the districts north of the Danube Canal swarmed with a people which through its appearance alone had no resemblance to the German people." He continued:

> The moral and physical cleanliness of this race was a point in itself. It was extremely apparent that these were not water-loving people, and unfortunately one

4. Adolf Hitler, *Mein Kampf* (Boston: Houghton Mifflin, 1939), p. 613.
5. Bullock, *Hitler*, pp. 11, 13.

could frequently tell that even with eyes closed . . . aside from the physical unclean-liness, it was repelling suddenly to discover the moral blemishes of the chosen people. Nothing gave me more cause for reflection than the gradually increased insight into the activities of Jews in certain fields. Was there any form of filth or profligacy, above all in cultural life, in which at least one Jew did not participate? When carefully cutting open such a growth, one could find a little Jew, blinded by the sudden light, like a maggot in a rotting corpse. The Jews' activity in the press, in art, literature, and the theater, as I learned to know it, did not add to their credit in my eyes. . . . The fact was not to be denied that ninety percent of all literary and artistic rubbish and of theatrical humbug was due to a race which hardly amounted to one-hundredth of all inhabitants of the country . . . the glorified theatrical criticisms always dealt with Jewish authors, and never did they attack anyone except the Germans.[6]

Hitler the frustrated artist believed his creations were better than the Jewish "rubbish" that was successful. Hitler the nationalist believed that Germans could better run the Austrian political milieu than the rising Social Democratic Party, a workers' party "headed primarily by Jews." Throughout his life Hitler would pick and choose from all the nineteenth-century clichés in an effort to persuade an audience to support him.

Anti-Semitism was his consistently-held belief. He never developed a system-atized political, social, and economic program—not even when the Nazi party took the reins of German government. He believed firmly in the survival of the strong (a biologic-materialistic concept) and in the mission of the Germanic Aryan race. He used any propaganda technique or slogan to further these ob-jectives. Martin Broszat, a German research associate of the Institute for Recent History in Munich, emphasizes that even anti-Communism was not the con-stant driving force in Hitler's life, although he used its fear advantageously to motivate a nation. Broszat writes:

Only his anti-Semitic mania was stronger and grew to the proportions of a negative religion. Whatever psychological interpretations of his life experience may indicate, Hitler's hatred of the Jews made up the most constant factor in all his willful polit-ical life. It was the dominant aggressive drive, possibly the only one of his ideolog-ical "convictions" which was not open to opportunistic manipulation. While there are crass discrepancies between the ideological phraseology and the reality of Na-zism almost everywhere else, in this matter the singlemindedness of the possessed is evident. He was true to his idea and carried his anti-Jewish hate propaganda to the extreme of systematic, assembly line genocide.[7]

A good historical illustration of this obsession occurred as World War II drew to a close. At the end of 1944 the Soviet Union had penetrated Hungary. At a time when the Nazi armies should have been mustering forces to secure lines

---

6. Hitler, *Mein Kampf*, pp. 75–77.
7. Martin Broszat, *German National Socialism, 1919–1945*, trans. Kurt Rosenbaum and Inge Pauli Boehm (Santa Barbara, Calif.: Cleo Press, 1966), pp. 51–52.

and transport material to hold back the Soviets, Hitler enraged his generals by insisting they use the transports and tie up the railway lines to try to get the last one-third of Hungarian Jewry to the Auschwitz extermination camp.

THE EXCITEMENT OF WAR

When World War I broke out in 1914, Hitler was ecstatic. A chance photograph of a crowd in Munich shows his elation upon hearing the proclamation of war. He was twenty-five years old and knew where he belonged. Begging permission to enter a Bavarian regiment in spite of his Austrian nationality, he was enlisted in the 1st Company of the 16th Bavarian Reserve Infantry Regiment. Rudolf Hess, who became an early member of the Nazi Party (as well as Hitler's private secretary, deputy, and Reich minister), was also a member of that regiment. Soon they were sent to the front lines of the fierce First Battle of Ypres. During the war Hitler worked as a communications messenger between the field company and headquarters. His letters convey an astounding excitement with the war and a compulsive restlessness to do all he could for the fatherland. He exhibited massive release of pent-up emotion as he took part in approximately fifty military engagements. Certainly brave, he was wounded twice, received the coveted Iron Cross, yet never rose above corporal. His superiors agreed that he was an extremely odd individual who could not be made sergeant because of an inability to command respect. An impassioned soldier who never grumbled, Hitler was loathed by many of his comrades. One soldier has noted that Hitler would sit "in the corner of our mess holding his head between his hands, in deep contemplation. Suddenly he would leap up and, running about excitedly, say that in spite of our big guns, victory would be denied us, for the invisible foes of the German people [the Jews and Marxists] were a greater danger than the biggest cannon of the enemy."[8]

THE FORMING OF THE NAZI PARTY

When the war ended Adolf Hitler was in a military hospital recovering from temporary blindness incurred from a British gassing. He was devastated by the armistice and believed that Germany had been "stabbed in the back" by the "November criminals" who signed the surrender. In a period of massive unemployment due to the return of soldiers and a deteriorating economy, thirty-year-old Hitler was appointed as an "Enlightenment Commando," an instruction officer whose job was to educate soldiers against the "polluting philosophies" of democracy, socialism, and pacifism. In opposition to the new democratic Wei-

---

8. William L. Shirer, *The Rise and Fall of the Third Reich: A History of Nazi Germany* (Greenwich, Conn.: Fawcett, 1959), p. 54. Compare Werner Maser, *Hitler's Letters and Notes*, trans. Arnold Pomerans (New York: Bantam, 1976), pp. 39–95 for reproductions and translations of Hitler's letters from home. The chance photograph of Hitler in the crowd is reproduced by Maser on page 47, as well as a photograph of Hitler with a group on sick leave, p. 95.

mar Republic, the old conservative civil service and judicial system had remained intact. The army fostered the conservative views even though it had sworn to serve the new republic. In addition, radical groups to the right and to the left, armed initially to protect the eastern frontier, turned their attention to the overthrow of the government. Political murders took place, as well as coups in various states. Numerous small political parties were formed, and Hitler was sent to investigate one of them in September 1919.

A few days later, he became the seventh committee member of the German Workers' Party—soon to be called the Nationalist Socialist German Workers' Party. Hitler explained:

> I should never have joined one of the existing parties . . . however, this ridiculously small foundation with its handful of members seemed to me to have the advantage that it had not yet hardened into an "organization," but seemed to offer to the individual the chance for real personal activity. For this was the advantage which was bound to result: here one would still be able to work, and the smaller the movement was, the easier it would be to bring it into the right shape. Here the contents, the goal, and the way could still be fixed.[9]

In April 1920 Hitler resigned from the army to devote himself full time to the party. In August the party changed its name, and in July 1921 he became its permanent chairman.

The Nazi Party took on his character as he proved himself to be a rabble-rouser and a master of crowd psychology. In 1920 almost two thousand people crowded into the large auditorium where the fledgling party held its first mass meeting and announced the Twenty-Five Points of the Nazi program. Hitler held most of the audience in the palm of his hand as applause and shouts of joy drowned out the objections from demonstrators.[10]

The Twenty-Five Points were mainly an appeal to the masses. Although Hitler reaffirmed them in 1926, he dispensed with many once he was in power. They called for an end to the Versailles Treaty and demanded more land for the German population. They contained a strong appeal for German citizens to be represented in government and for foreigners to leave Germany, so that German citizens could have work. Equality for citizens, nationalization of business trusts, shared profits from wholesale trade, land reform, provision for the elderly, education for the poor, protection from child labor, organization of youth clubs, the death penalty for "sordid criminals" (such as usurers and profiteers), and a "ruthless prosecution of those whose activities are injurious to the common interests" made up this hodgepodge of promises designed to recruit a majority

9. Hitler, *Mein Kampf*, p. 300. It is interesting that Hitler was appointed an instruction officer *after* he stood up in an Army meeting and railed against a man defending the Jewish people (p. 289). Ironically, his ridicule of a professor at the meeting of the German Workers' Party he was to investigate brought him to the attention of the GWP Committee as well.

10. Ibid., pp. 511–14.

of the population to the Nazi cause. In a forewarning of things to come, Article Four stated: "None but members of the nation may be citizens of the State. None but those of German blood, whatever their creed, may be members of the nation. *No Jew, therefore, may be a member of the nation.*" Articles Five and Six then went on to state that a non-citizen was only "a guest," and that voting and appointments to government posts were "enjoyed by the citizen of the State alone." Article Twenty-Four displayed many loopholes in the religious views of the Party when it declared:

> We demand liberty for religious denominations in the State, so far as they are not a danger to it and do not militate against the moral feelings of the German race. The Party, as such, stands for positive Christianity, but does not bind itself in the matter of creed to any particular confession. It combats the Jewish-materialist spirit within us and without us, and is convinced that our nation can only achieve permanent health from within on the principle: THE COMMON INTEREST BEFORE SELF.

The proclamation ended with another half truth: "The leaders of the Party swear to go straight forward—if necessary to sacrifice their lives—in securing fulfilment of the foregoing Points."[11]

Hitler and his minions would indeed go forward. By 1921 there were three thousand members in the party; by 1923, the number had increased to seventeen thousand, including General Erich von Ludendorff of World War I fame.[12]

Hitler had an innate ability for political organization. For example, in 1921 he organized the *Sturm Abtelungen*, the "storm-troopers," soon nicknamed the SA or Brownshirts. This was formal recognition of squads of hoodlums that had been operating in 1920 under the command of ex-convict Emil Maurice. The SA were used as an offensive force, parading with swastikas unfurled and crushing demonstrations against the party. Soon notoriety accompanied their exploits against socialists and Communists, and the Nazi treasury began to grow through contributions to the cause.[13]

Workers for the Nazi propaganda mill distributed millions of leaflets in the early years, billing their party as the only true representative of the people's interests. They also advertised Hitler's mass meetings ("War invalids free, Jews not admitted"). They purchased their own weekly paper, the *Völkischer Beobachter* (the "Racist Observer"), and as inflation increased they continually fanned popular hatreds against the Weimar Republic, the Versailles Treaty, the Jews, the Marxists, and democracy. A large demonstration was called on Sunday, January 14, 1923, in Munich to protest the Weimar Republic in general and French

11. Roselle Chartock and Jack Spencer, eds., *The Holocaust Years: Society on Trial* (New York: Bantam, 1978), pp. 135–36. All Twenty-Five Points of the Nazi program are found on pages 132–36.
12. Joachim C. Fest, *The Face of the Third Reich: Portraits of the Nazi Leadership*, trans. Michael Bullock (New York: Pantheon, 1970), pp. 20–23.
13. Bullock, *Hitler*, p. 48.

occupation of the Ruhr district in particular. Advertising leaflets were addressed to "National Socialists! Anti-Semites!" Nearly eighty thousand people assembled to demonstrate.[14]

By November 1923 inflation in Germany was at its worst (4.2 trillion marks per dollar), and most people's life savings were wiped out. Other countries of Europe were also experiencing social and political turmoil. In 1921, Benito Mussolini founded the Fascist Party in an Italy that suffered from wartime debt, acute postwar depression, unemployment, social unrest, and weak government. In 1922, while threatening to march on Rome, he was invited by the king to form a new government. He did.

MEIN KAMPF

Hitler, aware of all this, believed the time was right to overthrow the Munich government. His plan was to march on Berlin after that. But the action in Munich was a near fatal error for Hitler. What later became known as the Nazi Beer Hall *Putsch* on Munich was a dismal failure. Hitler was one of the first to flee as eighteen Nazis were killed and many others wounded. Only the venerable General Ludendorff remained erect, bravely marching through the police line. None of the SA followed him and he was immediately arrested. Hermann Göring, a popular and highly decorated fighter pilot who had joined the Nazi Party, was badly wounded. He was carried to a nearby bank where a Jewish man administered first aid that probably saved his life (during the Crystal Night pogrom in 1938, Göring would reprimand Reinhard Heydrich for not killing *more* Jews, rather than destroying so much valuable property). Hitler was hysterical at his failure and contemplated suicide. Nevertheless, he pulled himself together, secretly blaming his men for the failure. He accepted responsibility and arrest, and he turned his trial for treason into a propaganda victory. The conservative tribunal of judges sentenced him to only five years in prison. He served less than a year.[15]

In the Landsberg Prison, Hitler was treated like a special guest, in a well-furnished private room with an impressive view. It was here he dictated the first drafts of *Mein Kampf* ("My Struggle"—a book he wanted to entitle, "Four and a Half Years of Struggle against Lies, Stupidity and Cowardice"). *Mein Kampf* was a reiteration of racial theory and nationalistic slogans developed in the nineteenth century and permeating the early twentieth. They appear on page after page as he rambles on a wide range of topics, including politics, culture, history, literature, art, and even sex. It explains how the superior German Aryan race must expand, and even includes a blueprint for the conquest of the world.

14. This leaflet is reproduced in the appendix to volume 1 of *Mein Kampf*, pp. 558–59. Note pp. 517–59 for many others.
15. Note Shirer, *The Rise and Fall of the Third Reich*, pp.104–19 for a detailed account of the Putsch and the trial. Compare Fest, *The Face of the Third Reich*, pp. 23–26, and Fritz K. Ringer, ed., *The German Inflation of 1923* (New York: Oxford U., 1969).

"TO CREATE A HIGHER HUMANITY"—THE STATE

Mein Kampf posits the state as the means by which the purity of the race is maintained (an idea we have seen in Chamberlain and others), portraying history as a struggle between pure and impure races. Hitler wrote:

> The State is a means to an end. Its end is the preservation and the promotion of a community of physically and psychically equal living beings. This very preservation comprises first the racial stock and thereby it permits the free development of all the forces slumbering in this race. . . . Thus the highest purpose of the folkish State is the care for the preservation of those racial primal elements which, supplying culture, create the beauty and dignity of a higher humanity. We, as Aryans, are therefore able to imagine a State only to be the living organism of a nationality which not only safeguards the preservation of that nationality, but which, by a further training of its spiritual and ideal abilities, leads it to the highest freedom.[16]

"Thus a folkish State primarily will have to lift marriage out of the level of a permanent race degradation," continued Hitler, "in order to give it the consecration of that institution which is called upon to beget images of the Lord and not deformities half man and half ape."[17]

Hitler criticized missionary organizations of Christian churches (Protestant and Catholic) for sinning "against the image of the Lord Whose importance is stressed most of all by them." He claimed that instead of spending time "annoying the negroes with missions" they should rather teach "unhealthy parents" to take in Aryan orphans and not to raise their own racially inferior children. "While our European peoples, the Lord be praised and thanked, fall into a state of physical and moral leprosy," Hitler mockingly complained, "the pious missionary wanders to Central Africa and established negro missions." The state, therefore, must make up for this neglect. Hitler stated:

> Thereby the State has to appear as the guardian of a thousand years' future, in the face of which the wish and the egoism of the individual appears as nothing and has to submit. It has to put the most modern medical means at the service of this knowledge. It has to declare unfit for propagation everybody who is visibly ill and has inherited a disease and it has to carry this out in practice. . . . He who is not physically and mentally healthy and worthy must not perpetuate his misery in the body of his child. Here the folkish State has to achieve the most enormous work of education. Some day it will appear as a greater deed than the most victorious wars of our present bourgeois era.[18]

Couched in moral and humanitarian language, and based on his zoological perspective of breeding, one can easily see the foundation of Hitler's later euthan-

16. Hitler, *Mein Kampf*, pp. 594–95.
17. Ibid., p. 606.
18. Ibid., pp. 608–9.

asia and extermination programs. Also ascertainable is his later use of the medical profession in eugenics programs intended to create the purest of pure Aryan specimens.

THE DEGRADATION OF JEWS AND BLACKS

As we noted in his earlier statements, Adolf Hitler in *Mein Kampf* portrays the Jewish people as a race of parasites and infectious vermin. He describes them as conniving and unscrupulous in their dealings with other "honest" but "naive" races. He says they are seeking control of other races—in fact, control of the world. Hitler maintained that the Jews, unable to hold their own land, were feeding on the lands of others.

Today, many of the anti-Semitic organizations in the United States use "Zionism" and "Israel" as code words for "Jews" when speaking of their "elimination" and "eradication" (see chapter 18). It is noteworthy that Hitler believed the Jewish race's inferiority rendered it incapable of holding (or even wanting to hold) its own land. He proclaimed:

> For while Zionism tries to make the other part of the world believe that the national self-consciousness of the Jew finds satisfaction in the creation of a Palestinian State, the Jews again most slyly dupe the stupid *goiim*. [Jewish colloquial expression: Gentile men or women.] They have no thought of building up a Jewish State in Palestine, so that they might perhaps inhabit it, but they only want a central organization of their international world cheating, endowed with prerogatives, withdrawn from the seizure of others: a refuge for convicted rascals and a high school for future rogues.[19]

Ironically, Hitler's negative role led to the founding of a Jewish state more than two decades after these words were penned.

Hitler used every propaganda ploy possible to inspire paranoia, fear, and hate toward the Jewish people. He falsely characterized Jews as prominent race polluters, while degrading blacks and others as well. *Mein Kampf* expounds:

> For hours the black-haired Jew boy, diabolic joy in his face, waits in ambush for the unsuspecting girl whom he defiles with his blood and thus robs her from her people. With the aid of all means he tries to ruin the racial foundations of the people to be enslaved. Exactly as he himself systematically demoralizes women and girls, he is not scared from pulling down the barriers of blood and race for others on a large scale. It was and is the Jews who bring the negro to the Rhine, always with the same concealed thought and the clear goal of destroying, by the bastardization which would necessarily set in, the white race which they hate, to throw it down from its cultural and political height and in turn to rise personally to the position of master.[20]

19. Ibid., pp. 447–48.
20. Ibid., pp. 448–49.

"For a racially pure people, conscious of its blood," affirmed Hitler, "can never be enslaved by the Jew."

THE "SPIRITUAL LEVEL" OF PROPAGANDA

In those difficult economic periods, Hitler was speaking to a receptive audience. And Europeans had been prepared for his message by centuries of Jewish stereotypes and caricatures. *Mein Kampf* gives insight into Hitler's method of propaganda—and to methods of his modern followers. He wrote:

> All propaganda has to be popular and has to adapt its spiritual level to the perception of the least intelligent of those towards whom it intends to direct itself. Therefore its spiritual level has to be screwed the lower, the greater the mass of people which one wants to attract . . .
>
> The great masses' receptive ability is only very limited, their understanding is small, but their forgetfulness is great. As a consequence of these facts, all effective propaganda has to limit itself only to a very few points and to use them like slogans until even the very last man is able to imagine what is intended by such a word.[21]

Hitler believed that propaganda and tight organization went together. "In every really great revolutionary movement propaganda will first have to spread the idea of this movement," he noted. "That means, it will untiringly try to make clear to the others the new train of thought, to draw them over to its own ground, *or at least make them doubtful of their own previous conviction.*"

Hitler believed in keeping the active membership of the Nazi Party minimal in relation to the total population. Most people would be kept in line because "they will quietly consider themselves followers, but they will decline to manifest this publicly by membership." This Hitler refers to as "passive" support. The few not thoroughly indoctrinated with the movement's slogans would have the "new view of life . . . forced upon them."[22]

APPARENT DEFEAT

Upon his release from prison in December 1924, Adolf Hitler was in no position to force the German people to do anything. The Nazi Party as well as its propaganda mill were banned. The leadership was fragmented, and Hitler was on probation. There was even a movement by Bavarian state police to deport him to Austria. To make matters for the Nazi movement worse, the German economy was beginning to pick up. A new currency, the "gold mark" (worth 1 trillion old marks), was introduced a week after the Beer Hall *Putsch*. Coupled with a new spurt of American investment, the massive inflationary spiral was

21. Ibid., pp. 232, 234.
22. Hitler conveyed these ideas in his section, "Propaganda and Organization," near the end of *Mein Kampf*. Note especially pages 849–53 for those statements quoted. Italics mine.

curbed. In 1925 the moderate right wing's candidate for president, Field Marshal Paul von Hindenburg, was elected. A trusted figure, he pledged to support the constitution of the Weimar Republic. His election, moreover, seemed to underscore economic recovery. Unemployment fell, real wages increased, and retail sales were up. During the good years from 1925 to 1929, moderate political parties did very well; extremist parties, both of the right and the left, fared badly. Germany seemingly was turning into a paradise. Journalist William L. Shirer reminisces:

> My own acquaintance with Germany began in those days. I was stationed in Paris and occasionally in London at that time, and fascinating though those capitals were to a young American happy to have escaped from the incredible smugness and emptiness of the Calvin Coolidge era, they paled a little when one came to Berlin and Munich. A wonderful ferment was working in Germany. Life seemed more free, more modern, more exciting than in any place I had ever seen. Nowhere else did the art or the intellectual life seem so lively. In contemporary writing, painting, architecture, in music and drama, there were new currents and fine talents. And everywhere there was an accent on youth. One sat up with the young people all night in the sidewalk cafés, the plush bars, the summer camps, on a Rhineland steamer or in a smoke-filled artist's studio and talked endlessly about life. They were a healthy, carefree, sun-worshiping lot, and they were filled with an enormous zest for living to the full and in complete freedom. The old oppressive Prussian spirit seemed to be dead and buried. Most Germans one met—politicians, writers, editors, artists, professors, students, businessmen, labor leaders—struck you as being democratic, liberal, even pacifist. One scarcely heard of Hitler or the Nazis except as butts of jokes.[23]

The "Roaring Twenties" were at a high point in the United States as well; no one seemed to lose on the stock market. In a vicious world economic cycle, investors poured money into Germany, Germany repaid debts to France and England, and France and England repaid debts to the United States. With the stock market crash in 1929, the economies of all of these nations were crippled, and the United States had no international trade to spare it from economic collapse.[24]

RESURGENCE

Hitler did not give up. He put his propaganda mill back in action and reorganized his party. No one, however, worried about him. In 1928 the Nazis received only 810,000 votes out of 31 million cast. They occupied only a dozen seats in the Reichstag out of 491.

---

23. Shirer, *The Rise and Fall of the Third Reich*, p. 168.
24. Note John K. Galbraith, *Great Crash, Nineteen Twenty-Nine* (Boston: Houghton Mifflin, 1979). Compare Charles P. Kindleberger, *The World in Depression, 1929–1939* (Berkeley, Calif.: U. of California, 1973).

Yet ominous signs appeared on the horizon. The Evangelical Church Congress, a newly formed body of elected representatives from all the churches of the provinces, met in 1927 in Königsberg. Their responsibility was to debate social and political problems of the day, and then issue a "Christian" statement. The theme was "*Volk* and Fatherland." They declared the *Volkstum* ("national character") to be of divine origin. In the present situation, no duty was more pressing upon the Christian than its exaltation. German Evangelical Christianity was to be recognized as possessing its own special national character. The church, the Congress's representatives said, must not remain silent when Christianity and German national character were being torn asunder. Service to the fatherland and service to God were identical. As one of the leading young theologians of the period, Paul Althaus, urged in the conference's major speech: "German-Christian and Christian-German coherence stands as a clear, a transparent and an evident fact. The greatest moments and the most splendid figures in our national history bear witness to this." He stressed that the church must be alive to the "Jewish menace to our *Volkstum*."[25]

When economic depression spread worldwide, the Nazis were ready. In their pursuit of the reins of government, they learned to be all things to all men. In stark contrast to the right-wing majority, a left-wing Nazism had developed, under the leadership of Gregor and Otto Strasser. It adopted the full propaganda value of the Nazi slogan, "the common good before individual gain." Left-wing Nazism forged inroads into the labor movement, and party "factory cells" were created. The central party organization had departments of foreign affairs, business alliance sections, and a very strong youth division—resembling our Boy Scouts and Girl Scouts. The Nazi political machine was systematized down to the city block. In 1928 the Nazis decided, in the words of *Der Angriff* (one of their forty-nine newspapers), to "enter Parliament in order to supply ourselves in the arsenal of democracy with its own weapons . . . If democracy is so stupid as to give us free meal tickets and salaries for this purpose, that is its affair . . . We come as enemies; as the wolf bursts into the flock, so we come."[26] In 1929, party membership rose to 178,000, increasing to 862,000 in 1931 and over one million in 1932. By that time there were many new party organizations, such as the Union of German Nazi Lawyers, the Nazi Teachers' Association, the Union of Nazi Physicians, the German Women's Order, and the Union of Nazi Students. Hitler continued to spew forth venom against the Jewish community and the republic, always forecasting imminent doom.[27]

The Nazi Party grew as the economy declined (much as racism and racist incidents rose in the United States during the recession of the 1980s). Germany

25. Richard Gutteridge, *Open Thy Mouth for the Dumb! The German Evangelical Church and the Jews, 1879–1950* (Oxford: Basil Blackwell, 1976), pp. 42–43.
26. Goebbels' warning may be found translated into English in Tony Edwards, *History Broadsheets: Hitler and Germany 1919–1933* (Edison, N.J.: Heinemann, 1972), 8:33.
27. T. L. Jarman, *The Rise and Fall of Nazi Germany* (New York: New American Library, 1961), pp. 116–17.

began once again to suffer numerous bankruptcies of small businesses. Two million were unemployed in 1929, four and one-half million in 1931, and six million in 1933. Unfortunately the government of the Weimar Republic was impotent to control the situation. No single party had enough votes to form a government or make policy on its own. Against this background of economic suffering, national humiliation, and political weakness, the Nazi Party shocked the world by polling six million votes in the 1930 elections. The Social Democrats won with eight million votes; but the Nazis had 107 seats in the Reichstag, compared to the Social Democrats' 143. Propaganda and organization paid off as Nazi Party membership in 1930 included disproportionately large numbers of white collar workers, small businessmen, civil servants, farmers, and teachers. It was a very broad base from which to work.[28]

The German people were dismayed that those parties committed to maintaining a democratic republic (i.e., the Social Democrats, the Democrats, and the Catholic Centre parties), were unable to agree on basic economic policy. They were also too conservative to protest en masse through the Communist Party (although this party had made some gains). As Stalinist Russia had shown, Communism could be a ghastly form of totalitarianism. The Nazis often repeated simplistic slogans that gave them the appearance of having the answers to unemployment and social upheaval. They asked only for the chance to show their ability.

In the 1932 elections, the Nazis obtained thirteen million votes, making them the largest party in the republic (the Social Democrats polled approximately the same eight million votes). The Nazis still did not have a majority. Advisors to the aging President Paul von Hindenburg believed they could "tame" the Nazis for use by the ailing, conservative party structure. They refused to exercise their other option of allying themselves with the democrats in opposition to the Nazis, hoping eventually to replace the "ungodly" parliamentary democracy with a more active conservative system.

Their miscalculation was disastrous. On January 30, 1933, a reluctant Hindenburg appointed Adolf Hitler Chancellor of the Weimar Republic—the very republic Hitler had sworn to destroy.[29]

28. A provocative discussion of the rise of Nazism during economic decline is found in Jurgen Kuczynski, *Germany: Economic and Labour Conditions under Fascism* (New York: Greenwood Press, 1968), pp. 11–92.
29. Arnold J. Heidenheimer, *The Governments of Germany*, 3d ed. (New York: Thomas Y. Crowell, 1971), pp. 22–24.

6

Consolidation of Power and the Nuremberg Laws

"Someday the world will know that Hitler was right. The white people in this country will get fed up with our rotting civilization, and we'll have the party and organization they can turn to," declared Chicago's Nazi leader Frank Collin, sitting at his desk amid racist signs and banners directed at blacks and Jews. "The majority of the people will just sit back and watch the world on television," he added, "and they won't care if they're watching Nazis or Martians, so long as they don't run out of pretzels and beer."

Collin spoke just as the Illinois Appellate Court ruled that his Nationalist Socialist Party of America could march in predominantly Jewish Skokie, Illinois—if they did not wear swastika armbands. This was not good enough for the modern follower of Adolf Hitler, who cursed the "Jew Court." "Execute them," a young aide replied, "Line them up and execute them." Collin agreed.

Although Collin denies it, his father is a Jewish survivor of the Dachau concentration camp. Max Collin immigrated to the United States, changing his name from Cohn when he became a naturalized citizen in 1946, a few months after son Frank was born. His wife was Catholic, and so Frank was raised a Catholic, attending the Infant Jesus of Prague Elementary School and Mendel Catholic High School. Under the influence of a Nazi student in his dorm at Southern Illinois University he soon quit college to work full-time for the National Socialist White People's Party. After rising in the ranks to Midwest coordinator, the NSWPP discovered he was "half Jew" and decided that he "obviously couldn't be a good Nazi." Collin responded by setting up his own party in Chicago, declaring himself the national leader of the "true American Nazis."

He noted to reporter Marv Wilson that "once I learned the truth, I had to make sacrifices . . . I have no life outside the party." Collin at that time claimed to have "the respect of millions of Americans."[1]

His *Führer* had actually gained such massive respect in 1933.

PROPAGANDA, INTIMIDATION, VICTORY

The Berlin opera celebrated Hitler's appointment as chancellor with an opera by Richard Wagner; consequently, Wagnerism blanketed the next decade. Through the Reich Chamber for Fine Arts, the Nazi state became a great patron of the arts, rewarding those participating in the official art of "national socialist realism" and legally restricting, as well as physically intimidating, those refusing to comply with the nazification of culture. As Hitler declared in a speech on September 1, 1933: "Art is a lofty mission that requires the artist to be fanatical; German artists must now answer the call to help undertake the proudest defenses of the German *Volk* by means of German art."[2] Nazi Germany became an adman's paradise, full of artistic illusions of grandeur and progress. Political enemies and racial "inferiors" were blacklisted, losing their teaching positions, professional memberships, and even freedom to express themselves in private studios. This was a pattern applied to other fields as the Nazis consolidated their power.

When Hitler took his oath of office, he declared that he would "employ [his] strength for the welfare of the German people, protect the Constitution and laws of the German people, conscientiously discharge the duties imposed on [him] and conduct [his] affairs of office impartially and with justice to everyone."[3] In actuality, he and his subordinates planned to turn the German nation into a totalitarian state under the guise of a national revival labeled the "Third Reich." The Nazi Party recognized neither constitution nor law, only a hierarchy of local and state political machinery under the direct domination of the Führer, Adolf Hitler.

It was imperative that the Nazis gain total control of the national government as soon as possible. They proposed to do this by spreading and aggravating the fear of a communist revolution in Germany—the "Red Terror." They sought to provoke Communists and socialists into violent anti-Nazi reprisals; reprisals that would serve strictly as propaganda. The ploy did not work. Nevertheless, on February 27, 1933 the Reichstag building burst into flames and burned to the ground. Historians debate whether or not the Nazis set the blaze, but it is clear

1. Marv Wilson, "Father of U.S. Nazi Is Dachau Survivor," *Youngstown Vindicator*, 25 July 1977.
2. Sybil Milton, "Artists In The Third Reich," in Henry Friedlander and Sybil Milton, eds., *The Holocaust: Ideology, Bureaucracy, and Genocide* (Millwood, N.Y.: Kraus International, 1980), p. 116. Every person involved in producing, exhibiting, or distributing any art form (from painting to landscape gardening) was required to have membership in the Reich Chamber of Fine Arts.
3. Lucy Dawidowicz, *The War Against the Jews, 1933–1945* (New York: Holt, Rinehart and Winston, 1975), p. 48.

that it provided the pretext to rid the state of the Communists. Hitler persuaded a dazed President Hindenburg to exercise his constitutional right of emergency powers and allow Chancellor Hitler to suspend civil liberties during the so-called state of emergency. He did so, and the Nazi SA (numbering 400,000) immediately commenced a spree of terrorism against political opponents and "legal" seizure of police powers not already controlled by the Nazi state bureaucracy. Hindenburg furthermore was convinced to dissolve the Reichstag (in which the Nazis did not have a majority) and to call for new parliamentary elections.[4]

The Nazis hoped to pick up a majority in the new elections. For the first time the radio and press of the national government were at their disposal. By outlawing the Communist Party and intimidating anti-Nazi politicians, they believed they could secure more than a hundred additional seats in the Reichstag. In addition, Hitler convinced mighty industrialists such as Karl Bosch and Georg von Schnitzler (of I. G. Farben, the giant chemical conglomerate) that he believed in big industry and was against "socialist" labor. Furthermore, he promised to rearm Germany, an act that would drastically increase the industrialists' profits. Big business, therefore, contributed heavily to the Nazi political campaign.[5]

In spite of all these pressures, the Nazis received only 44 percent of the total vote (17,277,200 out of 39,343,300 cast). This provided them with less than a majority in the Reichstag. To gain a majority would require forging alliances with the conservative nationalists. Hitler, however, in need of more than a majority, immediately asked for passage of the "Law for Removing the Distress of People and Reich," nicknamed the Enabling Act. It required the Reichstag to yield its legislative powers to the chancellor. In essence, it would cease to function during the issuing of emergency legislation. Because this was an alteration of the constitution, Hitler needed a two-thirds majority to pass it. By a combination of terror and lavish promises, he skillfully conned the Catholic Centre Party and the remaining liberals and conservatives to vote for it.

Only the Social Democrats, the moderate socialists, stood firm against him. This took a great deal of courage: on the day of the vote, March 23, 1933, the Reichstag deputies had to march in facing a huge swastika banner behind the podium, passing through solid rows of black-shirted SS (*Schutz Staffel*—an elite "protection" corps) on the outside and many brown-shirted SA on the inside. As Otto Wels, the leader of the Social Democrats, walked to the podium to

4. Note Hermann Göring's use of the "emergency powers" as Prussian Minister of the Interior in Joachim C. Fest, *The Face of the Third Reich: Portraits of the Nazi Leadership*, trans. Michael Bullock (New York: Pantheon, 1970), pp. 76–77. Compare Walter Goerlitz, *History of the German General Staff, 1657–1945*, trans. Brian Battershaw (New York: Frederick A. Praeger, 1962), pp. 276–77 on the SA, and William L. Shirer, *The Rise and Fall of the Third Reich: A History of Nazi Germany* (Greenwich, Conn.: Fawcett, 1959), pp. 267–73 on the Reichstag fire.

5. Note Shirer, *The Rise and Fall of the Third Reich*, p. 265. Compare Martin Broszat, *German National Socialism, 1919–1945*, trans. Kurt Rosenbaum and Inge Pauli Boehm (Santa Barbara, Calif.: Cleo Press, 1966), p. 85.

speak, the chants of Nazi stormtroopers could be heard from the halls: "We want the Bill—or fire and murder." Speaking firmly and with dignity, he reaffirmed that his party would not vote for such a law. To be stripped by the Nazis of their power was one thing, but he explained that his party would still maintain its "dignity." Hitler flew into a rage at this defiance, revealing his savage temper to the delegates. The vote was then taken and Hitler was given emergency powers for four years.[6] By 1937 the Nazis would have the power to renew the Enabling Act. Hitler would not even have to suspend the constitution of the Weimar Republic. He could just circumvent it by its own emergency clause, a good deal of public support, and the treachery of naive Reichstag deputies. He had legally become dictator of Germany.

EARLY PERSECUTION OF THE JEWS

True to his character, Hitler did not abandon his anti-Jewish policy. A rash of legislation and violence ensued. For months the SA had been given free rein to terrorize the Jewish community. On March 11, 1933, in Breslau, for example, the SA looted a department store. When the police interfered, the SA broke into the courtrooms, abducted Jewish judges and lawyers, beat them, and dragged them through the streets. In other cities the same violence took place. Pulled from the sidewalks, Jews were forced to wash the streets, and professionals (doctors, lawyers, teachers, etc.) were pulled from their place of business and tortured. Even when the police wanted to help they could do little, because the SA troops were four times as large as the entire German army. Nazi leader Hermann Göring, Prussian Minister of the Interior at the time, discouraged police protection by stating: "I will ruthlessly set the police at work wherever harm is being done to the German people. But I refuse to make the police the guardians of Jewish department stores."[7] On April 1, 1933 Hitler's government, under the auspices of the SA, initiated an economic boycott against all Jewish businesses. It was followed on April 7 with the "Law for the Restoration of the Professional Civil Service" and the "Law Regarding Admission to the Bar."

"Civil servants who are not of Aryan descent are to be retired," declared the civil service law in section 3:1. This applied "to clerical employees and workers" as well (3:15). The admission to the bar law gave the Third Reich the right to revoke the licenses of lawyers of "non-Aryan descent." In deference to a plea from President Hindenburg on behalf of war veterans, the laws excluded those in positions before August 1, 1914, or those "who fought at the front during the World War for the German Reich or her allies, or whose father or sons were killed in action in the World War." The question immediately arose concerning who was a non-Aryan. The implementation decree on April 11, 1933, clarified:

6. Alan Bullock, *Hitler: A Study in Tyranny*, rev. ed. (New York: Bantam, 1961), pp. 228–29.
7. Lucy Dawidowicz, *The War Against the Jews*, p. 52. The Treaty of Versailles limited the German armed forces to 100,000 men.

"A person is to be regarded as non-Aryan if he is descended from non-Aryan, especially Jewish, parents or grandparents. It is enough for one parent or grandparent to be non-Aryan. This is to be assumed especially if one parent or one grandparent was of the Jewish faith." From this time forward, proof of "Aryan descent" had to be supplied to officials of the Third Reich, resulting in a great scramble to provide proper genealogical trees. Political dissidents were also hurt by these laws. The civil service law, for example, stated that those "whose political activities to date afford no assurance that they will at any time unreservedly support the national state may be dismissed from the service" (4:1). The message quickly went forth to the Aryan German government workers: "Unreservedly support the Nazis or lose your job."[8]

Within three months thirty thousand heads of families were out of work because of the new laws and administrative orders. These included 3,500 of the 7,000 Jewish doctors, 1,200 of the 2,800 Jewish lawyers, and 5,000 of the 6,000 Jewish government employees. Thousands of Jewish musicians, actors, dentists, pharmacists, and merchants were also affected. Soon approximately 20 percent of the members of the German Jewish population had lost their jobs. Jews were even excluded from being judges or jurors. The German public, fully aware of what was going on, rather than protesting en masse the gross infringement of civil rights, vied with one another to obtain the jobs left by vacated Jewry. Local communities, in fact, put further restrictions on Jews in order to alleviate the economic suffering of Aryan Germans. Some communities erected signs at their borders that proudly proclaimed they were now "Jewish free."

On April 25, 1933, the Nazis struck at two firm loves of the Jewish community—their children, and education. In the "Law Against the Overcrowding of German Schools and Institutions of Higher Learning," a quota system was imposed on Jewish students, setting into motion a system that would eventually exclude the Jewish child from German schools and colleges.[9]

It is a common misconception that Hitler began a policy of Jewish extermination as soon as he became dictator. He considered Jews literal vermin, an infectious bacteria that he wanted out of Germany. Accomplishing this proved a perplexing problem for the Third Reich. The rest of the world, being in economic depression, would not take all of Germany's Jews. In addition, most German Jews were unwilling to leave their land of culture. They felt that justice and decency would return, that good German people would soon see Hitler for what he was. The 37,000 Jews who left the country in panic in the spring of 1933 were regarded as deserters by some in the Jewish community. Jews began to adapt to their persecution, finding a false sense of security in the thought that perhaps the worst was over. An organization of Jewish war veterans de-

8. These Laws are translated in a number of anthologies. See for example Lucy Dawidowicz, *A Holocaust Reader* (New York: Behrman House, 1976), pp. 38–42.
9. Arthur D. Morse, *While Six Million Died: A Chronicle of American Apathy* (New York: Random House, 1968), pp. 157–58.

clared: "Nobody can rob us of our German fatherland."[10] They believed that as long as there were laws they could function. After all, Jews had been compromising for centuries.

Anti-Semitic activity at this time was not a matter of clear policy, but was mainly the result of mob activity or the whims of the SA. This is because the nazification of German culture demanded most of the Nazi government's time and energy.

THE NAZIFICATION OF CULTURE

Hitler did not persecute only Jews. Early 1933 concentration camps were filled with more non-Jews than Jews. Hitler was out to stifle the free press, break the trade unions, dismantle other political parties, and keep the church in line—in sum, to silence all opposition. Editors unfriendly to the Nazi regime were replaced (on October 4 a National Press Law would exclude Jews). Intellectual intolerance in the form of massive book burnings took place with pomp and fanfare—books by pacifists, socialists, and Jews were destroyed. Labor was betrayed a day after the May 1, 1933, national celebration of a "Day of National Labor," ostensibly an occasion to show the Nazi government's love for the workers. Trade union leaders were arrested, records and treasuries confiscated, and a giant Nazi German Labor Front organized. The Law for the Reorganization of National Labor was to go into effect January 24, 1934. During the summer of 1933 the Nazi Party became the only legal political party in the nation. Nazi-indoctrinated clergy were encouraged to take over Protestant churches; a deal was struck with the Vatican through more of Hitler's empty promises (more on this in chapter 15). The Gestapo, a secret political police force, penetrated all levels of German society.[11]

THE ECONOMY

Hitler had lowered wages; state governments and economies were consolidated under the totalitarian regime; and Germany began to rearm. The economy began to recover and men were put back to work, but at the high price of personal freedom. Virtually every area of German life was under the control of the Nazi regime, yet most citizens did not seem to care. Fed a steady dosage of propaganda by the press and entertained with massive rallies, parades, and "gifts" from the Führer, the German people swelled with pride at their nation's apparent comeback. Momentum was building.

We must be careful in condemning German citizens for their complicity with

10. Nora Levin, *The Holocaust: The Destruction of European Jewry, 1933–1945* (New York: Thomas Y. Crowell, 1968), p. 60.
11. T. L. Jarman, *The Rise and Fall of Nazi Germany* (New York: New American Library, 1961), pp. 151–68.

nazification; it is all too easy to over-estimate what would have been our own courage under such circumstances. As the Arab oil embargo reached a fervid pitch in the United States during 1973–74, a bumper sticker reading "We Need Oil Not Jews" was spotted on a surgeon's car in a hospital parking lot. (Many more read, "We Need Oil Not Israel.") The unemployed in the United States today, from auto workers to steelworkers, from new Ph.D.'s to engineers, can well empathize with the six million unemployed in Germany who, upon receiving jobs to feed their families, felt gratitude to the Führer.

EDUCATION

The realm of education proved as susceptible to nazification as any other. For years the Nazis had been indoctrinating university students across the nation. Academic youth, in fact, was in the vanguard of the Nazi movement, placing an extraordinary amount of pressure on professors, who, being civil servants, had to parrot the party line or lose their positions. A number of famous academicians, such as Martin Heidegger, the esteemed existentialist philosopher of Freiburg University, gave speeches that helped the Nazis immensely. Richard Strauss, one of the world's great living composers, served as president of the Reich Music Chamber. Book burnings at universities were attended by professors suitably capped and gowned for the auspicious occasions. So thorough was the winning over of Germany's intellectual community that only ten percent of the university teaching force was dismissed during the Nazi purge.[12]

In fact, the educated mind seemed to succumb as quickly (if not more quickly) as the uneducated. Theologian Helmut Thielicke lived through the Holocaust period as a young German pastor, and he testified to this phenomenon:

> At that time I had to learn to revise my ideas about the role of education and intelligence in political matters. The fact is that the intelligent person had at his disposal enough arguments and associations to prove to himself that what he fears isn't true at all. He is also much smarter at assessing the opportunistic chances of getting ahead than the naive spirits. Thus precisely in the intellectual class one could observe lamentable examples of character failure and delusion. In times which demand the utmost of men, intellectual enlightenment is of very little help.[13]

"The uncommitted mind, though it has been highly trained and perhaps has even achieved the eminence of a renowned academic chair," Thielicke warned from personal experience, "all too easily succumbs to the law of least resistance."

12. Note Richard Grunberger, *The 12-Year Reich: A Social History of Nazi Germany, 1933–1945* (New York: Holt, Rinehart and Winston, 1971), pp. 307–8. Compare Beate Ruhm von Oppen, "The Intellectual Resistance," in *The Holocaust: Ideology, Bureaucracy, and Genocide*, pp. 212–13.
13. Helmut Thielicke, *Between Heaven and Earth: Conversations with American Christians*, trans. and ed. John W. Doberstein (New York: Harper & Row, 1965), p. 153.

THE RISE OF THE SS

Those who have dedicated their lives to racist organizations should be reminded that even the most indoctrinated follower is not completely safe in a totalitarian organization of hate. To consolidate his power and avoid losing the support of the general army, Hitler murdered hundreds of his SA leaders during the summer of 1934, including Ernst Röhm, commander of the SA—a man who had stood by Hitler's side during the Beer Hall *Putsch*, served a prison sentence for him, and encouraged him during times of defeat. From this time forward, the elite SS, under Heinrich Himmler, a former chicken farmer responsible only to the Führer, played a more important role than the purged SA. The SS murdered many members of the SA during the purge, a grisly harbinger of its role during the Holocaust. While murdering loyal followers, Hitler instructed that others be destroyed as well—among them, the anti-Semitic Father Bernhard Stempfle, the priest of the Hieronymite Order who helped in the editing of *Mein Kampf*.[14]

On August 3, 1934, Hindenburg died, and Hitler proclaimed himself President as well as Chancellor. Members in the armed forces were now required to take an oath of allegiance, stating: "I swear by God this sacred oath, that I will render unconditional obedience to Adolf Hitler, the Führer of the German Reich and people, Supreme Commander of the Armed Forces, and will be ready as a brave soldier to risk my life at any time for this oath."[15] Hitler signed a treaty of neutrality with Poland earlier in the year, as the Nazi Propaganda Ministry continued successfully to portray Hitler as a prophet of peace in a Europe threatened by atheistic Communism. On the home front, Hitler was described as an advocate of law and order.[16]

THE NUREMBERG LAWS

SEGREGATING JEWS

On September 15, 1935, the notorious Nuremberg Laws, laws that attacked every Jew in Germany, were enacted. They were the culmination of the first phase of measures intended to sever the Jewish people from German society. A massive propaganda campaign in earlier months humiliated Jewish children in classrooms. Those remaining Jews—the ones who had not been intimidated

14. Goerlitz, *History of the German General Staff*, pp. 284–89.
15. The oath may be found in many sources. Note Shirer, *The Rise and Fall of the Third Reich*, p. 314.
16. In 1939 the Nazis would use their lawyers and foreign specialists to compile a document of over seven hundred pages seeking to prove that they were within their legal rights in attacking Poland. In fact, they asserted that Poland and Britain wanted war, and the Nazis were only defending themselves. For this facade of law and order on the international scene, note *Documents on the Events Preceding the Outbreak of the War*, compiled and published by the German Foreign Office in Berlin, 1939; and by the German Library of Information in New York, 1940. On the home front, refer to Broszat, *German National Socialism*, pp. 88–89.

into leaving—were moved to the back of the room to sit on "ghetto benches." Borrowing from laws used at times in the Middle East and in the American South, the Nazis segregated parks, even labeling park benches "only for Aryans" or "only for Jews." Jews were not permitted to walk on certain streets and had to fear sporadic hostile reactions from the noble Teutons. If any Jew complained to the police, he was often treated with contempt—in some cases whitewashed to the knees and paraded through the streets with signs that read: "I am a Jew, but I will never again complain about the Nazis." Jews found themselves no longer welcome in homes of former friends or organizations they once attended. On May 21, 1935, Jews were totally excluded from the armed forces.[17]

The Nuremberg Laws officially deprived the Jewish people—even those whose families had lived there for centuries—of citizenship in Germany. The thirteen supplementary decrees to those laws (the last published July 1, 1943) would systematically eliminate Jews from Germany altogether.

Both of the Nuremberg Laws were given by direct order from Hitler and were adopted unanimously by the Reichstag. The "Reich Citizenship Law" declared in part that a "citizen of the Reich is only that subject, who is of German or kindred blood and who, through his conduct, shows that he is both desirous and fit to serve faithfully the German people and Reich" (2:2). Only such "citizens" could from this time forward enjoy "full political rights in accordance with the provisions of the Laws" (2:3). Article three declared that supplemental decrees would follow to clarify this law.[18]

The "Law for the Protection of German Blood and German Honor" began:

> Thoroughly convinced by the knowledge that the purity of German blood is essential for the further existence of the German people and inturned by the inflexible will to safeguard the German nation for the entire future, the Reichs Parliament (Reichstag) has resolved upon the following law unanimously which is promulgated herewith:
> 1. Marriages between Jews and nationals of German or kindred blood are forbidden. Marriages concluded in defiance of this law are void, even if, for the purpose of evading this law, they are concluded abroad. . . .
> 2. Relations outside marriage between Jews and nationals of German kindred blood are forbidden.

Jews were also forbidden to employ female domestic help "of German or kindred blood" (3) and "to hoist the Reichs and national flag" (4). Marriage and sexual violations of these laws were to be punished by hard labor and imprisonment

---

17. Levin, *The Holocaust*, pp. 68–73. To review signs, documents, and pictures of this humiliation and propaganda campaign, see Zosa Szajkowski, *An Illustrated Sourcebook on the Holocaust*, 3 vols. (New York: KTAV Publishing, 1977–79), vol. 1.
18. "The Reich Citizenship Law of 15 Sept. 1935," Nuremberg Document PS 1416, National Archives Record Group 238, Washington, D.C., reproduced in John Mendelsohn, ed., *The Holocaust*, 18 vols. (New York: Garland Publishing, 1982), vol. 1, *Legalizing the Holocaust: The Early Phase, 1933–1939*, p. 23.

(later on one could be sterilized for an infraction; it was a serious offense). Other provisions initially provided for penalties of fines and up to one year's imprisonment.[19]

DEFINING JEWS

But the Nazis had a problem that had plagued racial theorists for decades: Who was a Jew? How much Jewish blood does it take to make one Jewish? After much debate and deliberation between their officials and their lawyers, they drew up the first supplementary decree on November 14, 1935. Its articles shed light on the *mischling*, the person of mixed blood. It explained:

> 2. (2) An individual of mixed Jewish blood, is one who descended from one or two grandparents who were racially full Jews, insofar as does not count as a Jew according to Article 5, paragraph 2. One grandparent shall be considered as full-blooded Jew if he or she belonged to the Jewish religious community. . . .
>
> 4. (1) A Jew cannot be a citizen of the Reich. He has no right to vote in political affairs; he cannot occupy a public office. . . .
>
> 5. (1) A Jew is anyone who descended from at least three grandparents who were racially full Jews. Article 2, par. 2, second sentence will apply.
>
> 5. (2) A Jew is also one who descended from two full Jewish parents, if:
> (a) he belonged to the Jewish religious community at the time this law was issued, or joined the community later.
> (b) he was married to a Jewish person, at the time the law was issued, or married one subsequently.
> (c) he is the offspring from a marriage with a Jew, in the sense of Section 1, which was contracted after the Law for the protection of German blood and honor became effective . . . September 15, 1935.
> (d) he is the offspring of an extramarital relationship, with a Jew, according to section 1, and will be born out of wedlock after July 31, 1936.[20]

This detailed code is illustrative of a proper, educated, cultured people gone racially mad. In some areas the absurdity reached epidemic proportions, labeling dogs owned by Jews as "Jewish." Under those circumstances, a Jew had to make sure his "Jewish" dog did not mate with an "Aryan" dog, or he would be in for a great deal of trouble!

In spite of this legal mumbo jumbo, the *mischling* problem did not go away; it continued to plague the Nazi bureaucrats. Further decrees defining half-Jews and quarter-Jews, "first degree" and "second degree" *mischling* were added to the law code, tying up law enforcement agencies and court agendas for years.

19. "Law for the Protection of German Blood and German Honor of 15 September 1935," Nuremberg Document PS 2000, ibid., p. 24.
20. "First Regulation to the Reich Citizenship Law of 14 November 1935 pertaining to Jews," PS 1417, ibid., pp. 31–32.

Mischling status was thought to be more favorable than that of full Jew, and many people did almost anything to obtain a more acceptable genealogical tree. Religious affiliation meant nothing now—a second generation German Christian might be labeled Jewish with a stroke of a pen, eliminating his citizenship and later marking him for deportation.

For many the time, energy, and struggle was all for nought. In the end, *mischling* were exterminated as well.[21]

---

21. Some of the legalistic hair splitting involving the Nazi courts is discussed in Levin, *The Holocaust*, pp. 472–76. The effect of "paradigms of punishment" on the victims of a "legal" Holocaust is analyzed by Helen Fein, *Accounting for Genocide: National Responses and Jewish Victimization During the Holocaust* (New York: The Free Press, 1979), pp. 316–18.

7

From the Olympics to the Crystal Night

"The crime is beyond exaggeration," declared *Newsweek* magazine on March 28, 1983, regarding the crowd of white patrons who watched silently as four white men in a New Bedford, Massachusetts, bar repeatedly raped a woman. "Didn't they at least owe her a phone call to the police?" the periodical questioned. Legally, no. There is no national law against sins of omission toward a stranger. Brooklyn Law School professor Jerome Leitner noted: "A baby slips off a dock into three feet of water. All an adult had to do to save him is get his feet wet. Can he stand there with impunity? Yes. Is he his brother's keeper? Anglo-Saxon law says no."[1]

In every decade since World War II, such accounts of horror abetted by apathy have been publicized. In 1964, in a residential area of New York City, twenty-eight-year-old Catherine Genovese was stabbed in three separate attacks within a forty-minute period while neighbors refused to get involved. No one even called the police during the prolonged assault and final murder.

Psychologists suggest that when a number of strong, able-bodied individuals (as opposed to only one) partially populate such a crowd, the strong people are less likely to initiate a rescue.

"WITHOUT ANY INDICATION OF ABATEMENT"

The "Night of Broken Glass," or Crystal Night, and the events leading up to it exemplify the many occasions of crowd passivity in the midst of Jewish suf-

---

1. "The Duties of a Bystander," *Newsweek*, 28 March 1983, p. 79.

fering. The *New York Times* reported on November 10, 1938, that the Nazi vandals "hacked away at windows [of Jewish shops], accompanied by the laughs and jokes of onlookers . . . large crowds followed the proceedings and were politely asked by the raiders and their accompaniers not to block the sidewalks." The reporter noted in passing: "However, that the onlookers were not wholly sympathetic to the proceedings was evidenced by the faces of some of them."[2] On November 11 the newspaper reported that "generally the crowds were silent and the majority seemed gravely disturbed by the proceedings . . . in one case a person in the crowd shouted, 'Why not hang the owner in the window?'"[3]

Even before the Nuremberg Laws, the conscience of the German population had been seared by a constant barrage of anti-Semitic Nazi propaganda. On August 6, 1935, the American consul general in Berlin, Douglas Jenkins, sent a leaflet found on the street to his Secretary of State because it "resembled the sort of propaganda published regularly in Streicher's weekly *Der Stürmer*." The translation of the leaflet read:

GERMAN CITIZEN, DO YOU KNOW:

THAT THE JEW—oppresses . . . your Child, rapes . . . your Wife, rapes . . . your Sister, rapes . . . your Fiancée, murders . . . your Parents, steals . . . your Property, ridicules . . . your Honor, derides . . . your Manners, destroys . . . your Church, spoils . . . your Culture, corrupts . . . your Race.

THAT THE JEW—lies to you, robs you, deceives you, calls you a beast.

THAT JEWISH—doctors slowly murder you, lawyers never help you attain your right, stores sell you spoiled foodstuffs, butcher shops are dirtier than pig-sties.

THAT THE JEW—has to do all the above according to the laws of the Talmud as it is for him a deed pleasing to his God.

GERMAN CITIZENS—THEREFORE DEMAND: Hard labor, cancelation of civil rights, confiscation of property and deportation for Germans who have sexual intercourse with non-Aryans. In cases of repetition, the death penalty. Their children are to be sterilized and cannot become citizens. They and the non-Aryan parent are to be deported. Women and girls who of their own free will start an affair with a Jew, are never to be granted legal protection. Hard labor for deceit and frauds.

THE JEW LIVES OF LIES AND WILL DIE OF THE TRUTH.[4]

Jenkins in his confidential report noted that the anti-Jewish campaign was being continued "without any indication of abatement," and that the German government prided itself in saying the campaign would be carried on "in a legal and orderly manner." "Signs 'Jews are not Wanted Here' are still displayed at the

2. "Berlin Raids Reply To Death of Envoy," *New York Times*, 10 November 1938.

3. "Nazis Smash, Loot and Burn Jewish Shops and Temples Until Goebbels Calls Halt," *New York Times*, 11 November 1938, p. 4. This report was continued from page 1.

4. Douglas Jenkins, "Anti-Jewish Propaganda," Report to the U.S. Secretary of State, 6 August 1935, Dept. of State Central Decimal File 862.4016/1533, National Archives Record Group 59, Washington D.C., reproduced in John Mendelsohn, ed., *The Holocaust* (New York: Garland Publishing, 1982), vol. 4, *Propaganda and Aryanization, 1938–1944*, pp. 112–16.

entrance of many villages and smaller towns," Jenkins wrote, "and considerable anti-Jewish activity has also been noted at seashore resorts along the Baltic."

Jenkins cited one example of "Miss Berta Gordon, a naturalized American of the Jewish race." While on vacation, she drove to Kolberg, Germany "where there was a large sign 'Jews Not Wanted' hung across the highway leading into the town." She and her party decided then to go to Henkenhagen, where there was "no indication of anti-Jewish activity." A hotel manager assured her they would be safe, but in the afternoon they "were required to turn in their passports to the police." The hotel manager asked them to leave the next day because the SA had warned him that "Jews could not remain in Henkenhagen." The woman stated that she would have been "maltreated regardless of her American citizenship," but refused to have the U.S. consulate take action because "she was afraid a protest from this office might result in the persecution of her relatives" in Berlin.[5]

Her fears were justified, because sporadic violence did occur. On the evening of July 15 two hundred Nazis attacked Jews in restaurants and theaters in the heart of Berlin's West End, shouting "The best Jew is a dead Jew." Bloody, wounded bodies were strewn on the sidewalks. An Annapolis midshipman, Ernest Wood, Jr., glared at a husky Nazi who was beating two women. When the Nazi pointed to the women and asked him what he thought of that, the American promptly knocked him down. Wood was fined $20 for his act of heroism. During that same evening, however, the Nazis were made painfully aware once again that their "science" of physiognomy was far from full proof. A tall blond Nazi leader mercilessly beat a short, dark-complexioned man he thought was a Jew. The man proved to be a Bavarian SA leader![6]

THE 1936 OLYMPICS

The world was aware of both the Nuremberg Laws and the anti-Semitism in Germany. The 1936 Summer Olympic Games were scheduled for August in Berlin. Throughout the United States, Christians and non-Christians debated whether one could morally participate in such a spectacle at the risk of adding credibility to the Nazi regime. The issues were similar to those raised over the 1980 Summer Olympic Games in the Soviet Union. Adolf Hitler had for years looked forward to the international prestige the games would lend to a resurrected Germany. He made every assurance to the American Olympic Committee that Jewish athletes in Germany would be treated according to the equal oppor-

---

5. Ibid., pp. 113–14. Marvin Lowenthal completed his book *The Jews of Germany: A Story of Sixteen Centuries* (Philadelphia: Jewish Publication Society, 1936) during this time and mentioned the boycotts, Jewish economic ruin, social stigma, and the many signs. One sign he spotted on a dangerous bend near Ludwigshaven read: "Drive Carefully, Sharp Curve—Jews, 75 miles an hour!" (p. 411).
6. Arthur D. Morse, *While Six Million Died* (New York: Random House, 1968), p. 182.

tunity statutes of the Olympic rulebook. In the end, however, the Nazis circumvented these rules in the same manner that they had circumvented the German constitution. They required "ideological fitness" as well as physical fitness from their athletes. In spite of the horrible conditions that prevailed in Nazi Germany, the United States participated in the 1936 Olympics in the name of international sports and cooperation.

Hitler turned the games into one of his greatest propaganda triumphs. The German exhibition electrified the world with the flight of the *Hindenberg* dirigible over the stadium, the show of military strength, the goose-stepping German soldiers, the bold Nazi flags and banners, the "Heil Hitler" salutes of the multitude, and the more than one hundred thousand Hitler Youth involved in the sensational torch relay. Avery Brundage, president of the American Olympic Committee at the time, exclaimed: "No nation since ancient Greece has captured the true Olympic spirit as has Germany!"[7]

Brundage had been taken in by the Third Reich's facade of German social and economic paradise. The national campaign to clean up Germany included temporary removal of anti-Jewish signs and literature, massive building renovation, and careful orchestration and censorship of the foreign press. Citizens were strongly encouraged to emphasize only the pleasant aspects of German life. Each was to become a host, an emissary of Germany to dispel foreign prejudice. Nevertheless, black American athletes (including the great Jesse Owens, who won four gold medals) were downgraded by the German press and snubbed by Hitler. And although the Nazis toned down somewhat their anti-Semitic campaign for the Olympics, during the next three years (1936–39) it progressed at an alarming pace. The Nazis were still aiming to expel the Jewish "vermin" from Germany. They did not yet have an organized effort to destroy all Jews, but there was talk to that effect.[8]

ENCROACHMENT

The month following the Olympics, Julius Streicher spoke to a group of editors and writers for anti-Semitic newspapers in Europe and America who were assembled in Nuremberg for the Nazi Party Congress. He explained that some believed the Jewish question could be solved without bloodshed; but he believed that if a final solution was to be reached, "one must go the bloody path." Streicher stated that such measures would be justifiable "because the Jews always attained their ends through wholesale murder and have been responsible for

7. Note Frederick W. Rubien, ed., *Report of the American Olympic Committee: Games of the XIth Olympiad, Berlin, Germany, August 1–16, 1936 and IVth Olympic Winter Games, Garmisch-Partenkirchen, Germany, February 6–16, 1936* (New York: The American Olympic Committee, 1936), for reports, pictures, and events. Brundage's report is on pages 27–38. Compare Morse, *While Six Million Died*, pp. 178–93.
8. Yehuda Bauer, *A History of the Holocaust* (New York: Franklin Watts, 1982), pp. 104–12.

wars and massacres." He concluded with a statement quoted in newspapers throughout the world: "To secure the safety of the whole world they [the Jews] must be exterminated."[9]

The world was worried about safety—that is, safety from the onslaught of another global war. The United States, still in the grip of the Great Depression, maintained a policy of absolute isolation. Britain and France, concerned about Germany's military growth, followed a policy of appeasement. Meanwhile Hitler, sensing British and French weakness, pursued a policy of gradual encroachment.

Playing on the hopes and fears of the democratic nations, he would rage in a speech, conjure up an injustice, and arouse the fear of war; he would take a little territory, then emphasize that he wanted no more, and inspire hope that war had been averted. On March 7, 1936 he reoccupied the Rhineland. In March 1938 he moved his forces into Austria, declaring that he only wanted the "German" part. In September 1938 he convinced the British and French to let him have the Sudeten, an area in Czechoslovakia with a large percentage of Germans. British Prime Minister Neville Chamberlain happily reported that "Mr. Hitler" had assured him this area was all he wanted. Chamberlain gloated over how he had secured "peace in our time." In the article "Democracies Hasten To Appease Dictators," *New York Times* London correspondent Harold Callender reported on Chamberlain's current diplomatic theory that "there is no reason why the democracies and the dictatorships should not be the best of friends." "In Britain the Chamberlain spirit has been manifest in hints to the press and others not to irritate the sensitive dictators," he wrote, "and while the press and radio continue to give news such as that of the wholesale deportation of Polish Jews from Germany and such as the Italian editorials proclaiming that Hitler and Mussolini now run Eastern Europe, comment has been somewhat restrained."[10]

With the claiming of each new territory, more Jews were brought under Nazi control—and ultimately, under Nazi persecution. As the Third Reich moved into Austria, Nazis and their sympathizers in Vienna smashed windows of small Jewish businesses and tormented Jews on the streets. Within days, Jews were dismissed from their places of employment in what the Nazi press called "the great spring cleaning." Soon after, the Nuremberg Laws were instituted in Austria.[11]

On the home front 1938 was a dismal year for German Jews. In January the Nazis required them to add "Jewish" names for better identification. Women were to add the name "Sarah"; men the name "Israel." It was to be legally ac-

---

9. Note "Streicher Advises Foreigners on Jews," *New York Times*, 16 September 1936.
10. Harold Callender, "Democracies Hasten To Appease Dictators," *New York Times*, 6 November 1938.
11. These actions were highly publicized as well. Note "Nazis Seize Austria After Hitler Ultimatum," *New York Times*, 12 March 1938, and "Action By Himmler," *New York Times*, 18 March 1938. 180,000 out of the 200,000 Austrian Jews lived in Vienna.

complished by August. In October the letter "J" was added to Jewish passports. In April the registration of Jewish businesses and "hidden" Jewish wealth was prescribed. This was the first step toward total Aryan control over all Jewish businesses. In June the Great Synagogue in Munich was destroyed by the Nazis; the property was turned into a parking lot. Jewish cemeteries were desecrated. Fifteen hundred Jews were arrested for their "criminal records" (most had minor infractions such as parking violations). They were sent to concentration camps until they promised to emigrate.[12]

Unfortunately, emigration was very difficult. German Jews tried desperately to get out of Germany. An international conference in Evian, France called in July 1938 to discuss the refugee situation ended in dismal failure, most countries (including the United States) maintaining their strict and stingy immigration quotas. In October thousands of Polish Jews were expelled from Germany. Telegrams to the U.S. State Department underscored the plight of these refugees, many beaten, hungry, forced to walk for miles. A. J. Drexel Biddle, Jr., of the U.S. embassy in Warsaw wrote:

> At Zbaszyn, on the main railway line from Berlin to Warsaw, it has been learned that the refugees were handled very roughly and that as a result they arrived in Poland in great disorder. Many had lost what few belongings they had managed to bring with them including their travel documents. Many were hysterical, and it is said that a few died of fright and several cases of temporary insanity were reported.[13]

More than five thousand refugees were forced to stay in this inadequate camp in the small Polish frontier village of Zbaszyn.

Herschel Grynszpan, a German-born Polish Jew staying with relatives in Paris, was informed by his sister Berta that his family had been deported from Germany to Zbaszyn. The message and subsequent reports in the French press filled the seventeen-year-old with intense anxiety. Feelings of revenge welled up inside the young man. He purchased a gun, intending to murder the German ambassador in order to avenge the persecutions against Jews. Upon reaching the German embassy on November 7, 1938, he was led instead to the office of the third secretary, Ernst vom Rath (ironically, a man who despised the Nazi regime). He fired five shots; two hit vom Rath. The secretary died on November 9. In a card to his parents found on his person, Grynszpan explained his actions:

> My dear parents. I could not do otherwise. May God forgive me. My heart bleeds at the news of 12,000 Jews' suffering. I must protest in such a way that the world will hear me. I must do it. Forgive me. Herschel.

12. Nora Levin, *The Holocaust: The Destruction of European Jewry, 1933–1945* (New York: Thomas Y. Crowell, 1968), pp. 75–76.
13. A. J. Drexel Biddle, Jr., "Mass Expulsion of Polish Jews from Germany," Report to the U.S. Secretary of State, 5 November 1938, Dept. of State Central Decimal File 862.4016/1824, National Archives Record Group 59, Washington, D.C., reproduced in Mendelsohn, ed., *The Holocaust*, vol. 3, *The Crystal Night Pogrom*, pp. 23–24.

Before the examining magistrate, Grynszpan described the nightmare of being Jewish in Germany and then added: "To be Jewish is not a crime. We are not animals. The Jewish people have a right to live."[14]

The Nazis intended to exploit the assassination to the fullest. The day before vom Rath's death, the German press demanded retaliation against German and foreign Jews in the Reich, declaring that the attempted assassination was "a new plot of the Jewish world conspiracy against National Socialist Germany, an attempt to torpedo Franco-German relations and a plot against European peace." Anti-Jewish riots commenced in many German cities, and storm troopers searched the streets for Jews, smashing windows of Jewish businesses (by law, these businesses had to be clearly marked). Ironically, in Berlin, the police had only a few weeks before the riots confiscated all Jewish weapons. When vom Rath died on November 9, a carefully designed rampage of destruction was planned for that evening under the guise of "spontaneous demonstrations." Under the leadership of Reinhard Heydrich, chief of security forces, a storm of terror was carried out by SA and SS dressed in civilian clothes. Heydrich reported to Reichs Marshal Göring that at minimum 815 Jewish shops were destroyed, 171 dwellings set on fire or destroyed, 191 synagogues set on fire, 76 more completely demolished, and 20,000 Jews arrested (the number would rise to at least 30,000, who would then be sent to concentration camps). Thirty-six Jews were killed and many injured. Heydrich noted: "The urgency with which the reports had to be prepared made it necessary to restrict them to general statements, such as 'numerous' or 'most shops destroyed.' The numbers, therefore, will greatly increase."[15]

The night of November 9 was called the "Crystal Night" because the broken windows of imported Belgian glass from shops and synagogues filled the streets. It was the largest nationwide pogrom in German history, spreading to nearly every town and city. The American consul general in Stuttgart prefaced his detailed report to the American ambassador in Berlin by declaring that "the Jews of Southwest Germany have suffered vicissitudes during the last three days which would seem unreal to one living in an enlightened country during the twentieth century if one had not actually been a witness of their dreadful experiences."[16] Göring was also upset, but for a different reason. The Jewish businesses were insured by German insurance companies. The Nazis would have to pay for their

14. Rita Thalmann and Emmanuel Feinermann, *Crystal Night: 9–10 November 1938*, trans. Gilles Cremonesi (New York: Holocaust Library, 1974), pp. 48–49.
15. Reinhard Heydrich, "*Kristallnacht*: A Preliminary Secret Report to H. W. Goering," in Paul R. Mendes-Flohr and Jehuda Reinharz, eds., *The Jew in the Modern World: A Documentary History* (New York: Oxford U., 1980), p. 496. Compare *New York Times* articles: "Nazis Ask Reprisal in Attack on Envoy," 9 November 1938; "Berlin Raids Reply to Death of Envoy," 10 November 1938; "Nazis Smash, Loot and Burn Jewish Shops and Temples," 11 November 1938.
16. Samuel Monaker, "Anti-Semitic Persecution in the Stuttgart Consular District," Report to American Ambassador in Berlin, 12 November 1938, Central Decimal File 862.4016/2002, reproduced in Mendelsohn, ed., *The Holocaust*, 3:182. Compare "American Press Comment on Nazi Riots," *New York Times*, 12 November 1938. For Nazi response, note "Nazis Warn Foreign Press 'Lies' Will Hurt Reich Jews; Arrests Run to Thousands," 12 November 1938.

"spontaneous demonstration." Göring told Heydrich, "I would have preferred if you had slain two hundred Jews instead of destroying such property values." Meeting with his staff, Göring decided that as punishment for vom Rath's death, the Jews would pay for the destruction of their own property. A one billion mark "atonement fine" ($400 million) was levied on the Jewish community.[17]

Terrified Jewish people responded by lining up at foreign consulates in a desperate attempt to get out of Germany. The Nazis only permitted them to take approximately two percent of their savings, sending them out penniless. Alas, they were not welcome anywhere. At the end of 1938 the joke was popular that "there were only two kinds of places in the world. One where Jews could not live and the other where Jews could not enter."[18]

17. "Staff Evidence Analysis: Protocol of the Discussion on the Jewish Problem Under the Leadership of Hermann Goering," 12 November 1938, Nuremberg Document PS 1816, National Archives Record Group 238, reproduced in Mendelsohn, ed., *The Holocaust*, 3:81.
18. For the Jewish refugees' plight see John George Stoessinger, *The Refugee and the World Community* (Minneapolis: U. of Minnesota, 1956), pp. 34–44. Compare Malcolm J. Proudfoot, *European Refugees, 1939–1952: A Study in Forced Population Movement* (Evanston, Ill.: Northwestern U., 1956), pp. 25–31.

8

Steps to World War

A link between Christians and Jews in the 1980s is their joint persecution under the communist regime of the Soviet Union. Between 1927 and 1953 Joseph Stalin killed twenty-five million Russians, including many Christians and Jews. The U.S.S.R. continues to be an enemy of biblical religion. Both Jews and Christians are forbidden to hold worship services in their homes or to "indoctrinate" their children. Soviet prisons, mental hospitals, and work camps slowly exterminate men and women of faith.

Although there is blatant use of bloody execution squads that bludgeon to death "enemies of the state," Russia spends much more time on propaganda campaigns, presenting itself as an angel of light. The Soviet Union's constant barrage of false statements, misquotes, and misrepresentations of the United States and Israel over shortwave radio and in the press are what its Committee for State Security (KGB) refers to as "Active Measures." Major Stanislav Aleksandrovich Levchenko, who worked in the headquarters of the KGB, defected to the United States late in 1979. He explained how decent people could be sucked into such a campaign, testifying:

> Few people who understand the reality of the Soviet Union will knowingly support it or its policies. So by Active Measures, the KGB distorts or inverts reality. The trick is to make people support Soviet policy unwittingly by convincing them they are supporting something else. Almost everybody wants peace and fears war. Therefore, by every conceivable means, the KGB plans and coordinates campaigns to persuade the public that whatever America does endangers peace and that what-

ever the Soviet Union proposes furthers peace. To be for America is to be for war; to be for the Soviets is to be for peace. That's the art of Active Measures, a sort of made-in-Moscow black magic. It is tragic to see how well it works.[1]

The irony of the situation is that in its anti-Israel, anti-Jewish campaign, the Soviet Union has unwitting accomplices in some of today's right-wing anti-Communist racist groups.

The Nazis knew these tactics well, and an understanding of their ploys during the Holocaust contributes to an enlightened perception of modern-day racist tactics.

"THE ESSENCE OF PROPAGANDA"

Joseph Goebbels, Hitler's Minister of National Enlightenment and Propaganda, once stated that "the essence of propaganda consists in winning people over to an idea so sincerely, so vitally, that in the end they succumb to it utterly and can never again escape from it."[2] Propaganda was the essence of National Socialism. Germany's experience shows how a daily diet of propaganda affected the spirit and intellect of good, decent, religious citizens. It serves as a warning to every one of us. Helmut Thielicke remembered:

> Good care was taken that one should not see this [massive injustice] happening to others. It either did not appear in the newspapers at all or in such a way that the readers (or those who listened to the speeches) were subjected by means of inflammatory accounts to the suggestion that the terrorist measures were simply retaliatory justice. When day after day for years there was nothing but talk of the crimes of the Jews, when one could read nothing but fictitious "documentary" accounts of Jewish owners of houses of prostitution, mass profiteering, exploitations, wars, and the multiplication of armaments, when the image of the Jews was obtained almost solely from caricatures and pornographic political newspapers, it required a very considerable inner substance, insight, and objectivity to arm oneself against it. Perhaps, then, one can understand that naive people (and how many such there are all around us!) would say what I heard said any number of times: "I know a decent Jew, for whom I feel sorry, but the others must be horrible!"[3]

How often have we in modern-day America heard similarly insensitive and naive statements about minority groups and refugees? Is it too hard for us to comprehend how we, like those poor souls, could be in the process of spirit hardening? By the time of Crystal Night many good citizens were silent, and a number gleefully participated.

1. John Barron, "The KGB's Magical War for 'Peace,'" *Reader's Digest* 121 (October 1982): 207.
2. Joachim C. Fest, *The Face of the Third Reich: Portraits of the Nazi Leadership*, trans. Michael Bullock (New York: Random House, 1970), p. 97.
3. Helmut Thielicke, *Between Heaven and Earth: Conversations with American Christians*, trans. and ed. John W. Doberstein (New York: Harper & Row, 1965), pp. 152–53.

"Crocodile Tears"—Hitler's Challenge to the Democratic Nations

In a two-hour-and-fifteen-minute speech on January 30, 1939—a speech anxiously awaited by the world—Adolf Hitler used the propaganda tactic of distorting and inverting reality to persuade the public that he was an apostle of peace "suffering from a campaign of defamation" by the world Jewish conspiracy that controlled the press, films, and radio.[4] He explained that Germany's relations with the United States suffered under such propaganda, but he believed millions of American citizens could not fail to realize "that there is not one word of truth in all these assertions. Germany wishes to live in peace and on friendly terms with all countries, including America." His speech contrasted the decline and stagnation of Germany before the Third Reich with the "tremendous events" of his regime. Hitler even added a little religion at the beginning of his speech, noting of those events: "We are, indeed, perhaps better able than other generations to realize the full meaning of those pious words, 'What a change by the grace of God.'" Hitler then sought to justify Germany's activities through a nazified view of history and to turn the tables on the world democracies. He asserted:

> In certain democracies it is apparently one of the special prerogatives of political-democratic life to cultivate an artificial hatred of the so-called totalitarian States. A flood of reports, partly misrepresentations of fact, partly pure inventions, are let loose, the aim being to stir up public opinion against nations which have done nothing to harm the other nations and have no desire to harm them, and which indeed have been for years the victims of harsh injustice.

"All it [Germany] wants is peace and quiet," Hitler promised.

Hitler spent considerable time talking about the "Jewish world enemy," who he claimed was constantly trying to provoke war by lying about his "intended attacks on other nations." Thus, the world was given insight into his hatred for Jewish people. He chastised the world for crying crocodile tears over the plight of the Jews—Adolf Hitler accused the world of being hard-hearted toward the Jews! He declared:

> On the contrary, in connection with the Jewish question, I have this to say: It is a shameful spectacle to see how the whole democratic world is oozing sympathy for the poor tormented Jewish people, but remains hard-hearted and obdurate when it comes to helping them, which is surely, in view of its attitude, an obvious duty. The arguments that are brought up as an excuse for not helping them actually speak for us Germans and Italians. For this is what they say:

4. The text of Hitler's speech was made available in newspapers and magazines across the country. Note "Excerpts from the Official Translation of Hitler's Speech Before the Reichstag," *New York Times*, 31 January 1939. It filled pp. 6 and 7.

First, "We"—that is, the democracies—"are not in a position to take in the Jews." Yet in these empires there are not even ten people to the square kilometer. While Germany with her 140 inhabitants to the square kilometer is supposed to have room for them!

Secondly, they assure us: "We cannot take them unless Germany is prepared to allow them a certain amount of capital to bring with them as immigrants." For hundreds of years Germany was good enough to receive these elements [the Jews], although they possessed nothing except infectious political and physical diseases. What they possess today, they have to by far the largest extent gained at the cost of the less astute German nation by the most reprehensible manipulations. Today we are merely paying this people what they deserve.

Hitler taunted the nations crying out against the barbaric expulsion of Jews from Germany by saying: "For how thankful they [the United States and others] must be that we are releasing apostles of culture and placing them at the disposal of the world."

Hitler told the world that if it really wanted the Jews, he would hand them over. He was very clear about his plans for the Jewish people if war should break out. He reminded his listeners that he had often been a "prophet" in the past, and firmly proclaimed: "Today I will once more be a prophet. If the international Jewish financiers in and outside Europe should succeed in plunging the nations once more into a world war, then the result will not be the bolshevization of the earth, and thus the victory of Jewry, but the annihilation of the Jewish race in Europe!"

"First Things First"—The United States and the Refugees

In spite of the world's horror over Crystal Night and Hitler's challenge in his January 30th speech, the United States government remained unwilling to ease immigration quotas to help the Jewish people. Franklin D. Roosevelt refused to provide leadership for the refugees, believing that it would hamper his domestic and defense programs. When his wife, Eleanor, pressed him on the issue, he declared: "First things come first, and I can't alienate certain votes I need for measures that are more important at the moment by pushing any measure that would entail a fight."[5] Public opinion polls conveyed to Roosevelt that although the American people were becoming very sympathetic to the plight of the Jews, they continued to believe that the United States's economy was not yet strong enough to assimilate the refugees. When the SS *St. Louis*, carrying 907 refugees, sailed slowly up the American coast in June begging the U.S. government for help, Coast Guard ships were sent out to prevent its landing. These European passengers had been given visas to enter Cuba, but Cuba reneged on her re-

5. Saul S. Friedman, *No Haven for the Oppressed: United States Policy Toward Jewish Refugees, 1938–1945* (Detroit: Wayne State U., 1973), p. 50. Friedman's excellent survey details the politics involved in our failure to help.

sponsibility. As the *St. Louis* sailed past Miami's skyline and beaches, refugee Max Korman, who had been deported to Zbaszyn and by a miraculous sequence of events obtained a Cuban visa, related his feelings to his wife in a letter:

> Here lived our uncle; this was the land to which I was supposed to [eventually] come. And here I was so near, but oh so far. I was not alone. The moment of truth arrived. What rotten merchandise we must be if no one is prepared to accept us. . . . Are we really so bad and so rotten? Are we really humanity's vermin and thus to be treated as lepers? Or has mankind ceased to be human?[6]

At the very same time, immigration opponents in Congress tied up and slowly destroyed the Wagner Bill, a bill that would have admitted twenty thousand refugee children from Germany and its occupied territory. New York Senator Robert Wagner delivered an impassioned nationwide radio address on June 7, 1939, using the *St. Louis* incident in a final effort to save his bill. "One by one, these incidents impress themselves on our consciousness, until they disappear from the public prints, and a merciful curtain of obscurity is drawn over their ultimate outcome," he chided. He called for public support as "a token of our sympathy" and also "as a symbol of our faith in the ideals of human brotherhood."[7] The widespread public outcry he envisioned never materialized.

William E. Nawyn in his recent study *American Protestantism's Response to Germany's Jews and Refugees, 1933–1941* has pointed out individual American clergymen, both conservative and liberal, who spoke out forcefully against Hitler, Crystal Night, and the *St. Louis* debacle. Organizations such as the American Christian Committee for German Refugees (ACCGR) tried desperately to garner support to alleviate the plight of the refugee. Unfortunately, the deeply concerned actions of these few individuals and organizations were unable either to help the refugees or pressure the government. Nawyn explained about the ACCGR:

> The fundamental reason why it received but minimal support is the failure of American Protestantism to become thoroughly aroused over the plight of the victims, Jewish or Christian, of the Nazi racial policies and, even more basically, about the moral issues involved in these policies. Latent anti-Semitism among Americans may well have played a role here. Undoubtedly too, fears that admission of refugees would have a negative economic impact served to dampen, or outweigh, compassion. But whatever the reason, the fact remains that American Protestants did not rush forward to extend a generous welcome to the refugees from Germany—not even [to] Christian non-Aryans, much less Jews.[8]

6. Max O. Korman, "On Being a Refugee," in Gerd Korman, ed., *Hunter and Hunted: Human History of the Holocaust* (New York: Dell, 1973), p. 52.
7. Friedman, *No Haven for the Oppressed*, p. 103. Note pp. 91–104 for the total scenario of the bill introduced ten days after Hitler's January 30 speech.
8. William E. Nawyn, *American Protestantism's Response to Germany's Jews and Refugees, 1933–1941* (Ann Arbor, Mich.: UMI Research Press, 1981), pp. 179–80.

"When human rights became endangered and the facts were clearly established," he concluded about the period, "few Protestant churchmen were ready to defend the defenseless or help the needy."[9]

The outbreak of World War II did not bring an end to the United States's golden opportunity to save the majority of remaining German Jews. Nevertheless, Congress and the American people remained firm in their opposition to bending the national-origins quota system. Between 1933 and 1945, two million visas that could have been issued under existing laws were not issued, but were held in reserve in case other groups should want them. The United States government refused their being shifted from one group to another.[10]

"To Take Care of the Jews"—The Invasion of Poland

Hitler invaded Poland on September 1, 1939. Within a month he had conquered it, and approximately 3.5 million more Jews were trapped by the Nazi regime. France and Britain declared war on Germany September 3 (the United States would not be pulled in until December 1941); but both the British and French were very slow to help Poland, which caused tremendous suffering. The Polish people underwent a torturous and inhumane occupation by the Nazi regime. Germany and Russia (who had signed a treaty of friendship and non-aggression on August 23) divided the spoils. The Nazi regime, which had attempted to rid Germany of Jewish "vermin" through emigration, now found itself swamped with the "worst kind" of Jew possible—orthodox Jews, poorly dressed Jews with the earlocks Hitler had detested in the inner city of Vienna and the districts north of the Danube Canal. The Nazis made sure not to take a single step backwards in their attempt to rid their domain of Jews. On September 21 Heydrich announced the Führer's determination to cleanse the new territories of Jews as soon as possible.[11]

Whereas German Jews were the most assimilated in Europe, having had a rather comfortable economic life before the Nazis impoverished them, Polish Jews were a stark contrast. Most were destitute and poverty-stricken. Poland had suffered economic instability since its independence at the end of World War I, and the Jews there were on the lowest end of the economic spectrum.

Nevertheless, Polish anti-Semitism flourished. Between 1935 and 1937 sixteen pogroms occurred, killing 118 Jews and wounding 1,350. Anti-Jewish riots, hundreds of separate mass assaults, and forced expulsions of Jews took place before the Nazis entered the country. Unassimilated and maintained by a strong community structure, Polish Jews clung tenaciously to their traditions, preserv-

9. Ibid., p. 183.
10. Note Charles Herbert Stember, et al., *Jews in the Mind of America* (New York: Basic Books, 1966), pp. 144–55 for American public attitudes on refugees.
11. Christopher Browning, *The Final Solution and the German Foreign Office* (New York: Holmes and Meyer, 1978), pp. 6–7. The earlocks *(pe'ot)* were sidelocks of hair grown by traditional Jews of the period in accordance with Leviticus 19:27, "You shall not round off the side-growth of your heads."

ing a thousand-year heritage of intellectual acumen and culture in Poland. (It is estimated that during the Middle Ages 80 percent of the world's Jews lived in Poland.) In spite of poverty, Jewish schools flourished and synagogues abounded.

Polish Jews in 1939 made up 10 percent of the population of Poland, and 40 percent of its urban population. By 1945 the Nazis had exterminated 90 percent of this community, virtually wiping out a millennium of Jewish civilization. In 1939 there were 3.3 million Polish Jews; by 1948, only 70,000 remained. Today, the mostly aged Jewish community is but a minuscule percentage of the total population.[12]

Photographs of Nazi troop trains entering Poland clearly show signs stating, "We are traveling to Poland in order to take care of the Jews." In a concentrated effort to dehumanize the Jews, the Third Reich immediately targeted Jewish institutions for destruction. Cemeteries were desecrated, synagogues were blown apart with heavy artillery or turned into stables and latrines. Jewish people were tortured and kicked around by German soldiers as well as by Polish collaborators. The barbarously sadistic actions in the early months of occupation were nearly beyond belief, the SS squads energetically at work in their *blitzpogroms* ("lightning massacres"). Julian Gross witnessed one such incident in Cracow and reported:

> At seven o'clock in the morning, SS men surrounded the Jewish community and demanded that three of its officials be surrendered to them. There was sporadic shooting in the street, and the Jewish officials were afraid to go out. At last my uncle and two of his associates volunteered to go. They were taken to the synagogue on Isaacs Street and ordered to set fire to the Scrolls of the Law. When my uncle refused to comply with the command, he was promptly shot and killed . . . A little Jewish boy was also taken from the street and [an] old man was ordered to throw hot coals and ashes upon him. The little fellow died of the burns, and the oldster became mentally deranged. On the same day, the SS killed the daughter of the proprietor of a toy store, while ransacking the establishment for gold.[13]

In a medieval style reminiscent of the Inquisition, a garden hose was sometimes plunged down a Jew's throat to fill his stomach until it ruptured. Those resisting the Teutons were tortured, hung, or shot, their bodies left as examples.

In 1935 Marvin Lowenthal finished a book he had been working on for years, *The Jews of Germany: A Story of Sixteen Centuries*. Viewing the first few years of the Hitler regime, he seemed to sense the impending doom, noting as he closed his volume:

12. Earl Vinecour and Chuck Fishman, *Polish Jews: The Final Chapter* (New York: McGraw-Hill, 1977), pp. 1–7. Compare Yehuda Bauer, *A History of the Holocaust* (New York: Franklin Watts, 1982), pp. 142–45. An excellent background text is Celia S. Heller, *On the Edge of Destruction: Jews of Poland between the Two World Wars* (New York: Columbia U., 1977).
13. Julian Gross, "City of Cracow," trans. Moshe Spiegal, in Jacob Glatstein et al., eds., *Anthology of Holocaust Literature* (New York: Atheneum, 1980), p. 32.

As the German Jew sinks from the stage of history, he leaves in the very process of his demise a heritage richer perhaps than anything his genius or days of vigor achieved. He leaves a lesson for every minority—racial, religious, political, or economic. . . . No land can remain half-bigot and half-tolerant. The fight against fanaticism is one fight, no matter who the victims are. In waging the fight to save himself or his kind, everyone must be prepared to shed his prejudices as well as his blood to save even those whom he feels impelled to despise. . . . And no majority is free so long as it holds a minority enslaved. The liberty of no individual can rise higher than its source; and this source is the general liberty of man.[14]

"Scant choice or time remains," he concluded. "The world, and Germany, has but a few years to decide whether it will choose liberty, or—in battlefields too horrible to contemplate—it must choose death."

The world had chosen death.

---

14. Marvin Lowenthal, *The Jews of Germany: A Story of Sixteen Centuries* (Philadelphia: The Jewish Publication Society of America, 1936), pp. 420–21.

9

The United States and Nazism

"Most of the professors [at Cleveland State University] are Jews. Who runs the state [of Ohio]? The Jews. They run the United Nations. They run the president. They run the whole show," declared Frank G. Spisak, Jr., a thirty-two-year-old former Cleveland State student during his trial for murder in July of 1983. "The Black people are overbreeding. They're going to take over and kill all the white people. They're doing it all the time. The streets aren't safe anymore," Spisak continued. Professing his constant love for and devotion to Adolf Hitler, he claimed that his "immediate superior is God," that he was part of the "forces of lightness" against the "forces of darkness" (Satan and his children, the Jews). He emphasized that Satan's creation was the "dark races." While on a "search and destroy mission" he killed black teenager Brian Warford at a bus shelter. "Fate," he said, brought him together with the popular and beloved black pastor Horace Rickerson, of the Open Door Baptist Church, when the two happened to be in a Cleveland State restroom. Rickerson was "punished by God" according to Spisak, who shot him three times in the abdomen. Realizing that no one heard the shooting, Spisak noted, "It was like the protective hand of God was with me—like God made me invisible and God stuffed everybody's ears." He did admit however to being sorry about killing Timothy Sheehan, assistant superintendent of buildings, in another restroom. He had mistakenly believed that Sheehan was a Jewish professor.[1]

1. For a written account of Spisak's testimony see John F. Hagen, "Spisak Tells of Waging Race War at CSU," *The Plain Dealer* (Cleveland), 6 July 1983. On the Reverend Horace Rickerson

Spisak's lawyers felt that by putting him on the witness stand the jury would certainly return an insanity verdict. However, the psychiatrist called by the defense testified under questioning that Spisak was not mentally ill or suffering from mental disease at the time of the murders. Thwarted, the defense lawyers could not find a reputable and qualified witness to testify that Spisak was mentally ill. Moreover, Spisak himself claimed to be sane, and the jury agreed. They sentenced him to die in the electric chair. Asked earlier if he felt he had failed God by being caught, Spisak asserted: "I don't think so. I can give my testimony, and that's helpful. That was what we needed all along, someone to take the stand and give a reasonable, logical concise explanation of what has to be done, and that's not been done until now."[2]

At the time of Spisak's arrest, a list was found of prominent Jewish businessmen he planned to exterminate. As a finale, his aim was to enter a black convention to be held a few weeks later with a machine gun he kept in his apartment and kill as many as possible. "That's why I say there's a lot of work that's got to be done," he said, regarding his dual role of liberating people from Jewish "control" and black "overpopulation." "Unfortunately there's not enough people to get it done."

But there were a startling number of Frank Spisaks living in the United States during the rise and triumph of Adolf Hitler. Thousands of hard-core Hitler followers populated the nation in the 1930s, men and women who were willing to take to the streets and carry out a fascist revolt if necessary. They and millions of others who were imbued with racial hatred give cause to pause and reflect on the success Hitler may have had if he had emigrated to *our* nation.

RACIST GROUPS IN THE UNITED STATES

Here too, racial prejudice has a long history; during the 1920s groups such as the Ku Klux Klan (KKK) enjoyed their most significant growth. Membership in the Klan prospered from a paltry five thousand in 1920 to five million in 1925. Lynchings and racial outbursts occurred even in northern states such as Minnesota. In the southern states the Klan maintained a foothold in both political parties. The Klan of the twentieth century was not only anti-black, but also anti-Jewish and anti-Catholic. A KKK pamphlet in 1925, "Christ and Other Klansmen," insisted that "God is the author of Klanism" and that Jesus Christ was the Klan's "first real member," embodying the true ideal of a Klansman. It also blamed the Jews for killing Christ. During the "Roaring Twenties" Jews, along with blacks, were restricted from beaches, hotels, universities, and from buying homes in certain sections of cities or suburbs. The president of Harvard

---

compare Greg Garland, "Pastor Slain at CSU, Mourners Ask 'Why,'" The *Cleveland Press*, 2 February 1982, and Margaret Williams, "'He Did So Much'—Ministers, Church Members Mourn Reverend Rickerson," *Call and Post* (Cleveland), 6 February 1982.

2. *The Plain Dealer*, 6 July 1983, p. 6a. Compare John F. Hagen, "Spisak Defense Dealt Big Blow," ibid., 12 July 1983, and "Jury Recommends Death for Spisak," ibid., 21 July 1983.

University called for a quota on Jewish admission, which was "unofficially" adopted after being narrowly defeated by the board of trustees.[3]

THE INFLUENCE OF THE *PROTOCOLS*

After World War I an intense fear of Communism spread through the United States in much the same fashion as in Germany. Nothing did more to link anti-Communism with anti-Semitism at that time than the publication of the spurious *Protocols of the Elders of Zion*. Purporting to be the dialogue from a conference of world Jewish leaders, the *Protocols* discloses a Jewish plot to take over the world under the guise of democracy, and claims that Jews already control the policies of a number of European states. Plagiarized from a treatise written by Maurice Joly in 1864 that attempted to show that Napoleon III had illusions of world conquest, the forger inserted all the references to Jews and Judaism. It is believed that the Russian secret police copied large sections of Joly's pamphlet in the 1890s, fabricating the Jewish plot in order to impress Czar Nicholas II. The Czar dismissed the *Protocols* as forgery and, although the first Russian public edition was released in 1905, it was not taken seriously until after the Bolshevik Revolution in 1917 and the subsequent bloodshed initiated by the Communists. Those fleeing the new government of Russia spread the document throughout Europe, where it had substantial effect, especially on Germany. The emphasis of the *Protocols* upon the alleged Jewish conspiracy to undermine German-Christian culture fit well into the mentality that opposed the Weimar Republic. Hitler and the fledgling Nazi party used it effectively.

In 1920, when the document was translated into English, the *Times* of London immediately called for an investigation. Philip Graves, a *Times* correspondent in Constantinople, fortuitously had purchased an old copy of Joly's French manuscript, finding that whole pages were practically identical to the *Protocols*. Unfortunately, Henry Ford, the beloved automobile magnate, published excerpts of the forgery in his *Dearborn Independent* newspaper and subsequently in a book entitled *The International Jew*. This gave it enormous credibility in the eyes of the American public. Even after Ford apologized in 1927 for supporting such false anti-Semitic literature, the *Protocols* continued to have great influence throughout the 1930s. In the mid-1930s, the period of the infamous Nuremberg Laws, Hugo Valentin wrote:

> The so-called "Protocols of the Elders of Zion" are among the most politically significant and symptomatically interesting documents in the history of Antisemitism. They are significant in that they were the chief means employed after the

---

3. Paul E. Grosser and Edwin G. Halperin, *The Causes and Effects of Anti-Semitism: The Dimensions of a Prejudice* (New York: Philosophical Library, 1978), pp. 249–51. Compare John Turner, *The Ku Klux Klan: A History of Racism and Violence* (Montgomery, Ala.: Southern Poverty Law Center, 1982), pp. 14–19; and Morton Rosenstock, "Are There Too Many Jews at Harvard?" in Leonard Dinnerstein, ed., *Anti-Semitism in the United States* (New York: Holt, Rinehart and Winston, 1971), pp. 102–8.

World War to promote savage hatred of the Jews in Eastern Europe and Germany. It is not exaggeration to say that they cost the lives of many thousands of innocent persons and that more blood and tears cling to their pages than to those of any other mendacious document in the world's history. They are symptomatically interesting from the fact that this gross fabrication in spite of its absurdities was taken seriously in such wide circles. . . . The very fact that people could believe for a moment in the fabled existence of a powerful Jewish secret world-conspiracy, which had for its object the destruction of the Christian States and the foundation of a Jewish world-monarchy on their ruins, shows the truth of Shaw's saying that our age is just as credulous as the Middle Ages, though its credulity finds other objects.[4]

Valentin, though perceptive, had no idea how many additional Jews would lose their lives partially due to the *Protocols*. The Nazis and anti-Semitic groups in America continued to circulate copies throughout World War II.

After the Nazi defeat, West Germany passed a law forbidding incitement to racial hatred and the spreading of racist literature. But today in the United States the *Protocols* and Henry Ford's *The International Jew* are marketed by publishing houses of racist organizations. In fact, West German neo-Nazis obtain much of their literature from the U.S.[5]

FRITZ KUHN AND THE GERMAN-AMERICAN BUND

While on the payroll as a chemist for the Ford Motor Company, Fritz Kuhn, leader of the German-American Bund, was allowed time off to travel around the country espousing the fascist cause. (After taking power in Germany, the Nazis allocated funds to pro-Hitler movements around the world.) A former officer of the German army during the First World War, Kuhn immigrated to the United States and was responsible for enlisting the support of German Americans to the Nazi cause once Hitler was in power. Collecting a portion of the $300 million the Nazi Ministry of Propaganda spent annually on worldwide revolution, the Bund circulated anti-Semitic materials, had a national radio program, and operated twenty-four "retreat facilities" across the nation. Saul S. Friedman relates that the Bund "attempted to frustrate [Roosevelt] administration policies which they construed as prejudicial to the Fatherland, including any proposals for the harboring of refugees from Germany."[6] Friedman's detailed scholarship

---

4. Hugo Valentin, *Antisemitism Historically and Critically Examined*, trans. A. G. Chater (New York: Viking, 1936), pp. 165–66. Note pages 165–83 for his chapter "The Protocols of the Elders of Zion—The Greatest Forgery of the Century." Professor Valentin taught at the University of Uppsala in Sweden and commented in his preface: "Antisemitism is no longer a problem which concerns only the Jews and their enemies. It concerns everyone" (p. 5).
5. A recent use of the law in West Germany involved an anti-Semitic game called "Jew, Don't Get Angry." Circulated by German neo-Nazis, the game was played on a board shaped like a Star of David, having names of extermination camps on each corner. See "Anti-Jewish Game in Germany," The *Jerusalem Post*, international edition, 19–25 June 1983.
6. Saul S. Friedman, *No Haven for the Oppressed: United States Policy Toward Jewish Refugees, 1938–1945* (Detroit: Wayne State U., 1973), p. 26.

leaves no doubt that the combination of political clout and propaganda by racist organizations was a significant reason for the American government's passivity toward the plight of the Jewish refugees.

The zenith of Bund activities occurred at its mass meeting in New York's Madison Square Garden on February 20, 1939. Nearly twenty thousand packed the large auditorium to hear Kuhn scream, "Keep America free from the Jewish menace!" amid banners reading "Smash Jewish Communism," "Stop Jewish Domination of Christian America," and "1,000,000 Bund Members by 1940." The Bund claimed to have twenty-five thousand active members; and when the war began, many of these filtered into other organizations. In 1936 Kuhn met Hitler in Berlin, subsequently seeing not only substantial growth of the Bund in major American cities the following year but also the birth of new fascist organizations.[7]

WILLIAM PELLEY AND THE SILVER SHIRTS

Working hand in hand with the Bund were organizations such as William D. Pelley's Silver Shirt Legion of America. A popular movie script writer in the 1920s, Pelley claimed to have died and gone to heaven in 1928. He said he was given instructions to found the Silver Shirts, which he did January 31, 1933, the day after Hitler was appointed chancellor. The Silver Shirt Legion, led by the self-acclaimed "American Hitler" Pelley, patterned itself after the Nazi SS. As the United States plunged deep into the Depression, the Silver Shirts reported a membership of one hundred thousand in twenty-two states. They called their fascist program "Christian Democracy," and wore Ls on their shirts, signifying "Liberation." Pelley advocated imprisonment for Jews who attempted to use "Gentile" names, prosecution on the grounds of sedition for those supporting a Jewish state in Palestine, and ghettoization of the American Jewish population. Between 1936 and 1938, Pelley mailed approximately three and one-half tons of anti-Semitic literature from his $80,000 publishing plant located in Asheville, North Carolina. The Dies Committee on Un-American Activities in 1938 cited the Silver Shirts as the largest, best publicized, and most highly financed fascist movement in the nation.[8]

THE FEELINGS OF THE GENERAL POPULATION

More than 120 American organizations were actively disseminating anti-Semitic propaganda between 1933 and 1940. Anti-Semitic fliers blanketed the United States. One declared: "Jesus Christ—Martin Luther—Mohammed—Pope Clement VIII—Benjamin Franklin—Ulysses Grant—James A. Garfield,—and Henry Ford unite with 50 other famous personages in saying: JEWS are TRAITORS to Amer-

---

7. Sheldon Marcus, *Father Coughlin: The Tumultous Life of the Priest of the Little Flower* (Boston: Little, Brown, 1973), pp. 149–50.
8. Friedman, *No Haven for the Oppressed*, p. 27.

ica and should not be trusted. BUY GENTILE." Another purported to trace President Franklin Roosevelt's "Jewish ancestry" and began:

> Christian Vigilantes Arise! BUY Gentile, EMPLOY Gentile, VOTE Gentile. Boycott the Movies! HOLLYWOOD is the Sodom and Gomorrha where INTERNATIONAL JEWRY controls VICE—DOPE—GAMBLING where young Gentile girls are raped by Jewish producers, directors, casting directors who go unpunished. The Jewish Hollywood Anti-Nazi League controls COMMUNISM in the motion picture industry. Stars, writers and artists are compelled to pay for communistic activities.[9]

Such labor bore fruit. A Gallup poll in April 1938 indicated that 58 percent of the U.S. population believed the persecution of European Jews to be entirely or at least partially the Jews' own fault. The results of another in July 1939 showed that 31.9 percent believed Jews had too much power in business, agreeing that steps should be taken to prevent its accumulation. Aviation hero Charles Lindbergh, an avowed pacifist, spoke to an audience of 7,500 in Des Moines, Iowa on September 11, 1941, charging the Jews with seeking to force the United States into war with Germany and threatening them with dire consequences if they "succeeded." Even in 1942, when the United States was in the war, 44 percent of those surveyed believed Jews had too much power and influence. This kept members of the American Jewish community's hands tied proving they were "good Americans" when they should have been demanding government relief for their European brethren.[10]

FATHER COUGHLIN

The charismatic personality who might have drawn the fascist, anti-Semitic sentiment together—were it not for anti-Catholicism—was the fiery radio priest, Father Charles E. Coughlin. A man who spoke to fifteen million listeners each Sunday (making his program more popular than entertainment shows of the time), Coughlin moved to the extreme political right after a disappointing defeat of his independent Union Party in 1936. There he joined Protestants Gerald Winrod and Eugene Sanctuary. Like them, he attacked the Roosevelt New Deal as a "Jew Deal" for Communism. He quoted from the *Protocols*, justifying Nazi treatment of Jews as a necessary "political defense mechanism." He became a popular figure in Germany and was quoted by the Nazi press.

Coughlin's Christian Front, organized in 1938, excluded Jews from membership and drew from the most ungodly of the Catholic and Protestant population. Chapter meetings turned into drinking fests, praising Coughlin and curs-

9. Reproductions of these anti-Semitic fliers and others may be found in Zosa Szajkowski, *An Illustrated Sourcebook on the Holocaust*, 3 vols. (New York: Ktav, 1977–79), 1:12–13.
10. Yehuda Bauer, *American Jewry and the Holocaust: The American Jewish Joint Distribution Committee, 1939–1945* (Detroit: Wayne State U., 1981), pp. 41–42. For Charles Lindbergh's attack note Carey McWilliams, *A Mask for Privilege: Anti-Semitism in America* (1948; reprint, Westport, Conn.: Greenwood Press, 1979), pp. 45–46.

ing Jews and their leader, Franklin Delano "Rosenfeld." Gangs of these drunken bullies beat up Jews and organized "buy Christian only" campaigns. Initially, Coughlin praised the zeal and courage of the Christian Fronters, explaining that the United States was a Christian country taken over by the non-Christians. His support for them by late 1939 faltered, however, due to bad publicity over Nazi-like activity. Through his periodical *Social Justice* and his radio program he continued his anti-Semitic, anti-Communist harangue until silenced by the Roman Catholic Church May 1, 1942 on the eve of government action against him. Coughlin blamed his censure not on the war nor on Roosevelt ("the President was only taking orders") but on "that small group of people who run the world." Nevertheless, Father Coughlin was content, knowing that in his heyday the polls had always affirmed that most of his listeners were "in his corner."[11]

"TRUE CHRISTIANS'" ACCEPTANCE OF HITLER—THE TESTIMONY OF OSWALD J. SMITH

A number of Christians have said that "true, Bible-believing Christians" in Germany never supported Adolf Hitler. Others have even claimed that there were *no* "true Christians" in Germany; only the liberal higher critics with their watered down theology fell for Hitler's propaganda. I wish this were true, but it is not.

Oswald J. Smith, pastor of the missionary-minded Peoples Church in Toronto, was an evangelist, preacher, missionary statesman, author of nearly thirty books published in thirty-five languages, poet, hymn-writer, radio preacher, editor, and avid traveler. Billy Graham, recounting how Smith's books have touched his life, states: "The name, Oswald J. Smith, symbolizes worldwide evangelization." Millions of Americans would agree. This pastor knew "true believers," and in 1936 he made one of his fifteen world tours, traveling to eighteen countries, including Germany. His article "My Visit To Germany" shows how effective Adolf Hitler was in his "Clean Up Germany" campaign before the Olympics (Smith left July 8 from Paris to Berlin) and in his brainwashing of good, decent Christians. Even forty-six-year-old Smith was taken in by the fervent testimony of the German Christians.[12]

Smith emphasized he was writing about "the New Germany, not the Germany I had seen in 1924 and 1929, but the Germany of Adolph Hitler"; and if anyone doubted his statements, all that person had to do was "to visit Germany for himself and he will find what I have found, for *seeing is believing*." He believed he had "inside information" because he talked to German Christian lead-

---

11. See Marcus, *Father Coughlin*, especially 154–65, 208–18. Compare David J. O'Brien, "American Catholics and Anti-Semitism in the 1930s," *Catholic World* 204 (February 1967), pp. 270–76.

12. Oswald J. Smith, *The Peoples Church and Its Founder* (Toronto: The Peoples Press, 1961), p. ii. See page 95 for his travels in 1936.

ers who had lived in Germany since the days of the Kaiser and were not afraid to speak frankly with him. The safety and security Smith felt in Germany as well as the optimism and courtesy of the people deeply impressed him. "Germany has awakened," he exuberantly reported and then continued:

> What, you ask, is the real attitude of the German people toward Hitler? There is but one answer. They love him. Yes, from the highest to the lowest, children and parents, old and young alike—they love their new leader. Their confidence in him cannot be shaken. They trust him to a man.
>
> "What about your elections?" I asked. "You have no choice. It is Hitler or no one. There is no opponent." "We don't want another party," they replied with indignation. "We have had enough of parties. We want a true leader, a man who loves us, and works for our good. We are satisfied with Hitler." And that feeling exists everywhere. Every true Christian is for Hitler. I know, for it was from the Christians I got most of my information, and right or wrong, they endorse Adolph Hitler.[13]

Smith added that German Christians did not like all the "Little Hitlers" serving under Hitler. These men did not have their Leader's spirit. But the people rationalized, saying that Hitler could not "personally attend to everything" and "must of necessity leave much to those under him."[14]

The Christians immediately impressed upon Smith the desperate situation of Germany in 1932, with more than seven million unemployed and gross immorality abounding everywhere. Smith explained:

> The Bolshevicks were preparing to take over the country. When their offices were raided, lists of the pastors of Berlin were found, marked for death. There was no hope, no future. Germany was doomed.
>
> Then came Hitler, and just in time. Two days later, and Communism would have been in complete control. Now all is changed. All is different. It is German freedom instead of Soviet slavery. Hitler has saved Germany. He has put new hope into the hearts of seventy million people. . . . Now only one million are unemployed and "everybody is busy."

Smith listened "spellbound" to the contented, happy people. "All must work. There is no time for dissipation," he wrote. "They have a saying in Germany now—'Strength through Joy' . . . Hitler knows well the value of holidays, and he has made abundant provision. For again it is 'Strength through Joy.'"[15]

Smith mentioned that the "ideal family consists of four children" and "all girls

---

13. Oswald J. Smith, "My Visit to Germany," *The Defender* 11 (September 1936), p. 15. Circulation of this periodical was 94,000 in September 1936.
14. Ibid. This would correspond to Helmut Thielicke's testimony that German Christians continued, even when the worst occurred, to believe that the Führer would do nothing wrong and that he was a good Christian. Note Helmut Thielicke, *Between Heaven and Earth*, trans. and ed. John W. Doberstein (New York: Harper & Row, 1965), pp. 151–52.
15. Ibid.

are trained to be mothers." Furthermore, mass immorality was being corrected. He explained:

> Before the days of Hitler, women, like the women of the United States, used paint and lip-stick. "We don't need these things," declared their new leaders, and cosmetic firms had to close for lack of trade. In all my travels through Germany I never saw a German girl with artificial color on her face or lips. And oh, how fresh and natural they looked! How much more attractive.
>
> Before Hitler's days, Spiritism flourished. Almost every corner had its medium. Now occultism of every description is banned. Hitler has enforced the laws of Saul. Spiritism was sending the people to the asylums. Today it is no more.[16]

Smith was more than thrilled that Russellism (Jehovah's Witnesses) was banned as dangerous to the nation. He suggested that the "United States and Canada could learn a valuable lesson in this regard."

In actuality, both Smith and the German church were to learn that when one person's religious freedom is violated, all religious freedom is on the chopping block as well.

Smith was sorry "that the good Jews have had to suffer with the bad. But who can differentiate in an hour of mob rule and violence? Even Hitler could not restrain his followers." He testified: "Not for a moment would I say anything against the orthodox God-fearing Jews. I would be the last to make their lot harder than it is, for I love them. But they have been betrayed by their renegade brethren who have become their worst enemies, and they know it not."[17]

As for the persecution of Catholics by the Nazi regime, German Christians assured him that "Hitler has nothing to say about Roman Catholicism as a religion. He himself is by birth, a Roman Catholic. But he is against the political influence of the priests and the vile practices that have been proven against them."

"But the most favorable sign of all," Smith concluded positively, was "the spiritual awakening that is coming to the German people." The Dom Cathedral in Berlin was full, with a minister who "preaches the old-fashioned Gospel. He spares no one. And none interferes with him. He deals openly with sin and salvation." The Christian leaders assured him that as long as there was such preaching and praying "Germany is safe." This gave Smith confidence for he believed America and England faced similar problems. He ended:

> Let us pray for Germany. I am convinced that this nation is bound to play an important part in the immediate future of Europe. France, I do not trust. France is Red, immoral and godless. Germany is Protestant. It was from Germany that Luther came. There are signs of a growing friendship between Germany and Great

---

16. Ibid., p. 16. The Nazis, however, actually drew heavily from the pagan Teutonic rites in an effort to capture the early history of the Germanic tribes.
17. Ibid., p. 17.

Britain. I am glad. If England and Germany stand together the present peace of Europe is assured.[18]

Germany, however, was not "safe." The church itself had taken the Führer and his misdeeds into her bosom and shortly would receive the consequences. Revival never did come to Germany when the church failed to love her neighbor.

Gerald Winrod published Smith's article in his *Defender* magazine. Winrod published the articles of many fine Christians in this magazine, as well as advertising some respectable Christian literature. Followers of Winrod called themselves "Defenders." Their theme song was "Faith of Our Fathers"; their motto was "Back to the Bible." The Defenders experienced an agonizing period when they finally discovered that their leader had become a fascist, an anti-Semite, and a secret follower of Adolf Hitler. Like the Communists with their "Active Measures," Winrod did not come out directly and declare himself as such, but he steadily injected his racist poison into the periodical and the organization.

It should be noted that this anti-Semitism has since been rooted out. Elmer A. Josephson, a graduate of Bethel Institute (Baptist General Conference) with additional courses at the Moody Bible Institute, experienced a spiritual crisis after succumbing to the world conspiracy theory and the *Protocols*. He joined Winrod in 1937 because Winrod was "one of America's top communist-fighters." Soon after, Josephson took a second glance at his life in the light of Scripture and found he was "traveling a very perilous path." He left Winrod and has since operated Bible Light, a ministry supportive of the Jewish people and Israel. He explained in a note accompanying a short testimony of his ordeal: "The parent organization, The Defenders, has since disassociated itself from any form of anti-Semitism and is a friend and supporter of Israel."[19]

CHRISTIANS WHO SAW AND SPOKE THE TRUTH

Fundamentalists and evangelicals have received considerable bad press because of anti-Semites such as Winrod. Many scholars have taken for granted that the more theologically conservative one is, the more anti-Semitic one becomes. My research has shown that nothing is historically further from the truth. The fundamentalist-evangelical movement has traditionally been a firm supporter of the Jewish people and has staunchly opposed anti-Semitism. During the Holocaust, conservative Christians tended to believe that the Jewish people were being exterminated, while more liberal Christians were labeling the reports "atrocity propaganda."[20]

18. Ibid., p. 18.
19. Elmer A. Josephson, *Israel, God's Key to World Redemption* (Hillsboro, Kansas: Bible Light, 1974), p. 15. Note also pages 16–17 for his experience with Winrod.
20. Note my book, *Zionism Within Early American Fundamentalism, 1878–1918: A Convergence of Two Traditions* (New York: Edwin Mellen, 1979). Chapters 1 and 8 discuss the modern period. Compare Hertzel Fishman, *American Protestantism and a Jewish State* (Detroit: Wayne State U., 1973). Pages 178–83 provide a good summary of his total research on liberal Protestant anti-Jewish attitudes.

Arno C. Gaebelein, the great fundamentalist prophetic teacher, perceptively saw Adolf Hitler for what he was. Gaebelein wrote as early as 1930 about the dangers of Hitler coming to power, and even earlier about patriotic civil religion in Germany and its possible evil consequences. After the 1936 Olympic Games, Gaebelein was flabbergasted that the English statesman David Lloyd George "brought back a glowing report of the bettered conditions in Germany and that the people are happy." Gaebelein's periodical *Our Hope* consistently detailed the anti-Semitism of the Nazi regime throughout the 1930s and during World War II.[21] When anti-Semite Colonel E. H. Sanctuary tried to use The American-European Fellowship, an interdenominational missionary society of which Gaebelein was president, in the same manner that Winrod used the Defenders, Gaebelein forced him to resign. Sanctuary was as subtle as Winrod, spouting the proper Christian clichés, but Gaebelein labeled his literature "malicious and slanderous" against the Jewish people. After a group including Sanctuary, Winrod, and Pelley had been indicted for sedition by the Attorney General's Office, Gaebelein explained of Sanctuary and his deceitful crew: "And now he is in the clutches of the Law. He was an admirer and supporter of the seditious German Bund, a co-laborer with Pelley, Winrod and other secret followers of Hitler."[22] (Sanctuary was very active in the Ku Klux Klan in the 1930s as well and was the author and publisher of its official history, *Knights of the Ku Klux Klan*.) In the latter 1930s Donald G. Barnhouse circulated a petition repudiating the *Protocols*. It was signed by Gaebelein, Harry Ironside, Keith Brooks, and many other leading evangelicals.

Hitler's atheistic persecution of the Christian church was clearly manifested two years after the Olympics, when he seized control of the German Evangelical Church and began a program of persecution and silencing. Only then were many Christians made aware of their error in believing that Nazi Germany was Christian. At the end of the war, when Nazi atrocities were exposed to the world, Christians were finally convinced that the "possible" inhumanity of man to man was an actuality.

On many, however, the primary lesson was lost. It was lost because they viewed it as "Hitler's problem," "liberalism's problem," "conservatism's problem" or a "German problem." They failed to see that it was and is *our problem*. It could have happened here, and it could have happened to us. The groups, the deception, and the hatred were and are here. When in April 1938 Hitler announced his detailed program for the German church, Gaebelein shuddered and declared

---

21. See my article, "Our Hope: An American Fundamentalist Journal and the Holocaust, 1937–1945," *Fides et Historia*, 12 (Spring 1980), pp. 89–103, and my book, *Arno C. Gaebelein, 1861–1945: Irenic Fundamentalist and Scholar* (New York: Edwin Mellen, 1983), which also includes conversations with his son the late Frank E. Gaebelein on this topic.
22. Note Rausch, *Arno C. Gaebelein*, pp. 273–74.

that it was "viciously anti-Semitic and therefore anti-Christian."[23] It was a statement he had uttered for years about Nazi Germany, containing a kernel of truth that the Holocaust case study provides for us. Today, we must affirm: *If it is even mildly racist, it is anti-Christ.*

23. Ibid., p. 169.

10

The Ghetto

In vivid color photographs, the world viewed the ghastly horror of the Cambodian atrocities. The November 12, 1979 cover of *Time* magazine displayed a mother with agony and desperation on her face, holding her starving baby. The caption read: "STARVATION: Deathwatch in Cambodia." "A starving baby minutes away from death has no responsibility or knowledge of Cambodian politics," said veteran *Time* correspondent Marsh Clark in anguish. "What human cruelties and failings, one wonders, have reduced tens of thousands of people to the state of dumb, brute animals?"[1] Out of a population of eight million people, approximately four million had died. In their effort to establish a new Cambodia, the communist Khmer Rouge lashed out at the intelligentsia, killing even those suspected of being able to read or write. Children classified as offspring of undesirables were chained together and buried alive under mounds of suffocating dirt bulldozed on top of them. In horrors reminiscent of the medieval period, those deemed slackers received a hatchet blow to the back of the head or, as some refugees reported, were disemboweled. Moreover, widely-read American news magazines contained photographs of skulls from a mass grave and children with irreparable bone deformation as a result of malnutrition. Other

---

1. "A Letter from the Publisher," *Time*, 12 November 1979, p. 2. "There is no serious question that the Khmer Rouge . . . committed a form of genocide unknown to mankind since the Holocaust," Clark prefaced. See "Deathwatch: Cambodia" in the same issue for photographs and their detailed analysis of the suffering (pp. 42–48). Page 48 included an excerpt on the medical aspects of starvation entitled: "The Body Eats Itself."

photographs revealed emaciated adults and corpses—thousands of corpses.

When the Vietnamese took over the country and began to battle the Khmer Rouge, food became a weapon and racism was rampant. Hanoi regarded the Cambodians as treacherous barbarians who had rebelled against their authority in the nineteenth century. Consequently, they favored the massive starvation of the Cambodian people, obstructing the relief efforts of a concerned world.

For Marsh Clark, who watched the progression of Khmer Rouge leader Pol Pot's army, there was one modern precedent: the Holocaust. For Holocaust survivors, the stark photographic documentation of Cambodian starvation and humiliation served as a harrowing reminder of a time that was never supposed to surface again. In amazement they said: "Why it's just like the Ghetto!" It was the Jewish community who spearheaded relief efforts to help alleviate the suffering of the Cambodian victims.[2]

THE ESTABLISHMENT OF POLISH GHETTOS

German armies on September 1, 1939 poured across the Polish border, bringing sudden death and destruction. Fighter planes and bombers destroyed most of the Polish air force before it could get off the ground; divisions of German tanks raced toward Warsaw, leaving fire, carnage, and destruction in their wake. The world had never witnessed a scene quite like this, as a Nazi infantry numbering one and one-half million men equipped with the most sophisticated weaponry, electronic gear, and mobile units available devastated Poland in a surprise attack. Hitler, aware of the unprovoked nature of the offensive, prepared his German people a week prior to the attack with heavy propaganda that spoke of Polish "atrocities"—atrocities that never occurred. As Poland lay prostrate before the Nazis, Hitler explained that the Polish state had turned its back on peace and that he was just meeting "force with force."[3]

Restrictions and pogroms against the Jews began almost immediately. On September 21, 1939, Reinhard Heydrich instructed the chiefs of the *Einsatzgruppen* (Special Action Groups) of the Security Police that their first assignment was "the concentration of the Jews from the countryside into the larger cities." Heydrich wrote that "Jewish communities of fewer than 500 persons are

2. For a discussion of the historical events of this atrocity note William Shawcross, *Sideshow* (New York: Simon and Schuster, 1979). Relief efforts are noted in "Racing to Save the Hungry," *Time*, 12 November 1979, p. 50.
3. Detailed Nazi propaganda was even circulated throughout the United States on Polish (and British) responsibility for the war. Refer to *Documents on the Events Preceding the Outbreak of the War*, compiled and published by the German Foreign Office in Berlin, 1939; and by the German Library of Information in New York, 1940. Compare *Allied Intrigue in the Low Countries: Further Documents Concerning the Anglo-French Policy of Extending the War*, published by the German Library of Information in New York, 1940, justifying Nazi movements into Belgium and Holland. The United States, of course, did not enter the war until December 1941.

to be dissolved and to be transferred to the nearest city of concentration." He decreed that a *Judenrat*, a Jewish Council, was to be set up, stating:

> In each Jewish community, a Council of Jewish Elders is to be set up, to be composed, as far as possible, of the remaining personalities and rabbis. The council is to comprise up to 24 male Jews (depending on the size of the Jewish community).
>
> The council is to be made fully responsible, in the literal sense of the word, for the exact and punctual execution of all directives issued or yet to be issued. . . .
>
> For general reasons of security, the concentration of Jews in the cities will probably necessitate orders altogether barring Jews from certain sections of cities, or, for example, forbidding them to leave the ghetto or go out after a designated evening hour, etc. However, economic necessities are always to be considered in this connection.[4]

At the outset, Heydrich emphasized that "the planned overall measures (i.e., the final aim) are to be kept strictly secret," and that "Distinction must be made between: (1) The final aim (which will require extended periods of time), and (2) The stages leading to the fulfillment of this final aim (which will be carried out in short terms)." Historians debate whether or not Heydrich was actually at this time referring to the "Final Solution" (*Endlösung*, the total extermination of the Jewish people) by his reference to "final aim" (*Endziel*). When the Final Solution was clearly enacted, Heydrich zealously pursued it.[5]

German forces entered Warsaw on September 29, 1939. The Jewish population was approximately 394,000 (over one-third of the city's population). On October 26 Jews were required to join forced-labor teams to clean up the debris remaining from the Nazi bombardment (eventually, they would also dig anti-tank ditches to prevent the Russians from overrunning Poland when Germany attacked her "new found friend" on June 22, 1941). Throughout Poland similar encroachments were instituted; Jewish males between the ages of twelve and sixty were rounded up for fourteen-hour-a-day slave labor. To stigmatize the Jewish people and facilitate identification, a November 23 decree announced that Jews "over ten years of age are obliged, beginning December 1, 1939, to wear a white band, at least 10 centimeters wide, with the Star of David on the right sleeve of their inner and outer clothing." Failure to comply was punishable by imprisonment. Further edicts confining Jews to a single section of Warsaw led to detention in a quarantine area, so that by October 16, 1941 the penalty for leaving this area (the Warsaw Ghetto) without authorization was death. In a noteworthy parody on American history, some of these sections, reserved for mass expulsions, were referred to by the Nazis as "reservations."[6]

---

4. Heydrich's written instructions translated into English may be read in many sources. Note, for example, Lucy Dawidowicz, *A Holocaust Reader* (New York: Behrman House, 1976), pp. 59–64. On page 61 she has a fine map of the German partition of Poland.
5. See Yehuda Bauer, *A History of the Holocaust* (New York: Franklin Watts, 1982), p. 151.
6. Dawidowicz, *A Holocaust Reader*, pp. 65–68 for these decrees and one establishing the Warsaw Jewish Council.

The Polish People

A FEW RESISTERS

The new and restrictive laws against Jews often made clear that Gentiles who helped or hid a Jew were liable to the *same punishment* as a Jew, namely, death. In spite of this, a few Poles risked their lives to hide Jews. Leon Wells, a survivor who testified at the Nuremberg trials and other Nazi war criminal trials, praised the Kalwinski family, who lived in the outskirts of Lvov, Poland. He wrote:

> Most of us were hidden in their basement for over two years. The Kalwinskis did not do it for money in spite of the fact that they themselves were not well-to-do people. They were small farmers who owned two or three pigs, a horse, and a cow. Mrs. Katarina Kalwinska had three sons and one daughter. The oldest, twenty-three years old, was never told by his parents that they were hiding Jews as he was already married and as such he might tell his wife who in turn might tell her family, and this was much too risky. The youngest son who at this time was about seven years old knew together with his older brother and sister about the Jews hidden in the basement, but he also knew that if he said anything that he would not only be punished, but together with his family he would be hanged. This fact was brought home even more when the Germans discovered thirty-five Jews hidden only a few blocks away at the house of the cattle dealer Jozefek. Jozefek was hung in a public square and his body left dangling for several days as a warning to others. After a full day's work taking care of the farm house and her children, Mrs. Kalwinska continued late into the night after everyone had gone to sleep, cooking and washing for twenty-three Jews in the basement. All of this had to be done in the night so as not to arouse suspicion in the daytime when the neighbors could drop in.[7]

After the war Mrs. Kalwinska asked the survivors to refrain from visiting her because "she did not want some of her anti-Semitic neighbors to know what she had done."

MANY WHO COMPLIED

Such acts of bravery stand in bold contrast to those of the majority of the Poles. It must be remembered that the Polish people suffered terribly under Nazi domination, enduring rationing, poverty, hunger, rape, and murder. But we cannot deny that their anti-Semitism over the decades grew into a Jew-hatred that fashioned them into key collaborators with the Nazi regime.

Simcha Berg, a Jew from Lodz, responded to the call to defend Warsaw along

---

7. Leon W. Wells, "A Survivor's Testimony," in Michael D. Ryan, ed., *Human Responses to the Holocaust* (New York: Edwin Mellen, 1981), p. 76. This book contains the papers delivered at the 1979 Bernhard E. Olson Scholars' Conference on "The Church Struggle and the Holocaust," sponsored by The National Conference of Christians and Jews. Compare Stanley Bors testimony in Sylvia Rothchild, *Voices from The Holocaust* (New York: New American Library, 1981), p. 223 on the thousands that Poles refrained from saving in the ghetto.

with many other Polish citizens. Bombed and strafed by Nazi planes on his way among thousands to the city, stumbling over the corpses of the less fortunate, Simcha survived. When Warsaw surrendered, the Nazis introduced soup kitchens for starving Poles. As thousands lined up, Polish Gentiles pointed to Jews and shouted, "Away from the line!" Simcha and other Jews were turned away, as the Poles informed the Nazis that they were Jews. Simcha reflected: "When the war started and the Germans came into Poland, they didn't know the difference between a Jew and a non-Jew . . . the Poles went with them and pointed out, 'This is a Jew and this is a Jew.'"[8] Prejudiced acts such as these occurred even before the Nazis had a chance to institute their anti-Semitic measures!

The Nazis intended to appropriate this intrinsic anti-Semitism utterly. They determined that the Poles received a portion of the goods plundered from Jews. Furthermore, a primary objective of the German papers printed in the Polish language was to deepen hatred toward the Jews by blaming them for Poland's problems. Even the anti-Nazi Polish underground press spewed forth the same hatred, leaving the Jewish people no recourse but to either establish their own underground combat organizations or to quietly pretend (if they were fortunate enough to join a Polish partisan group fighting the Nazis) not to be Jewish. While the Germans deliberated concerning the area to be restricted to Jews, Poles fought to keep as many streets as possible "Aryan." The first year, mobs of Polish hooligans swept down on Jewish streets, beating Jewish men, women, and children with clubs, having no fear of Polish police who refused to intervene.

THE DILEMMA FOR JEWISH LEADERSHIP

As late as July 9, 1942, when Jews of the Warsaw Ghetto had seen almost three years of bitter persecution, Adam Czerniakow, leader of the Warsaw Jewish Council, complained in his diary:

> In the afternoon Polish urchins [keep] throwing stones over the little wall to Chlodna Street. Ever since we removed the bricks and stones from the middle of Chlodna Street, they have not got much ammunition left.
> I have often asked myself the question whether Poland is Mickiewicz and Slowacki [two Polish Romantic poets of the nineteenth century] or whether it is that urchin. The truth lies in the middle.[9]

In the same entry Czerniakow noted: "At 8 in the morning I went to the little square at Ceglana Street to see about 800 deportees from Rawa Mazowiecka and surroundings, who were brought there during the night. Small children,

8. Saul S. Friedman, *Amcha: An Oral Testament of the Holocaust* (Washington, D.C.: University Press of America, 1979), p. 110.
9. Adam Chernikow, *The Warsaw Diary of Adam Czerniakow*, ed. Raul Hilberg, Stanislaw Staron, and Josef Kermisz; trans. Stanislaw Staron and the staff of Yad Vashem (New York: Stein and Day, 1979), p. 377.

babies, women. The sight would break my heart, had it not been hardened by 3 years of misery." Czerniakow, however, was not as hardened as he believed. When the Nazis announced massive "deportations to the East" regardless of age or sex, he committed suicide.

The Nazis had formed the Jewish councils to make their administrative tasks easier. Leadership unwilling to work with the Nazis was immediately eliminated. Those who tried to negotiate for the lives of their people were frustrated at every turn. Czerniakow was able to gain a few concessions, but in the end lost all. Nazi cunning and deception was diabolical. Jewish community leaders were faced with questions as to how far they should go along with the Nazis before saying a strong *No!* If they say no, who would take their place if they were shot? Would their people be better off without them? Could they save some if they compromised the lives of others? Whose life should be negotiated? For some the question became basic: "Can I save my life and my family's?"

The question of the Jewish Council members' integrity is complex. Isaiah Trunk in his monumental study, *Judenrat: The Jewish Councils In Eastern Europe Under Nazi Occupation*, suggests that the critical test of the council members' moral standards, integrity, and personal responsibility for the community came at the precise moment they knew of the destination for "resettlement." Those not resigning their post and continuing to participate in the deportation process to the death camps were, according to Trunk, Nazi accomplices. Trunk, however, also stressed the declaration of some in Warsaw: "No Council, no police, nothing at all; do whatever you wish, we will not cooperate. You want to catch [for forced labor]—all right, catch. You want to kill, so kill. Passive resistance. You can rule over us—maybe fate so ordained—but never will we become a willing, cooperating subject."[10] And so it was, the choices of leadership demonstrated themselves to be both futile and fatal.

LIFE IN THE GHETTO

MISERY AND DEATH

The Warsaw Ghetto is a case study in man's inhumanity to man. Like the rest of Poland's ghettos in major cities, the history of the Warsaw Ghetto is a mixture of atrocity and misery; perfidy and exploitation; the will to live and human dignity in the midst of suffering. An adult's starvation level is 900–1,000 calories per day; a child's growing body requires more than 2,000 calories. Aryan Germans in Warsaw received 2,300 calories a day. The Nazis instituted rationing in the Ghetto: legal consumption for a Jew was approximately 200 calories— mandatory starvation! Life in a ghetto was potentially worse than in a concentration camp, for hunger could linger indefinitely. The Jews, starving, sold any

10. Isaiah Trunk, *Judenrat: The Jewish Councils in Eastern Europe Under Nazi Occupation* (New York: Macmillan, 1972), p. 17.

possession to get food. Some resorted to selling themselves. Smuggling operations permeated the Ghetto scene. The Polish community and German soldiers took advantage of the situation; portions of the Warsaw Ghetto gained reputations for "terrific buys" and "good times."[11]

In Warsaw 400,000 Jews were compressed into an area once populated by 150,000 poor Jews and Gentiles. Joined by additional Jewish refugees from rural areas, this number swelled to approximately 500,000. Disease broke out; death was rampant. Emmanuel Ringelblum, a young and promising social historian who chose to return to his people in Poland from Geneva, wrote as early as January 1940: "The mortality among the Jews in Warsaw is dreadful. There are fifty to seventy deaths daily." The average number of Jews per room in the Ghetto was thirteen, with many left on the streets.

There were not enough orphanages for children, and temperatures dipped well below zero during the winter of 1941–42. Ringelblum recorded in 1941:

> The first frosts have already appeared, and the populace is trembling at the prospect of cold weather. The most fearful sight is that of freezing children. Little children with bare feet, bare knees, and torn clothing, stand dumbly in the street weeping. Tonight, the 14th [of November], I heard a tot of three or four yammering. The child will probably be found frozen to death tomorrow morning, a few hours off. Early October, when the first snows fell, some seventy children were found frozen to death on the steps of ruined houses. Frozen children are becoming a general phenomenon. The police are supposed to open a special institution for street children at 20 Nowolipie Street, meanwhile, children's bodies and crying serve as a persistent background for the Ghetto.[12]

"People cover the dead bodies of frozen children with the handsome posters designed for Children's Month," Ringelblum wryly noted, "bearing the legend, 'Our Children, Our Children Must Live—A Child Is the Holiest Thing.'" Thousands of pages could be used to document atrocities committed against adults and little children. The misery of the Ghetto is perhaps summed up by the child who tried to collect an additional lunch at a public "soup" kitchen. Ringelblum recorded, "When discovered, the child begged with tears in his eyes to be allowed to have two lunches, because he did not want to die like his little sister."[13]

11. Note Yisrael Gutman, *The Jews of Warsaw, 1939–1943: Ghetto, Underground, Revolt*, trans. Ina Friedman (Bloomington, Ind.: Indiana U., 1982), pp. 66–72. Compare Chaim A. Kaplan, *Scroll of Agony: The Warsaw Diary of Chaim A. Kaplan*, ed. and trans. Abraham I. Katsh (New York: Macmillan, 1965), pp. 225–26; 290–96.
12. Emmanuel Ringelblum, *Notes from the Warsaw Ghetto*, ed. and trans. Jacob Sloan (New York: Schocken Books, 1974), pp. 233–34.
13. Ibid., p. 230. This account continues: "The bare Jewish graveyard, next to the Evangelical and Catholic ones, which still have their trees, is a symbol of Jewish woe. Living and dead, the Jewish populace suffers evil.—The beginning of November, 1941, news from Lodz [Ghetto] that the Lodz Jews had been prohibited from marrying and having children. Women pregnant up to three months have to have an abortion. In a word—Pharaoh's laws revived by the Prussians."

PROTECTING A SPARK OF CIVILIZATION

Ringelblum and many others felt compelled to record what was happening in the Ghetto. Even young people drove themselves to recount their struggle and the evil that was forced upon them. This was true of most ghettos, as well as the concentration camps. Although the penalty was death, the Jewish community as a literate and proud people wanted the world to know what had happened to them.

Secret archives with numerous contributors were established. Emmanuel Ringelblum's "Oneg Shabbat" (a code name for the Warsaw Ghetto archives) employed the efforts of economists, journalists, social scientists, rabbis, historians, and research assistants to investigate special topics. They used code names and concealed their information in varied forms, sometimes in the body of a personal letter or note. While most of these individuals in Warsaw were deported to the death camps in the summer of 1942, Ringelblum and his family hid with a Polish family in the Gentile section of Warsaw. He buried the Oneg Shabbat collection in three milk pails and continued to write his memoirs. Alas, he was discovered by the Nazis in March 1944. He, his family, and the Poles who helped them were executed. Two of the three milk pails were later found.

Many Holocaust memoirs have been lost to us; but those documents that did survive bear testimony to the courage and fortitude of a resilient people who sensed in their suffering condition a *mission* to warn men and women of the hardening of conscience among civilized peoples. Although these accounts underscore the depravity of mankind, they never neglect to emphasize those who helped them, such sporadic occurrences radiating as beacon lights in a dark world. The difficulty of their task and the enormity of their mission was conveyed by Warsaw historian Dr. Ignacy Schipper, who declared to Alexander Donat:

> History is usually written by the victor. What we know about murdered peoples is only what their murderers vaingloriously cared to say about them. Should our murderers be victorious, should *they* write the history of this war, our destruction will be presented as one of the most beautiful pages of world history, and future generations will pay tribute to them as dauntless crusaders. Their every word will be taken for gospel. Or they may wipe out our memory altogether, as if we had never existed, as if there had never been a Polish Jewry, a Ghetto in Warsaw. . . . But if *we* write the history of this period of blood and tears—and I firmly believe we will—who will believe us? Nobody will *want* to believe us because our disaster is the disaster of the entire civilized world.[14]

The Nazis hoped to achieve total dehumanization of Jews in the ghettos. Instead, the Jewish people formed underground social, educational, and reli-

14. Alexander Donat, *The Holocaust Kingdom* (New York: Holt, Rinehart and Winston, 1965), p. 211.

gious organizations, foiling in part Nazi intentions. Schools and theaters were established; reading circles and sewing circles abounded. Craftsmen taught the young trades, and scientists gathered research statistics on the effects of malnutrition on the social milieu as well as on the human body, including their own bodies: Artists painted pictures of flowers and fruit, and they held competitions and exhibitions. Clandestine newspapers abounded, and news about Palestine was gladly received. Facts about conditions in other ghettos and camps were collected. Religious life was maintained and Jewish holidays celebrated. Dr. William Glicksman, who was in the Czestochowa ghetto in Poland, testified that "Jewish culture was strengthened a thousand times. We had secret schools, secret *minyans* for praying. The libraries were burned down so we shared out private books."[15] For many who were tortured and bruised in the ghetto, their faith in God was vibrant. Even during the terror of deportation in the Warsaw Ghetto in July 1942, a lone voice cried out to crowds of anxious people: "Take heart, Jews. You'll see, with God's help we'll overcome this new misfortune too!"[16]

A Nazi Laboratory

Conditions in the ghettos continued to deteriorate. Typhus raged, taking a monthly toll of 6,000 to 7,000 in the Warsaw Ghetto, where a wall eight to ten feet high was constructed in 1941 to separate Jews from the rest of the city. The streets were strewn with naked corpses thrown out during the night with dirty paper covering their faces. Corpses were gathered in heaps and tossed into collective graves. Bernard Goldstein recalled:

> Half-dead, half-naked swollen human beings, with lacerated, parchment-yellow bodies are scattered alongside the wall of the Catholic church on Lezno Street. Sickly infants with pussy eyes breathe heavily, emitting gurgling sounds. The older ones, pale and emaciated beg with their last bit of strength: "A pi . . . ece of bread!" The street is already crowded. Everyone tries to make his way carefully for fear of touching someone infected with typhus. A bedraggled, filthy Jew, bare-footed and frothing at the mouth, is dragging a small wagonload of children who wail: "Bread, bread . . ."[17]

Many, unable to move, spent most of the day bedridden and writhing in pain from hunger and cold. To help ward off the cold and to boil meager rations (such as potato skins and cabbage roots), moldings of doors, windows, and

---

15. Rothchild, *Voices from the Holocaust*, pp. 236–37.
16. Vladka Meed, *On Both Sides of the Wall: Memoirs from the Warsaw Ghetto* (New York: Holocaust Library, 1979), p. 10.
17. Bernard Goldstein, "Hell in the Streets," in Jacob Glatstein et al., *Anthology of Holocaust Literature* (New York: Atheneum, 1968), pp. 109–10. Typhus is a highly infectious disease caused by a microorganism. It is characterized at the onset by nausea, headache, dizziness, and high fever, followed by a rash that may cover the entire body. The victim becomes lethargic and delirious.

floors were stripped from rooms and used in the stove. From ghetto to ghetto the dismal conditions were much the same.

With administrative precision and scientific scrutiny, the Nazis photographed the ghetto experience. Their aim in ghettoization was to destroy the Jewish people. Historian Philip Friedman in his essay, "The Jewish Ghettoes of the Nazi Era," explained:

> The ghettoes were designed to serve the Nazis as laboratories for testing the methods of slow and "peaceful" destruction of whole groups of human beings. Goebbels aptly characterized the ghettoes as *Todeskisten* (death caskets). The governor of Warsaw, Ludwig Fischer, was reported (in January 1942) to have made the following remark, giving away the secret of ghettoization: "The Jews must adjust themselves to all conditions, but we shall endeavor to create such conditions for them as will make the adjustment difficult." On another occasion, Fischer is reported to have said: "The Jews will disappear because of hunger and need, and nothing will remain of the Jewish question but a cemetery."[18]

Starvation, however, was too slow for the Nazis. On April 1, 1942, Governor-General Frank declared in an address in Lvov: "That we have sentenced 1.2 million Jews to die of hunger should be noted only marginally. It is clear that, if the Jews do not starve to death, this will result in the speeding up of anti-Jewish measures."[19] Deportations to the death camps would fulfill his grim prophecy.

AN AMERICAN DISGRACE

We must remember that war hysteria can easily magnify prejudice against a minority group even in a democracy. While Jews were ghettoized in Europe, the United States government "relocated" 110,000 Japanese Americans, the entire Japanese population of California, Oregon, and Washington. The very day Frank delivered his speech in Lvov, Poland, posters appeared in San Francisco declaring in part:

> All Japanese persons both alien and non-alien, will be evacuated from the above designated area by 12:00 o'clock noon Tuesday, April 7, 1942. . . . A responsible member of each family, preferably the head of the family, or the person in whose name most of the property is held, and each individual living alone, will report to the Civil Control Station to receive further instructions.[20]

18. Philip Friedman, *Roads to Extinction: Essays on the Holocaust*, ed. Ada June Friedman (New York: The Jewish Publication Society of America, 1980), p. 69.
19. Ibid., pp. 69–70.
20. Note Roger Daniels, *Concentration Camps USA: Japanese Americans and World War II* (New York: Holt, Rinehart and Winston, 1972), for facts and pictures on the period. The poster appears on page xvi.

After the attack on Pearl Harbor, years of hostility toward the Japanese surfaced into hysterical rage. Respected newspapers such as the *Los Angeles Times* referred to them as "yellow vermin," "Japs," "mad dogs," and "Nips." Japanese were accused of spying, even being charged in newspapers of planting their gardens to point secretly to American air bases! Signs in restaurants and stores read: "No Japs Served Here," "Japs Not Allowed" and "Japs Not Welcome."

Even though American relocation centers were not brutal, they were an unjustifiable confinement to both the young and the old. Japanese Americans suffered huge economic losses, being forced to sell homes and businesses within weeks. Moreover, the embarrassment and humiliation occasioned to second- and third-generation American citizens (including veterans from World War I), was a needless degradation. Most went quietly to the camps. In the relocation centers their young men signed up to serve in the military, and like blacks they were segregated into their own fighting units (except those in the intelligence division). Japanese American soldiers earned outstanding war records, and yet some who lived through treacherous battles were refused service at restaurants and referred to as "dirty Japs" even after the war. This dark page of American history, more clearly envisioned in view of the Holocaust, confronts the Christian. And the words of one Japanese American who in February 1943 protested at the Heart Mountain (Wyoming) Relocation Center, are hauntingly clear: "Although we have yellow skins, we too are Americans. We have an American upbringing. . . . We believe that our nation's good faith is to be found in whether it moves to restore full privileges at the earliest opportunity."[21] The year 1945 found Japanese Americans still incarcerated behind barbed wire.

In light of this history, the Associated Press release "Bias Fueled in Detroit at Japanese-Americans" is chilling. Angered over the effect Japan's automobile industry had on the United States (and especially Detroit's economy), autoworker prejudice erupted into violence. A Chinese American, Vincent Chin, was beaten to death in suburban Detroit in June 1982 after being mistaken for a Japanese. Japanese American policeman Mark Bando told a *Detroit Free Press* reporter in July 1983: "You see types that are strictly out for blood. They want to hurt you. We're walking targets." Lawyer James Shimoura spoke out in the same article declaring that unless attitudes changed, violence against Japanese Americans could increase. Meanwhile, the Japanese American community was appalled when Chin's attackers pled guilty to a reduced sentence, were fined $3,700 each and placed on probation. This tragic example gives only an inkling of what can happen if we consider our fellow man inferior, if we use him as a handy scapegoat on which to blame our misfortune, vent our anger, or unleash our frustration. Hatred in action is a frightening, dangerous reality.[22]

21. Edward H. Spicer, et al., *Impounded People: Japanese Americans in the Relocation Centers* (Tucson, Ariz.: U. of Arizona, 1969), p. 151.
22. Note "Bias Fueled in Detroit at Japanese-Americans," *The Plain Dealer* (Cleveland), 11 July 1983.

11

The *Einsatzgruppen*

"I can hardly find words to describe the tragedy," said a shaken Prime Minister Indira Gandhi as she viewed the March 1983 carnage in Assam. Burned out villages and fields strewn with hacked-up and bloated corpses of children attested to the slaughter of three thousand Muslims by angry and bigoted Hindus. The carnage had lasted eight hours and had killed mainly women and children. A young girl whose eye had been gouged out told Gandhi that the Hindu raiders used rifles, hatchets, and spears. The massacre showed that the causes of the Muslim-Hindu bloodshed during the partition of India in 1947 had not been resolved. Even among followers of a religious system as eclectic as Hinduism, murder could be perpetrated in the name of nationalism. "We have no contacts with the Assamese agitators [the executors of the bloodbath] at present, but we do sympathize with them," commented a Sikh militant. In the previous few decades, industrious and productive Muslims had emigrated from Bangladesh, angering residents because "foreigners" were competing for jobs and were permitted to vote. Corpses of innocent children arranged in rows, the bitter fruit of prejudice, were photographed; their faces and young bodies were graphically clear in *Newsweek* and *Time*.

"We don't know where the Assamese will attack us again," a fearful Muslim school teacher asserted. "We are in a minority. We have no other place to go. It looks as though we have to live in danger all our lives."[1]

1. The quotes may be found in "An Assam Massacre: Bad Blood for India," *Newsweek*, 7 March 1983, pp. 38–40. Compare "The Agony of Assam," *Time*, 7 March 1983, pp. 44–45. There are photographs and maps in each article.

As we have seen, special action groups or *Einsatzgruppen*, a division of the SS under the direction of Reinhard Heydrich, chief of the Security Police, had been active during Crystal Night and the invasion of Poland. Following the German army, they carried out "special tasks" in Poland, including actions against Jews and dissident Poles. These groups were small—six groups with less than two thousand total members—but they were helped in their violence and cruelty by members of the general army (*Wehrmacht*) as well as other SS.

In planning the surprise invasion of Russia, however, the Nazis thoroughly discussed an expanded role for the *Einsatzgruppen*. "Mobile killing units" became a more exact definition of their expanded role. Early in 1941 the Nazis decided that Soviet officials, Communists, and Jews should be murdered rather than held as prisoners of war. Hitler apparently gave the order to destroy European Jewry to Himmler (Heydrich's chief) long before the invasion of Russia on June 22, 1941, the invasion serving as a smoke screen for this "Final Solution" to the Jewish "problem." The Soviet campaign brought five million Jews under the Nazi domain. The *Einsatzgruppen* murdered an estimated two million Jewish men, women, and children in western Russia.[2]

For the invasion of Russia, four *Einsatzgruppen* with a combined total of about 3,000 men were formed. To give an idea of their configuration, consider *Einsatzgruppe* A, assigned to the Baltic states. It included 340 militarized formations of SS, 172 motorcycle riders, 133 Order Police, 89 State Police, 87 Auxiliary Police, 41 Criminal Police, 35 Security Service (SD), 51 interpreters, 18 administrators, 13 female employees, 8 radio operators, and 3 teletype operators.

Unlike the old SA, most of the *Einsatzgruppen* members were not criminals or sadists, but upstanding citizens with no criminal records. In fact, they had the right to transfer from the groups. Nor were they from the bottom of the social order—they were largely middle-class. The great majority of the officers were professional men, and most were intellectuals. Of the top four commanders, three had Ph.D.s. A large number of lesser officers were lawyers. There was a professional opera singer and a former pastor. Most were in their thirties. It was necessary to *train* these people to become killers.[3]

Otto Ohlendorf, commander of *Einsatzgruppe* D, explained during the Nuremberg Trials how the mobile killing units functioned. He was a young man of thirty-four when Heydrich selected him to command. Having studied at the universities of Leipzig, Gottingen, and Pavia, he held a doctorate in jurisprudence and had worked his way up to important directorships in the Institute for World Economy and Maritime Transport and in the German trade organization. The young intellectual treated his party activities as a mere sidelight until Hey-

---

2. Note Martin Gilbert, *The Holocaust* (New York: Hill and Wang, 1978), pp. 37–40 for a map and pictures of this destruction. Compare Yehuda Bauer, *A History of the Holocaust* (New York: Franklin Watts, 1982), pp. 193–95.
3. Raul Hilberg, *The Destruction of the European Jews* (Chicago: Quadrangle Books, 1967), pp. 187–90.

drich required his total devotion and Himmler stated "that an important part of our task consisted of the extermination of Jews—women, men and chidren—and of Communist functionaries." Ohlendorf emphasized that he was informed of the attack on Russia about four weeks in advance, and explained:

> When the German Army invaded Russia, I was leader of the Einsatzgruppe D in the southern sector [Bessarabia and the southern Ukraine], and in the course of the year, during which I was leader of the Einsatzgruppe D, it liquidated approximately 90,000 men, women and children. The majority of those liquidated were Jews, but there were among them some Communist functionaries too.
>
> In the implementation of this extermination program the Special Commitment Groups (Einsatzgruppen) were subdivided into Special Commitment Detachments (Einsatzkommandos), and the Einsatzkommandos into still smaller units, the so-called Special Purpose Detachments (Sonderkommandos) and Unit Detachments (Teilkommandos). Usually, the smaller units were led by a member of the SD, the GESTAPO or the Criminal Police. The unit selected for this task would enter a village or city and order the prominent Jewish citizens to call together all Jews for the purpose of resettlement. They were requested to hand over their valuables to the leaders of the unit, and shortly before the execution to surrender their outer clothing. The men, women and children were led to a place of execution which in most cases was located next to a more deeply excavated anti-tank ditch. Then they were shot, kneeling or standing, and the corpses thrown into the ditch. I never permitted the shooting by individuals in the group D, but ordered that several of the men should shoot at the same time in order to avoid direct, personal responsibility. The leaders of the unit or especially designated persons, however, had to fire the last bullet against those victims which were not dead immediately. I learned from conversations with other group leaders that some of them demanded that the victims lie down flat on the ground to be shot through the naps of the neck. I did not approve of these methods.[4]

It is noteworthy that *Einsatzgruppe* D was the smallest of the four groups, with approximately 400–500 men and 170 vehicles at its disposal.

Ohlendorf also admitted the implementation of gassing vans during his year as a commander. In his affidavit he asserted:

> In the spring of 1942 we received gas vehicles from the Chief of the Security Police and the SD in Berlin. These vehicles were made available by Amt II of the RSHA [Reich Security Main Office, the "functional" director of the *Einsatzgruppen*]. The man who was responsible for the cars of my Einsatzgruppe, was BECHER. We had received orders to use the cars for the killing of women and children. Whenever a unit had collected a sufficient number of victims, a car was sent for their liquidation. We also had these gas vehicles stationed in the neighborhood of the transient camps into which the victims were brought. The victims were told that

4. "Affidavit by S.S. *Gruppenführer* Otto Ohlendorf," Nuremberg Document PS 2620, National Archives Record Group 238, reproduced in John Mendelsohn, ed., *The Holocaust* (New York: Garland Publishing, 1982), vol. 10, *The Einsatzgruppen or Murder Commandos*, p. 28.

they would be resettled and had to climb into the vehicles for that purpose. When the doors were closed and the gas streamed in through the starting of the vehicles, the victims died within 10 to 15 minutes. The cars were then driven to the burial place, where the corpses were taken out and buried.[5]

Thus, in cold, concise language, Ohlendorf confirmed the testimony of survivors of the horrors.

The Jewish people in the Russian-controlled areas were deceived about the Nazi intentions for a number of reasons. First of all, the Germans that the older people remembered were the Germans of World War I—some of the best-behaved troops they had encountered. Secondly, Jews in Stalin's Russia had been persecuted by the communist regime, whereas Nazi anti-Semitism was not widely publicized. Thirdly, the Nazis sought to deceive the Jewish community by every conceivable ploy in order to conduct a systematic and thorough liquidation. The success and commitment of the *Einsatzgruppen* was exemplified at *Babi Yar* (the "Old Woman's Ravine") outside of Kiev. Nazi posters deluded Jews into gathering en masse for "resettlement." Helped by Ukrainian police, the Germans terrorized and herded men, women, and children into holding areas where they were stripped of possessions and clothes. Contrary to modern movie portrayals, the victims did not march like drones to the edge of the pit. Rather, they had to run a gauntlet between soldiers and dogs until they were so tired they could hardly move. A. Anatoli Kuznetsov, a survivor, described the scene in *Babi Yar*:

> At that moment they entered a long corridor formed by two rows of soldiers and dogs. It was very narrow—some four or five feet across. The soldiers were lined up shoulder to shoulder, with their sleeves rolled up, each of them brandishing a rubber club or a big stick. Blows rained down on the people as they passed through. There was no question of being able to dodge or get away. Brutal blows, immediately drawing blood, descended on their heads, backs and shoulders from left and right. The soldiers kept shouting: "Schnell, schnell!" [Hurry, hurry!] laughing happily, as if they were watching a circus act; they even found ways of delivering harder blows in the more vulnerable places, the ribs, the stomach and the groin.[6]

When people stumbled and fell to the ground, the dogs were set upon them. "The poor people, [were] now quite out of their minds." Naked, disoriented human beings were shoved in short lines to a ledge where they were shot. The field report for *Einsatzgruppe* C [the group involved in the *Babi Yar* massacre] stated: "In collaboration with the Einsatzgruppe staff and 2 commandos of the Police Regiment South, the Sonderkommando 4a executed 33,771 Jews on September 29 and 30 [1941]." Money, clothing, and other valuables "were confiscated and placed in part at the disposal of the NSV [National Socialist People's Welfare] for the use of *Volksdeutsche* [ethnic Germans living outside of Germany]

5. Ibid., p. 29.
6. A. Anatoli Kuznetsov, *Babi Yar* (New York: Farrar, Straus and Giroux, 1970), pp. 105–6.

and in part given to the city's administrative authorities for the use of the needy population."[7] This two-day total far surpassed Auschwitz and Treblinka in number killed per day.

The report also stated that public opinion against the Jews was "very strong," and the Nazis continually found willing accomplices among the Ukrainian people. The use of local populations became standard procedure among the *Einsatzgruppen* whenever possible. In Odessa in the Crimea, Romanians killed 144,000— mostly by drowning—without Nazi aid. Many smaller "actions" were also carried out; sometimes individuals and families were forced to dig their own graves before being shot.

When the German advance temporarily bogged down and the Russians regained some territory, reports of the mass murder reached the West. Unfortunately, these reports were often considered exaggerated, or "atrocity propaganda." The Nazis, however, were concerned that thousands of bodies might attract too much attention. Heydrich ordered Paul Blobel, Chief of Sonderkommando 4A, to remove "the traces of executions carried out by the *Einsatzgruppen* in the East." Blobel became an expert at exhuming and burning buried corpses, but his task was enormous. He confessed: "According to my orders, my duties should have covered the entire area in which the *Einsatzgruppen* were employed. However, owing to the retreat from Russia, I did not totally carry out my orders."[8]

In Lithuania the Nazis sought to enlist the local populace to commit the atrocities, but Franz Stahlecker, Commander of *Einsatzgruppe* A reported: "It was not a simple matter to organize an effective action against the Jews." Nevertheless, under the direction of an obscure journalist a band of 300 Lithuanian assassins killed more than 1,500 Jews in two days in June 1941, burning down a Jewish neighborhood and destroying several synagogues. The Nazis publicized their actions as a "spontaneous" reaction of the native population. The grateful Germans rewarded them well and enlarged their numbers. Stahlecker excitedly reported that the unit "did particularly well in extermination actions," and he assigned it to work in other areas with the *Einsatzgruppe*. In less than three months nearly 150,000 Jews were massacred in Lithuania, Latvia, and Estonia. Two battalions of Lithuanian snipers (about 500 men) were dispatched to cities such as Lublin and Minsk. Only isolated voices in Lithuania rose in protest; many ignored the plight of the Jews entirely.

And yet, there were those who spoke up and helped. Several church leaders protested, and a number of individuals and families hid Jews. A priest hiding thirty children in his church stood in front of German soldiers and shouted, "If you kill the children, you'll have to kill me first!" They killed him and extermi-

7. "Operations Situation Report, Einsatzgruppen C, October 7, 1941," in Lucy Dawidowicz, ed., *A Holocaust Reader* (New York: Behrman House, 1976), p. 90.
8. "Affidavit by S.S. *Standartenfuehrer* Paul Blobel," Nuremberg Document NO 3947, National Archives Record Group 238, Mendelsohn, ed., *The Holocaust*, 10:140–41.

nated all the children. To these few Christians, life—the lives of others particularly—was a precious commodity. As a poor Lithuanian peasant named Thad-
daeus explained to his Jewish guests in the forest: "I am not sheltering you for
the money . . . I only want to prove that not all Lithuanians are like Klimatis
[the murdering journalist]."[9]

The ghastly actions of the *Einsatzgruppen* reached into the ghettos of Poland.
The cruelty of the soldiers, hardened by mass death and indoctrinated to think
of Jews as contagious vermin, was appalling. These men could bash a child's
head into a wall to hear it pop, or throw little children into a red hot burning
pit—without a second thought. Historian Philip Friedman documented the story
of Zosia in the Warsaw Ghetto, and wrote:

> Zosia was a little girl, she was the daughter of a physician. During an "action"
> one of the Germans became aware of her beautiful diamondlike dark eyes.
> "I could make two rings out of them," he said, "one for myself and one for my
> wife."
> His colleague is holding the girl.
> "Let's see whether they are really so beautiful. And better yet, let's examine them
> in our hands."
> Among the buddies exuberant gaiety breaks out. One of the wittiest proposes to
> take the eyes out. A shrill screaming and the noisy laughter of the soldier-pack. The
> screaming penetrates our brains, pierces our heart, the laughter hurts like the edge
> of a knife plunged into our body. The screaming and the laughter are growing,
> mingling and soaring to heaven.
> O God, whom will You hear first?
> What happens next is that the fainting child is lying on the floor. Instead of eyes
> two bloody wounds are staring. The mother, driven mad, is held by the women.
> This time they left Zosia to her mother.
> Two weeks later I met the girl by chance. It was a quiet day, the girl was lying in
> her bed. A handkerchief was tied around her eyes. The girl was stroking her moth-
> er's hand and comforting her:
> "Don't cry, mother dear, it probably had to happen this way. It is still better that
> they took my eyes instead of killing me. After the war I will wander from town to
> town, from one country to another, and will tell everybody how the Germans tor-
> tured us, so that everybody will understand that revenge must be taken on the
> Hitlerites, and when I take the bandage off my eyes, nobody will have pity on the
> German children any more.". . .
> At one of the next "actions" little Zosia was taken away. It was, of course, neces-
> sary to annihilate the blind child.[10]

Waiting for deportation with his mother and older sister, a five-year-old boy

9. Note Philip Friedman, *Their Brothers' Keepers* (New York: Holocaust Library, 1978), pp. 136–
41.
10. Philip Friedman, ed., *Martyrs and Fighters: The Epic of the Warsaw Ghetto* (New York: Frederick
A. Praeger, 1954), pp. 166–67.

stuck his tongue out at the SS officer supervising the blockade. The Nazi reached into his pocket for his knife and cut the little pink tongue off. Blood gushed out of the boy's mouth "like heavy cream."[11]

Jews were not the only group dehumanized and treated brutally. The Gypsies of Europe were also declared aliens; the Nuremberg Laws defined them as non-Aryans, forbidden to marry Aryan Germans. In 1938 Himmler established the Central Office for Fighting the Gypsy Menace. By that time, two hundred Gypsy men were in the Buchenwald concentration camp. Over three thousand joined Jews in the ghettos of Poland in May 1940. Charged with crime, corruption, filth, and disease since the Middle Ages, the Gypsies lost all legal rights under the Nazis and died of starvation and sickness in concentration camps. By the end of the war 15,000 out of 20,000 Gypsies who had been in Germany in 1939 were dead. At least 200,000 out of the 700,000 living in Europe during the same period were murdered by the Nazis. Martin Bormann, head of the Nazi Party Chancellery, exhibited his extreme anti-Gypsy prejudice when he objected in a letter December 3, 1942:

> I have been informed that the treatment of the so-called pure Gypsies is going to have new regulations. . . . Such a special treatment would mean a fundamental deviation from the simultaneous measures for fighting the Gypsy menace and would not be understood at all by the population and the lower leaders of the party. Also the Führer would not agree.[12]

Today, the Gypsies continue to battle against prejudice in Europe. No country wants them.

The world on the whole remained silent during the genocide of the *Einsatzgruppen*; Hitler seemed to foresee this silence. After all, he was well aware that between 1915 and 1923, 1,500,000 Armenians had perished, and an additional 500,000 had been exiled at the hands of the Ottoman Turks while the world was silent. The Turkish government used murderers and criminals released from prisons throughout Asia Minor to form the *Teshkileti Mahsusa*, their own murder squads. Whole villages were massacred as the Turks sought to solve their "Armenian Question." Because of this extermination, less than 100,000 Armenians today reside in their ancestral homeland of Turkey.[13]

Hitler realized that the Turks had not completely destroyed the Armenians; and, in spite of the lightning strikes and successes of the *Einsatzgruppen*, he

---

11. Ibid., p. 167.
12. Donald Kenrick and Gratton Puxon, *The Destiny of Europe's Gypsies* (New York: Basic Books, 1972), p. 89. Compare Helen Fein, *Accounting for Genocide: National Responses and Jewish Victimization During the Holocaust* (New York: The Free Press, 1979), pp. 28–29, and Gilbert, *The Holocaust*, p. 21–22.
13. "Fact Sheet: The Armenian Genocide," Armenian Assembly of America, 1420 N. Street, N.W., Washington, D.C., 1983. Compare Fein, *Accounting for Genocide*, pp. 10–18.

knew the Final Solution to his "Jewish Question" was not progressing swiftly enough. The Nazi extermination machine decided to employ two inventions of the twentieth century: poison gas and the concentration camp. Utilizing the transportation system masterminded by Adolf Eichmann, it was an ominous decision.

12

The Concentration Camp

"I Saw Dachau in 1945 and Somebody is Lying" wrote Robert M. Bartell, Chairman of Liberty Lobby's Board of Policy, in the title of his article for *The Spotlight*. The article symbolized numerous essays in *The Spotlight*, a weekly tabloid from Washington, D.C. published by Liberty Lobby, which protest that the Holocaust never occurred. Bartell asked, "If there were no gas chambers at Dachau, were there any in occupied Poland—at Auschwitz, for example?" He suggests that deliberate falsification occurred so Israel could collect "reparations for 'crimes' against the Jewish people." Bartell complained, "Now, a judge in Los Angeles says the 'holocaust is a judicially recognized fact. It did in fact occur.'" "I was there," Bartell concluded, "and I don't believe it."[1]

The Spotlight thrives on conspiracy theory, from plots by the Trilateral Commission to take over the world to plots by the Internal Revenue Service to circumvent the Bill of Rights. Advertising itself as "The Paper You Can Trust," it purports to publish news the "establishment press" will not report with an honesty and straightforwardness of which the "establishment" is incapable. Such claims have bolstered sales to nearly 350,000 copies a week, and many Christians are convinced that *The Spotlight* gives them the "inside scoop."

An inordinate number of articles deal with Israeli "plots" and the Holocaust "hoax." Front page headlines include titles such as "Israel and Libya Join In Terror Campaign Aimed at Americans," "Israel Gives Our Secrets to Reds,"

1. Robert M. Bartell, "I Saw Dachau in 1945 and Somebody Is Lying," *The Spotlight*, 16 November 1981, pp. 26–27.

125

"Top French Government Officials Linked to Mossad [Israel's Secret Service], Acts of Terror," and "Israel Destroying U.S. Allies." When the Institute for Historical Review (a group of "scholars" whose main purpose is to convince the world that the Holocaust did not occur) held its third annual conference in 1981, *The Spotlight*'s December 14 headline read "Revisionists Defy Establishment" and asserted: "The Establishment said it [the conference] wouldn't happen—but it did." In a box above the headline another article was promoted: "'Skokie' Distorted the Truth."

Liberty Lobby, which publishes *The Spotlight*, denies that it is anti-Semitic— a fact disputed by both Jews and Christians.[2] While *The Spotlight* attributes charges of anti-Semitism to "aliens," "subversives," and "conspiratorial forces," the Anti-Defamation League proved that Willis Carto, the Lobby's founder, had not always sought the shelter of code words for Jews. The report quoted Carto's correspondence with the late columnist Drew Pearson in 1966, in which Carto asserted:

> Hitler's defeat was the defeat of Europe. And of America. How could we have been so blind? The blame, it seems, must be laid at the door of the international Jews. It was their propaganda, lies, and demands which blinded the West to what Germany was doing . . . If Satan himself, with all of his superhuman genius and diabolical ingenuity at his command, had tried to create a permanent disintegration and force for the destruction of the nations, he could have done no better than to invent the Jews.[3]

Liberty Lobby took Pearson to court, attempting to block the publication of Carto's statement. The U.S. Court of Appeals refused to ban the quote, Justice Warren Burger declaring in a note to his majority opinion that the Lobby had indeed engaged in a "calculated program of anti-Semitism with racist overtones."

After losing more court cases—both for libel—to William F. Buckley, Jr. and E. Howard Hunt, the Lobby frantically solicited monetary pledges from *The*

---

2. Jerry Falwell, who has been criticized in *The Spotlight* for his "manic Semitism," has pointed out numerous errors in one of *The Spotlight*'s articles. "This kind of journalism—if you can call it that," Falwell stated, "is inexcusable in any publication." Pat Robertson told viewers of the "700 Club" on April 14, 1983, that they should not buy or read *The Spotlight*. William F. Buckley, Jr., conservative editor of the *National Review* declared the Liberty Lobby "a hotbed of anti-Semitism and name-calling centered around the mysterious Willis Carto, who regularly poisons the wells of polemical discourse." R. Emmett Tyrell, Jr., editor-in-chief for the conservative *The American Spectator*, noted that Liberty Lobby "has always had a colorful collection of bigots and simpletons around it practicing the solitary vice of political extremism—namely, applying conspiracy theories to every vexatious public problem." The Anti-Defamation League published a report, "Liberty Lobby and the Carto Network of Hate," which disclosed that the Lobby's founder, Willis Carto, had "put together a wide and shifting network of extremist, racist and anti-Semitic publications and organizations" since the 1960s.
3. "Liberty Lobby and the Carto Network of Hate," *ADL Facts* 27 (Winter 1982): 18–19. Compare "Falwell Protests," *The Spotlight*, 2 May 1983, p. 27, and "Pat Robertson Bans Us," same issue, pp. 1, 3.

Spotlight readers, insisting that each American citizen's freedom of speech was under attack. "Here is the balance of my pledge," one form stated, "to assist in your efforts to protect our Constitutional rights." Bartell later noted that the response had been "heartwarming."[4]

The measure of trust given *The Spotlight* by its readership is heartrending to the student of the Holocaust. In the "Letters" section, numerous readers emphasize "the Establishment's assault upon Liberty Lobby" and tell the Lobby to "have faith," for it will prevail. Jerry Falwell and Pat Robertson are said to be on the payroll of sinister Zionists. Israel is castigated as a persecutor of Christians (and is even called the "anti-Christ" by one reader). Menachim Begin is said to "hate Christianity." And *Spotlight* converts continue to be tallied. One man writes from El Paso, Texas:

> Little did I realize how misinformed and uninformed I was, until I began reading The SPOTLIGHT. But the truth in the first several issues was so shocking that your newspaper generated skepticism and incredulity, including an impression that The SPOTLIGHT was radical and anti-Semitic.
>
> However, I had the patience to give you the benefit of the doubt. Now I clearly see that your stand is against political Zionism, not religious Judaism. That which I shamefully misconstrued as radicalism is, in reality, patriotism.
>
> Thank God for The SPOTLIGHT, that rarest of newspapers, which prints the whole shocking truth and nothing but the truth. It is the obligation of all decent Americans to read The SPOTLIGHT, so that they may wisely act to preserve our freedom.[5]

Within one month of this letter, *The Spotlight* announced that convicted Ukrainian guard John Demjanjuk (the notorious "Ivan the Terrible" at the Treblinka extermination camp), was "smeared" by Jewish witnesses.[6] Liberty Lobby's battle to whitewash the Holocaust is an endless confrontation with "The Establishment," a confrontation most of its readers endorse.

Bartell is correct in saying the gas chamber at Dachau never functioned for mass extermination. But, as with all propaganda, his is a half truth. For, as we have seen, a gas chamber is not required to murder other human beings.

A "Model" Camp—Dachau

The Nazis themselves registered 31,951 deaths at Dachau out of 206,000 registered prisoners from 1933 to 1945. The actual number may approach 50,000,

---

4. Note "Liberty Lobby Now Defendant," *The Spotlight*, 11 July 1983, p. 15. The letter appeal from Bartell for funds was dated June 17, 1983 and insisted: "We must act quickly. I'm hoping you will pledge an emergency contribution of $100 today. I know that is a lot of money in these difficult times, but this is really important and if we lose—the end of the SPOTLIGHT and LIBERTY LOBBY will be here."

5. Refer to "Letters," *The Spotlight*, 25 July 1983, p. 23. Compare similar sections, 23 May 1983, p. 27, and 11 July 1983, p. 23.

6. Mark Weber, "Nuremberg Document Shows Cleveland 'Nazi' Is Innocent," *The Spotlight*, 15 August 1983, p. 19.

as unregistered mass executions and death marches occurred near the end of the war. Still, a twenty-five percent death ratio was far below the norm for major Nazi camps.

Dachau, the first official concentration camp built, was considered a "model" camp. It was intended for Germans. Originally constructed to hold 5,000 prisoners, Dachau imprisoned political opponents of the Nazis (Communists, Social Democrats, and others) when it first opened in March 1933. Hitler explained that the camp would restore "calm to our country." The number of prisoners grew as clergymen, Jews, Gypsies, Jehovah's Witnesses and other "antisocials" were incarcerated. In 1937 prisoners were used for slave labor to enlarge the camp. Above the main gate, a sign proclaimed *Arbeit Macht Frei* ("Work Makes Free").[7]

Although this was an easy camp by Nazi standards, it was a nightmare. Brutal punishment, exhausting labor, inadequate food, and medical experimentation turned Dachau into a chamber of horrors. As the war progressed, Dachau gave birth to 165 subsidiary camps, where prisoners were hired out to armament manufacturers and housed in wretched barracks near the factories. Ragged, starving prisoners trudged to work in full view of the civilian population.

In Dachau itself, a new crematorium was built in 1942 to dispose of the dead. Cremation was a slow process (about two hours) and the smell of burning flesh permeated both the camp and the town. From the color of the smoke, inmates claimed to be able to determine how long the victim had been in Dachau: veterans with little flesh on their bones produced a thin green smoke as compared to new arrivals with more flesh, who engendered a yellow smoke. Construction on a gas chamber next to the crematorium began in 1942, but was sabotaged and not completed until 1945. It was never used for extermination; the SS transported prisoners to the Hartheim State Institution in Austria—secretly a center for euthanasia—for gassing. Nevertheless, Austrian wives whose husbands had been arrested by the Nazis in 1938 did receive small packages in the mail with a short note attached: "To pay, 150 marks for the cremation of your husband. Ashes enclosed from Dachau."[8]

Dachau was a model in many ways. Its example influenced procedures used in other concentration camps, from holding centers like Bergen-Belsen to labor camps such as Stutthof and Buchenwald. Even the extermination complexes, such as Sobibor and Treblinka, could point to lessons learned at Dachau. A number of SS officers moved through Dachau to higher positions in other camps, including four Commandants of Auschwitz. Adolf Eichmann began his camp career in Dachau. And it was with Dachau prisoners that the ghastly medical

7. Note Barbara Distel and Ruth Jakusch, eds., *Concentration Camp Dachau, 1933–1945* (Munich: International Dachau Committee, 1978), a 229-page catalog intended to accompany the visitor to the Dachau Memorial Museum. It contains numerous pictures and documents as well as history.
8. Konnilyn G. Feig, *Hitler's Death Camps: The Sanity of Madness* (New York: Holmes and Meier, 1979), pp. 47–54. Compare Nora Levin, *The Holocaust: The Destruction of European Jewry, 1933–1945* (New York: Thomas Y. Crowell, 1968), p. 99 on the Austrian wives.

experiments were initiated—experiments in which medical doctors moved from euthanasia to systematic research with human guinea pigs. Dr. Sigmund Rascher developed the standard cyanide capsule there (ironically, a capsule that both Himmler and Göring used to commit suicide). Rascher performed experiments on inmates with the objective of helping the war effort. Leo Alexander, a medical doctor and consultant to the U.S. Secretary of War during the Nuremberg Trials, reported in *The New England Journal of Medicine* of Rascher's experimentation at Dachau:

> When Himmler learned that the cause of death of most SS men on the battlefield was hemorrhage, he instructed Dr. Sigmund Rascher to search for a blood coagulant that might be given before the men went into action. Rascher tested this coagulant when it was developed by clocking the number of drops emanating from freshly cut amputation stumps of living and conscious prisoners at the crematorium of Dachau concentration camp and by shooting Russian prisoners of war through the spleen.
>
> Live dissections were a feature of another experimental study designed to show the effects of explosive decompression. A mobile decompression chamber was used. It was found that when subjects were made to descend from altitudes of 40,000 to 60,000 feet without oxygen, severe symptoms of cerebral dysfunction occurred—at first convulsions, then unconsciousness in which the body was hanging limp and later, after wakening temporary blindness, paralysis or severe confusional twilight states. Rascher, who wanted to find out whether these symptoms were due to anoxic changes or to other causes, did what appeared to him the most simple thing: he placed the subjects of the experiment under water and dissected them while the heart was still beating, demonstrating air embolism in the blood vessels of the heart, liver, chest wall and brain.
>
> Another part of Dr. Rascher's research . . . concerned shock from exposure to cold. It was known that military personnel generally did not survive immersion in the North Sea for more than sixty to a hundred minutes. Rascher therefore attempted to duplicate these conditions at Dachau concentration camp and used about 300 prisoners in experiments on shock from exposure to cold; of these 80 or 90 were killed. (The figures do not include persons killed during mass experiments on exposure to cold outdoors.)[9]

"In one report on this work," Alexander noted, "Rascher asked permission to shift these experiments from Dachau to Auschwitz, a larger camp where they might cause less disturbance because the subjects shrieked from pain when their extremities froze white."

"EVERY EVIL THE MIND CAN CONCEIVE"—AUSCHWITZ

More extensive medical experiments for the Third Reich were carried out at Auschwitz, a combined labor and extermination camp in Poland. The largest

9. Leo Alexander, "Medical Science Under Dictatorship," *The New England Journal of Medicine* 241 (14 July 1949): 42–43.

concentration camp the Nazis possessed, Auschwitz held a standing population of 100,000 men, women, and children on a grounds that covered twenty square miles. It was actually a complex of three major sections, a virtual city of destruction. Auschwitz I was established by order of Himmler on April 27, 1940, and it incarcerated mainly political prisoners. Auschwitz II (Birkenau) was established in October 1941. It was an extensive camp of wooden barracks, at first containing Russian prisoners of war, most of whom died because of wretched camp conditions. After March 1942 most new arrivals were Jews and some Gypsies. In less than five years, at least two million Jews died in Birkenau. Commandant Rudolf Hoess stated in his memoir that Adolf Eichmann estimated that a total of 2,500,000 human beings died in Auschwitz, many in the extensive gas installations and crematoria (no record being kept of those killed immediately upon arrival). Estimates run as high as four million, and Auschwitz/Birkenau ranks as the largest killing center in history, a place where murder was efficient and technological expertise modern. Auschwitz III (Buna) was an "industrial park" utilizing cheap slave labor to support Hitler's war effort. Private companies built factories there, led by the huge I. G. Farben chemical conglomerate, which manufactured synthetic rubber. Smaller factories and labor camps dotted the area surrounding Auschwitz as Aryans sought financial gain.

"The evidence of Auschwitz has demonstrated many things about humanity," wrote Otto Friedrich. "It has demonstrated that men (and women) are capable of committing every evil the mind can conceive, that there is no natural or unwritten law that says of any atrocity whatsoever: This shall not be done."[10]

Auschwitz was chosen for its isolation and accessibility. An early scouting team reported to Himmler that conditions in the area were deplorable, with swamps, mosquitoes, and a polluted water supply. But Rudolf Hoess convinced Himmler that the excellent railroad connections, centralized proximity to large Jewish populations, and solitary surroundings were unmatchable attributes. Dr. Rascher alluded to its isolation, which would hide the atrocities that occurred and so enhance medical experimentation. Professors and scientists clamored to use the human guinea pigs to further medical science. Dr. August Hirt, professor of anatomy at the University of Strassburg, requested human skulls for "certain anthropological experiments" and to be housed in his Strassburg Anatomical Institute. Hirt preferred that the skulls be measured while the individuals were alive. Wolfram Sievers, executive secretary of the Institute for Research into Heredity, wrote to Himmler's adjutant Dr. Rudolf Brandt on November 2, 1942:

> Dear Comrade Brandt! The Reichsfuehrer S.S. once ordered, as you know, that S.S. Hauptsturmfuehrer Prof. Dr. Hirt should be provided with all necessary material for his research work. I have already reported to the Reichsfuehrer S.S. that for

---

10. Otto Friedrich, "The Kingdom of Auschwitz," *The Atlantic* 248 (September 1981): 60. This article provides an overview of the history and conditions in Auschwitz based on primary sources from survivors.

some anthropological studies 150 skeletons of inmates or Jews are needed and should be provided by the concentration camp Auschwitz. It is only necessary that the Reich Main Security Office (Reichssicherheitshauptamt) will now be furnished with an official directive by the Reichsfuehrer S.S.; by order of the Reichsfuehrer S.S., however, you could advise so yourself.[11]

The response was that Dr. Hirt was to be given "everything necessary for his investigations." A later letter from Sievers to Eichmann noted that a "total of 115 persons were worked on, 79 of whom were Jews, 2 Poles, 4 Asiatics and 30 Jewesses." They had been "accommodated" in the hospital building at Auschwitz and quarantined to avoid "the existing danger of infectious diseases."[12]

EXPERIMENTATION

The "Scientific Department" in Block 10 of Auschwitz I conducted sterilization experiments on women. Dr. Horst Schumann experimented with X-rays and surgical techniques in this regard. Dr. Carl Clauberg, professor of gynecology at the University of Königsberg, was so excited at the prospect of using live women for experimentation that he took a sabbatical both from the University and from his position as chief physician of the University's Women's Hospital to work in Auschwitz. A famed authority with several books and scores of research papers to his credit, Clauberg injected substances into the ovaries to try to achieve sterilization. Other physicians in different blocks of Auschwitz transplanted cancer tissue into the uterus. Some removed sexual organs from both men and women; in contrast, others induced multiple pregnancies by artificial insemination, and then terminated them. After all, the master race must learn to increase rapidly while the inferior races were being sterilized. Dr. Koenig, an aspiring surgeon, practiced his surgical techniques; he was especially fond of amputations. German pharmaceutical firms sent drugs to test on inmates, and the I. G. Farben corporation structured a large and lethal nerve gas experiment using Auschwitz prisoners. Mass experimentation on the effect of electric current on the human brain killed many prisoners, and experiments infecting and treating malaria (originally begun at Dachau) abounded.[13]

11. "Letter by Wolfram Sievers to Rudolf Brandt on Professor Hirt's work with the skeleton collection, 2 November 1942," Nuremberg Document NO-086, National Archives Record Group 238, reproduced in John Mendelsohn, ed., *The Holocaust* (New York: Garland, 1982), vol. 9, *Medical Experiments on Jewish Inmates of Concentration Camps*, p. 217. This entire volume contains letters and affidavits regarding the Nazi medical experiments on Jewish inmates of concentration camps.

12. Note documents NO-089 and NO-087 reproduced in Mendelsohn, ed., *The Holocaust*, 9:219–225. Compare pages 226–31 for subsequent correspondence and notations about what should be done with the skeleton collection if Strassburg was endangered by Allied forces. Because of the meticulous nature of the testing, some of the skeletons had not yet been totally defleshed in September 1944.

13. Max Weinreich, *Hitler's Professors: The Part of Scholarship in Germany's Crimes Against the Jewish People* (New York: YIVO, 1946), pp. 197–99. Compare Philip Friedman, "Crimes in the Name of Science," in *Roads to Extinction: Essays on the Holocaust*, ed. Ada June Friedman (New York: The Jewish Publication Society of America, 1980), pp. 322–32.

The infamous Dr. Josef Mengele, an assistant at the Institute for Hereditary Biology and Race Research at the University of Frankfurt, was loaned to Auschwitz and from 1943–45 sent boxcar loads of new arrivals directly to the gas chambers. He was involved in choosing which of the incoming workers would be put to death because they did not appear healthy enough. He also carried on his research, searching out twins (especially twin children) and dwarfs for his experiments in heredity. Birth defects or malformations of any kind often intrigued his fancy. Dr. Miklos Nyiszli, a Jewish medical pathologist shipped to Auschwitz soon after the Nazis invaded Hungary in March 1944, was selected by Mengele as part of the *Sonderkommando* (a group of "privileged" prisoners who worked in the crematoriums). Nyiszli took charge of all the pathological work conducted in Auschwitz, working directly under Mengele. He wrote:

> Among malefactors and criminals, the most dangerous type is the "criminal doctor," especially when he is armed with powers such as those granted to Dr. Mengele. He sent millions of people to death merely because, according to a racial theory, they were inferior beings and therefore detrimental to mankind. This same criminal doctor spent long hours beside me, either at his microscopes, his disinfecting ovens and his test tubes or, standing with equal patience near the dissecting table, his smock befouled with blood, his bloody hands examining and experimenting like one possessed. The immediate objective was the increased reproduction of the German race. The final objective was the production of pure Germans in numbers sufficient to replace the Czechs, Hungarians, Poles, all of whom were condemned to be destroyed, but who for the moment were living on those territories declared vital to the Third Reich.[14]

Nyiszli learned that their reports were "forwarded to the Institute of Biological, Racial and Evolutionary Research at Berlin-Dahlem . . . checked by the highest medical authorities at one of the most famous scientific institutes in the world." After the war Mengele, who personally killed twin children in the "interest of science" and had no aversion to having a father and son killed and *cooked* so that the flesh could quickly be stripped from their bones (the skeletons sent immediately to the Berlin Anthropological Museum), lived under his own name in Bavaria until 1951. He then escaped to Argentina and has eluded capture under the protection of various South American countries to the present day.[15]

In Auschwitz, Jewish mothers tried frantically to pass their children off as twins because word was conveyed that they might save their children in that

14. Miklos Nyiszli, *Auschwitz: A Doctor's Eyewitness Account*, trans. Tibere Kremer and Richard Seaver (New York: Fawcett Crest, 1960), p. 52.
15. The bizarre story of father and son is found on pages 130–34 of Nyiszli's account as the entire Litzmannstadt (German for Lodz, Poland) Ghetto was liquidated in the gas chambers of Auschwitz. Nyiszli witnessed many such gassings. The Paris newspaper *Le Monde* reported in "Le Docteur Mengele Serait Conseiller Technique a la Prison 'Libertad,'" 28–29 December 1980, that Mengele was spotted in Uruguay in 1980, where he was serving as a technical consultant with the colonels of the political prison Libertad.

manner. Upon arriving on the trains, the young, the old, the pregnant, the sick, the handicapped were immediately separated from those able to work and were sent to the gas chambers. When slave labor was well stocked, men, women, and children suffered this fate regardless of health.

EXTERMINATION

Extermination of the Jewish people as the "Final Solution" to the Jewish "problem" was a decision made no later but possibly earlier than 1941. Rudolf Hoess, Commandant of Auschwitz from 1940–43 testified to that effect. After estimating totals of Jews arriving at Auschwitz from the beginning of 1942 into 1943 (Poland, 250,000; Greece, 65,000; Germany, 100,000; Holland, 90,000; France, 110,000; Slovakia, 90,000; Bulgaria, none; Belgium, 20,000; and in the end, Hungary, 400,000), a pre-trial interrogator asked Hoess, "Now you just told us you had facilities for 130,000. If you add all those figures they amount to a much greater number than 130,000. How could you accommodate all these people?" Hoess replied: "They were not supposed to be employed in work there, but they were supposed to be exterminated." "You had decided that?" asked the interrogator. "That order I received in mid year of 1941, I believe it was July, from the Reichs Führer SS [Himmler] in person," replied Hoess. Hoess related Himmler's saying that Hitler gave the order for the "final solution of the Jewish problem" and that the term meant "extermination." "By what means were Polish Jews [in Auschwitz] executed in 1941?" questioned the interrogator. "By gas," answered Hoess.[16]

As has been seen, murder by gas was employed by the Nazis against their own people during the euthanasia program as early as 1940. Gassing vans were used by the *Einsatzgruppen*, killing scores of people stuffed inside. The first experiment in wholesale murder by gas on Polish soil was at Auschwitz I in mid-September 1941. A group of Soviet prisoners-of-war and Polish political prisoners was killed. The first special extermination camp for Jews was a mobile killing center established at Chelmo, Poland in December 1941. Utilizing three gassing vans with a capacity of eighty to one hundred Jews, the Nazis convinced the victims that they were going to work in the east and would be treated fairly. Told that they must take a bath and that their clothes had to be disinfected, Jews undressed and walked a corridor to the van that would "take them to the bathhouse." The exhaust pipe was vented in the middle of the floor, asphyxiating

16. "Transcript of the pretrial interrogation of S.S. *Obersturmfuehrer* Rudolf Hoess, 1–2 April 1946," Pretrial Interrogation Series of the International Military Tribunal at Nuremberg, reproduced in Mendelsohn, ed., *The Holocaust*, vol. 12, *The "Final Solution" in the Extermination Camps and the Aftermath*, pp. 72–73. The entire interrogation is found on pp. 56–127. Compare vol. 11, *The Wannsee Protocol and a 1944 Report on Auschwitz by the Office of Strategic Services*, on the Final Solution. The Wannsee Protocol was the official Nazi summary of the first of three interagency meetings at the Wannsee headquarters of the Criminal Police to discuss the Final Solution of the "Jewish Question."

those inside as it drove to a wooded area where its cargo would be buried. Adolf Eichmann reported:

> I followed the van and then came the most horrifying sight I've ever seen in my life. The van drew up alongside a long pit, the doors were opened and the bodies thrown out; the limbs were still supple, as if they were still alive. They were thrown into the pit. I saw a civilian pulling out teeth with a pair of pliers and then I took off. I rushed to my car and departed and said no more. I was through. I had had it. A white-coated doctor said that I ought to look through the peephole and see what went on inside the vans. I refused. I couldn't speak. I had to get away. Frightful, I tell you. An inferno. Can't do it. I can't do it.[17]

The mobile killing center in Chelmo, Poland was kept strictly secret while it murdered an estimated 360,000 Jews from the Lodz Ghetto and the surrounding areas. It was joined on March 17, 1942 by the Belzec extermination center, equipped with six permanent carbon monoxide gas chambers that claimed the lives of approximately 600,000 Jews; and by Sobibor (May 1942), Treblinka (July 1942), and Majdanek (turned from a labor camp into an extermination center in the fall of 1942), which all together killed approximately 1.5 million Jews.[18]

From the inception of the Auschwitz/Birkenau complex, it was decided that Zyklon B, a crystalline hydrogen cyanide pesticide, should be utilized to kill Jews. As Hoess explained, Zyklon B "was used [around the camp] in order to gas rooms and to exterminate insects. Since it was very poisonous and had to be treated with great care we assumed that it was the proper thing to use against humans." This mode of extermination was free of the mechanical breakdowns of the carbon monoxide method of the other camps. Two barns were sealed and converted for use as gas chambers from March to August 1942. At that time there was no need to gas more than three hundred persons at a time. In August, however, transports began arriving from France, requiring up to seven hundred to be gassed in a day. As Birkenau continued to grow, new gas chambers were designed, disguised as shower rooms. Four crematoria were added that could burn thousands in one day. Still, the crematoria could not keep up with the mass killing in the chambers, and open pit burning was practiced as well.

Hoess decided that victims who came into Auschwitz should not know they were going to be gassed. They were forced to move quickly out of the cattle cars and to discard their luggage, as camp physicians made their selection in seconds, sending each to the right (work) or left (death). Each group was stripped of its possessions, including his or her clothes. An organized, efficient bureau-

---

17. Heinz Hoehne, *The Order of the Death's Head* (New York: Coward-McCann, 1970), p. 374.
18. See Feig, *Hitler's Death Camps*, for chapters on each of these camps and extensive bibliography on books and articles relating to the primary concentration camps and extermination centers. Most of Warsaw's Jews perished in Treblinka. Compare Jean-Francois Steiner, *Treblinka* (New York: Simon and Schuster, 1967); and Alexander Donat, ed., *The Death Camp Treblinka: A Documentary* (New York: The Holocaust Library, 1979).

cracy kept and used everything for the war effort, from mounds of hair for stuffing submarine mattresses to the gold fillings recorded by the camp dentist and later extracted from the corpses. Fake signs that read "To Delousing," "To Disinfecting," "To Bath," and "To the Showers" served to deceive and maintain calm as long as possible. In their new twenty-by-thirty-foot "showers," the Nazis prided themselves on being able to accommodate two thousand naked men, women, and children at a time.

As the victims waited for the water, the amethyst-blue Zyklon B crystals were poured down one of the shafts. Hoess explained:

> I saw it happen often enough. Generally it took from three to fifteen minutes. The effect varied. Wherever the gas was thrown into the chamber, the people standing right next to it were immediately anaesthetized. It gradually spread out to the far corners of the room and generally after five minutes one could no longer discern the human forms in the chamber. Everybody was dead after fifteen minutes, and the chambers were opened after a half an hour and not once was anybody alive at this time. . . . At first they all screamed, of course.[19]

Gerald Reitlinger explained how the victims crowded the huge metal door "with its little window, where they piled up in one blue, clammy, blood-spattered pyramid, clawing and mauling each other even in death. Twenty-five minutes later, electric pumps removed the gas-laden air, the great metal door slid open, and the men of the Jewish *Sonderkommando* entered, wearing gas masks and gum boots and carrying hoses, for their first task was to remove the blood and defecation before dragging the clawing dead apart with nooses and hooks."[20]

After one such gassing, the chief of the gas chamber *Sonderkommando* burst into Nyiszli's room. "Doctor," he said, "come quickly. We just found a girl alive at the bottom of the pile of corpses." Nyiszli recounted:

> I grabbed my instrument case, which was always ready, and dashed to the gas chamber. Against the wall, near the entrance of the immense room, half covered with other bodies, I saw a girl in the throes of a death-rattle, her body seized with convulsions. The gas kommando men around me were in a state of panic. Nothing like this had ever happened in the course of their horrible career.
>
> We removed the still-living body from the corpses pressing against it. I gathered the tiny adolescent body into my arms and carried it back into the room adjoining the gas chamber, where normally the gas kommando men change clothes for work. I laid the body on a bench. A frail young girl, almost a child, she could have been no more than fifteen. I took out my syringe and, taking her arm—she had not yet

19. Note Mendelsohn, ed., *The Holocaust*, 12:88.
20. Gerald Reitlinger, *The Final Solution: The Attempt to Exterminate the Jews of Europe, 1939–1945*, 2d ed. (New York: Thomas Yoseloff, 1968), p. 160. Compare David D. Brodeur, "Auschwitz Gas: Medical and Chemical Origins," *Faith and Thought* 102 (1975): 197–216. Note page 201, which refutes the Holocaust "revisionists" who declare that Zyklon B could not kill a human in a chamber.

recovered consciousness and was breathing with difficulty—I administered three
intravenous injections. My companions covered her body which was cold as ice with
a heavy overcoat. One ran to the kitchen to fetch some tea and warm broth. Everybody wanted to help, as if she were his own child.[21]

They saved the life of the bewildered child, who then tried to reconstruct in her
mind the experience. Nyiszli and the *Sonderkommando* frantically searched their
minds for a solution. Even the *Sonderkommando* never left the crematorium alive—
crews were replaced every few months. The SS officer in charge considered their
appeal, but he believed the girl had seen too much—that she would certainly
tell others. One-half hour later, the girl was dead, an SS bullet in the back of her
neck.

"A Nightmare"

Cruelty toward children abounded in the concentration camp. At the Auschwitz Trials, a witness testified to seeing a mountain of children's corpses, rats
scurrying over them. Others remembered SS breaking the spines of children
over their knees like kindling wood or smashing a child's skull against a wall.
Some threw little children into the fire alive, not bothering to waste a bullet.

One of the most heartbreaking scenes in the camp involved pregnant women
giving birth. The only way to save a mother from the gas chamber was to kill
the baby. One midwife sent to the camp especially for infanticide reported that
until 1943 all newborns were drowned in a small barrel. One horrified witness
recalled a female clerk taking a baby only three hours old and submerging its
body in cold water. It was two days after Christmas, Judith Newman remembered, and her joy over a Jewish child being born in her block turned to horror
as the "baby swallowed and gurgled, its little voice chittering like a small bird,
until its breath became shorter and shorter. The woman held its head in the
water. After about eight minutes the breathing stopped. The woman picked it
up, wrapped it up again, and put it among the other corpses." Newman wanted
to scream, "Murderess!" The clerk explained that it was the only way she could
keep the mother from being gassed. This kind of ethical decision faced each
person in the murky world of the concentration camp.[22]

Jews, from the time of their arrival at the camps, found themselves on a slide
of physical and moral decline in a world gone mad—where injustice, evil, and
suffering were the norm. Prisoners were subjected to shocks so terrible that they
could not be assimilated by normal psychological mechanisms. Elie Wiesel writes:

I pinched my face. Was I still alive? Was I awake? I could not believe it. How
could it be possible for them to burn people, children, and for the world to keep
silent? No, none of this could be true. It was a nightmare . . . Soon I should wake

21. Nyiszli, *Auschwitz*, pp. 88–89.
22. Note Feig, *Hitler's Death Camps*, p. 184. Compare pp. 346–47.

with a start, my heart pounding, and find myself back in the bedroom of my child-hood, among my books . . .

My father's voice drew me from my thoughts:

"It's a shame . . . a shame that you couldn't have gone with your mother . . . I saw several boys of your age going with their mothers . . . "

His voice was terribly sad. I realized that he did not want to see what they were going to do to me. He did not want to see the burning of his only son.

My forehead was bathed in cold sweat. But I told him that I did not believe that they could burn people in our age, that humanity would never tolerate it . . .

"Humanity? Humanity is not concerned with us. Today anything is allowed. Anything is possible, even these crematories . . . "

His voice was choking.[23]

Elie Wiesel, the young Hungarian boy, survived. His father, mother, and sisters died.

To him, as to so many prisoners, existence was clouded with unreality. Each inmate had to accept radically new values, an SS universe where atrocities were for pleasure, good was evil and evil good. Insensibility to hardship and callous-ness to extreme cruelty were necessary for survival. If a Jew did not remain strong and determined, defying the Nazis by his or her very existence, he would fall (as did the large majority) into a state of total mental languor and sometimes become known as a *Mussulman*. A former Buchenwald prisoner described such *Mussulmanner* transferred from Auschwitz to the Buchenwald labor camp:

When they could still walk, they moved like automatons; once stopped, they were capable of no further movement. They fell prostrate on the ground; nothing mat-tered any more to them. Their bodies blocked the passageway. You could step right on them and they wouldn't draw back their arms or legs an inch. No protest, no cry of pain came from their half-open mouths. And yet they were still alive. The Kapos, even the S.S. men, could beat and push them, but they would not budge; they had become insensible to everything. They were men without thoughts, without reac-tions, without souls, one might say. Sometimes, under the blows, they would sud-denly start moving, like cattle, jostling against each other. Impossible to get them to tell their names, much less the date of their birth. Even gentleness was not enough to make them talk; they would only give you an expressionless stare. And when they tried to answer, their tongues could not touch their dessicated palates to produce sounds. You smelled only a poisonous breath, as though it issued from entrails already in a state of decomposition.[24]

On the average, twenty-five percent of all Jews deported to the death camps

23. Elie Wiesel, *Night* (New York: Avon, 1960), pp. 42–43. Compare Randolph L. Braham's mas-sive two-volume work, *The Politics of Genocide: The Holocaust in Hungary* (New York: Columbia U., 1981), for details on Hungarian anti-Semitism and the resulting deportations and genocide.
24. Leon Poliakov, *Harvest of Hate: The Nazi Program for the Destruction of the Jews of Europe* (New York: Syracuse U., 1954), pp. 222–23. *Mussulman* comes from the German *Muselmann* (lit. "Moslem"), likening the numbed victims to the starving beggars of India.

survived the first selection, and yet scarcely two or three percent lived to see the end of the war. For example, only six hundred out of the ninety thousand Jews deported from the Netherlands survived; less than three thousand out of one hundred and ten thousand deported from France endured. "Among the different extermination methods perfected by the Nazi technicians of mass murder," Leon Poliakov summarized, "that of immediate death in the gas chambers was by no means the cruelest."[25]

It is impossible to describe an average day in the labor camps. Schedules varied by camp for each prisoner and each time period. Early morning roll calls, the parade-step marches to the music of a camp orchestra (formed by the SS from thousands of professional Jewish musicians who were imprisoned), the blows, the exhaustion, the meagre rations, the starvation, and the death were common phenomena to many. The repeated "selections," the hangings for minor offenses, the stench, the vermin, the thirst, hunger, and cramped wooden bunks three tiers high are often mentioned in testimonies. It is important to realize that in addition to the major camps and killing centers that the Nazis controlled (Konnilyn Feig refers to the "Big Nineteen" and covers them in her recent definitive study),[26] there were hundreds of smaller "tent" camps of fifty to one hundred workers (used for digging anti-tank ditches and other related purposes) that were just as abominable. Often in these camps, prisoners were worked to death as in the major centers, or machine-gunned during the Allied advance.

It is actually impossible to experience the realities of the camps—impossible, while well fed and comfortably seated, to comprehend the world of loneliness, terror, gas-filled lungs, naked corpses, burning flesh, fire drenched skies, billowing black smoke and ashes, where time is no more. Perhaps, the greatest accomplishment for which we can hope is to believe, to care, and to change.

25. Ibid., p. 223.
26. Feig emphasizes that the Nazis were quite clear and official about the camps they considered "major." She divides them on pp. 26–27: (1) the four killing centers (Chelmo, Belzec, Sobibor, Treblinka); (2) the official concentration camps: (a) the two labor/extermination centers (Auschwitz/Birkenau and Majdenak); (b) the eleven concentration camps given official status by Himmler (Dachau, Sachsenhausen, Ravensbruck, Buchenwald, Flossenburg, Neuengamme, Gross-Rosen, Natzweiler, Mauthausen, Stutthof and Dora/Nordhausen); (3) the official reception and holding center (Bergen-Belsen); (4) the unique fortress town (Therensienstadt).

Children of Lodz being marched away to meet death in an extermination camp.

Pitiful little children, cold and hungry, on a sidewalk in the Warsaw Ghetto.

Women, some with babes in arms, await extermination in Mizocz, Volyn (Ukraine), c. 1941.

Despair and desperation drove some Holocaust victims to suicide on the high voltage wires. (Dachau)

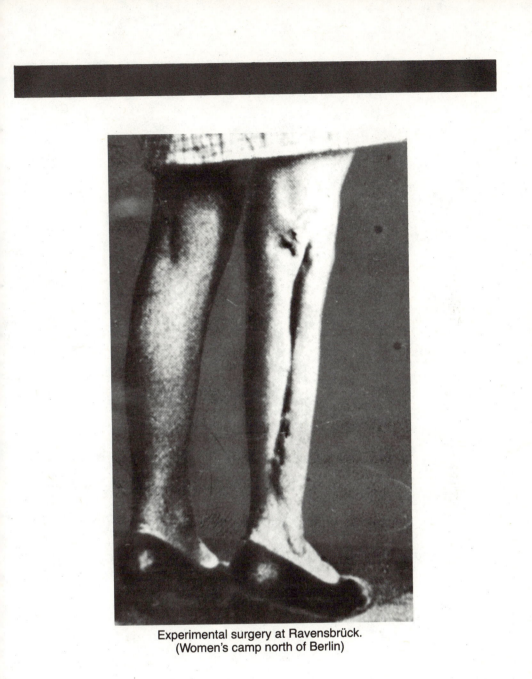

Experimental surgery at Ravensbrück.
(Women's camp north of Berlin)

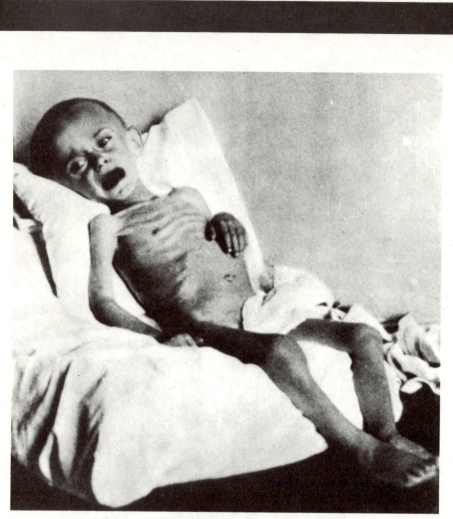

A tiny "guinea pig," eyes full of misery and terror. (Medical experiments at Auschwitz)

Elderly people and mothers with children, new arrivals at Auschwitz from Hungary, are selected for death. These people were immediately gassed after this was taken by an SS photographer. (Spring 1944)

Struggling to exist at Buchenwald.

The dead stacked like cordwood. (Buchenwald)

BUCHENWALD

A crematory oven gives back its scraps—a skull, a rib cage . . .
(Buchenwald labor camp)

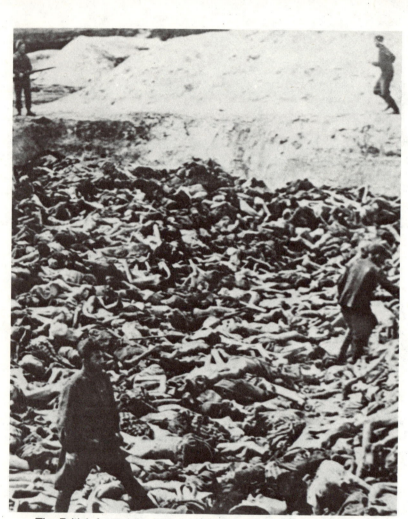

The British forced the infamous Dr. Klein, who killed thousands by injection, to stand among his victims in a mass grave. (Bergen Belsen)

13

The Christian Resistance Movement

On a hill in Jerusalem sits the Holocaust memorial Yad Vashem (Hebrew for "place and name," from Isaiah 56:5). Visitors walk through a museum exhibiting objects, pictures, and documents of the history of the Holocaust. The facility contains a massive central archive with millions of films, microfilms, photographs, and records of the Holocaust. Eyewitness accounts and a large library (including trial documents such as the Eichmann trial evidence) enhance any scholarly pursuit of the topic.

Article 9 of Israel's Martyrs' and Heroes' Remembrance Law (1953), which officially established the memorial and the archive, recognizes the "Righteous of the Nations" by organizing a department to perpetuate the names of "the high-minded righteous who risked their lives to save Jews." A judicial committee, always chaired by one justice of the Israeli Supreme Court, investigates every instance of a Gentile rescuer, commemorating that person with a certificate of honor, the right to plant a tree on the Avenue of the Righteous, and a silver medallion. This high honor is reserved for those who risked their lives for the Jewish people during the Holocaust. A few thousand have been honored thus far, a figure far from complete according to Jewish statisticians because of deaths and failures to report heroic deeds. Inscribed on the medallion is the talmudic maxim. "He who saves one life is considered as having saved the whole universe." The other side pictures a pair of emaciated hands clutching barbed wire wrapped around a globe.[1]

1. A representation of the medallion is found on page 184, vol. 14, of the *Encyclopedia Judaica* under "Righteous of the Nations" (Jerusalem: Keter Publishing, 1972). This reference encyclo-

The planting of a tree, like so many official acts in Israel, has biblical connotations. "How blessed is the man who does not walk in the counsel of the wicked," declares Psalm 1:1, affirming in verse 3:

> And he will be like a tree
> firmly planted by streams of water,
> Which yields its fruit in its season,
> And its leaf does not wither;
> And in whatever he does, he prospers.

Only an evergreen carob tree is planted in the Avenue of the Righteous, because it does not wither under the intense heat of summer or the cold, damp winds of winter. The tree is a symbol of both the Jewish and Christian emphasis on the importance of *deeds* in a righteous life—in contrast to lofty, inactive rhetoric.

In Nazi-ruled nations, the deed mattered and action was imperative. A state of neutrality, expressing sorrow for the plight of the Jew or even praying that God would deliver them, was not enough. Christians had to care enough to *act*.

"I DID NOTHING SPECIAL"

Many Christians who did help were more adept at actions than at broadcasting their heroic deeds. Peter Hellman found in writing his book *Avenue of the Righteous*, which details "inspiring true stories of heroic Christians and the Jews they saved from the Holocaust," that when asked *why* they acted as they did, most of them shrugged their shoulders and replied: "I did nothing special. Anybody would have done it." One exception was Jeanne Daman Scaglione, who as a young schoolteacher in Brussels, Belgium, saved hundreds of Jewish children. She responded:

> I became persuaded that it was imperative for a non-Jew to concern herself actively with saving Jewish lives under pain of indirect collaboration by default in the destruction of the Jewish community. To the extent that I could, I tried to come out of this war having refused, at least, to find refuge in an easy neutrality.[2]

However, Scaglione stated emphatically that she had no interest in seeing her portrait in the book. "So I had been put on notice," wrote Hellman, "that as a rule those who have earned a tree are loath to trumpet the news."

---

pedia of sixteen volumes and numerous yearbooks is one of the finest for illustration and explanation of Jewish life, thought, and history. Its article on the Holocaust, for example, includes over one hundred pages of photographs, maps, and exposition. Other articles detail the history of Jewish communities throughout the world (by town, city, or nation). Because of its penchant for accuracy and the listing of additional sources, it is highly recommended to the student of Judaica.

2. Peter Hellman, *Avenue of the Righteous* (New York: Bantam, 1980), p. viii. Note Hellman's observations about the memorial, the carob tree and the "Righteous" in his introduction, pp. v–xii.

HOLLAND—A "HIDING PLACE" FOR JEWS

The country with the highest per capita representation in the Avenue of the Righteous is Holland. Before World War II, Jewish refugees from Germany were generously aided by the Dutch (Anne Frank's family fled from Germany to Holland in 1933). There were approximately thirty thousand Jewish refugees in the country at the time of the Nazi occupation in May 1940. Nazi decrees against the Jews of Holland kindled deep resentment in the Dutch population. Considering it a prelude to the revocation of their own personal freedom, individuals from all classes of Dutch society opposed the Nazis. In February 1941 the Nazis tried their usual tactic of using local criminals and hooligans to carry out a "spontaneous demonstration" against the seventy thousand Jews in Amsterdam. The SS were amazed to find that both the Jews and the Dutch Gentiles fought back. Christians joined Jews in beating up the hoodlums, wounding at least half of them with iron bars and "knuckle-dusters." Factory workers and longshoremen formed patrols to repulse the subsequent assaults, and physicians pledged their assistance to the wounded. After such a humiliating defeat, the SS had to discard their fake role as observers. They were forced to bring three battalions of their own police, armed with tanks and automatic weapons, to inflict heavy casualties on the Jews. The Nazis in a later skirmish deported Jewish resisters to the Mauthausen concentration camp in Austria. The Dutch became outraged, calling for mass strikes that paralyzed the nation. The Nazis proceeded to arrest workers indiscriminately, sending many to concentration camps. The brutality of the Nazis prevailed, but the SS were put on notice that this nation was not going to stand idly by while racists attacked Jewish citizens.[3]

Protestant and Roman Catholic churches sought to save the Dutch Jews from deportation. They actively protested to the Germans and drew up a manifesto to be read in the churches. The manifesto, which included a protest against deportations, was condemned by the Nazis, who gave orders forbidding its reading in the churches. With the exception of the Dutch Reformed, all the churches ignored the Nazi order and read the manifesto to their congregations.[4] A large Christian resistance movement developed in the fall of 1942, when the Nazis began mass deportations. The Dutch people offered Jews the protection of their homes. It is estimated that through these efforts from ten to fifteen thousand Jews were saved. Corrie Ten Boom's family with "the hiding place" in their crooked little house was part of this movement. For the Ten Boom family there was no crisis of decision whether to risk their lives for the Jewish people—they simply did it because it *had* to be done.

3. Philip Friedman, *Their Brothers' Keepers* (New York: Holocaust Library, 1978), pp. 60–63. Compare J. Presser, *The Destruction of the Dutch Jews*, trans. Arnold Pomerans (New York: E. P. Dutton, 1969), pp. 45–57.
4. B. A. Sijes, "Several Observations Concerning the Position of the Jews in Occupied Holland During World War II," in Yisrael Gutman and Efraim Zuroff, eds., *Rescue Attempts During the Holocaust* (Jerusalem: Yad Vashem, 1977), p. 550.

Nevertheless, Nazi propaganda succeeded in spreading its racist cancer even in Holland. As Corrie noted:

> The true horror of occupation came over us only slowly. During the first year of German rule there were only minor attacks on Jews in Holland. A rock through the window of a Jewish-owned store. An ugly word scrawled on the wall of a synagogue. It was as though they were trying us, testing the temper of the country. How many Dutchmen would go along with them?
>
> And the answer, to our shame, was many. The National Socialist Bond [Dutch Nazis], the quisling organization of Holland, grew larger and bolder with each month of occupation. Some joined the NSB simply for the benefits: more food, more clothing coupons, the best jobs and housing. But others became NSBers out of conviction. *Nazism was a disease to which the Dutch too were susceptible, and those with anti-Semitic bias fell sick of it first.*
>
> On our daily walk [in the town of Haarlem] Father and I saw the symptoms spread. A sign in a shop window: JEWS WILL NOT BE SERVED. At the entrance to a public park: NO JEWS. On the door of the library. In front of restaurants, theaters, even the concert hall whose alley we knew so much better than its seats.
>
> A synagogue burned down and the fire trucks came. But only to keep the flames from spreading to the buildings on either side.[5]

"We talked often, Father, Betsie and I," Corrie remembered, "about what we could do if a chance should come to help some of our Jewish friends."

Other Christians worked with Jewish underground groups. Joop Westerville, son of a Plymouth Brethren elder in Holland, worked with an organization smuggling Jewish young people to Spain (from which they could reach Palestine more easily). The father of four children, Westerville was a noted educator and head of his own school. Nevertheless, when the opportunity arose to participate in the difficult journey of crossing the heavily guarded Dutch and Belgian borders, traveling through France and over the rugged mountain terrain, he gladly and with dedicated fervor led his young Jewish charges. In the summer of 1944 this Christian man was captured and sent to the Vught concentration camp. He was tortured daily and finally shot by the Nazis in a forest near Vught. The many survivors he helped remembered him, erected a monument in Israel, and planted a forest in his name.[6]

MORE WOMEN THAN MEN

Philip Friedman praises the courage of women in saving Jews from the Nazis.

> On the whole, women played an important role in the rescue of Jewish children. Many women were involved in the rescue activities. More easily moved by their

---

5. Corrie Ten Boom, *The Hiding Place*, with John and Elizabeth Sherrill (Washington Depot, Conn.: Chosen Books, 1971), pp. 67–78. Italics added.
6. Friedman, *Their Brothers' Keepers*, pp. 65–67. This book is an excellent source on the Christian resistance movement.

emotions than men, women very often acted on their first impulse and thought less of the consequences . . . gentile women also remained equally loyal to their employers and were hiding them, risking their own lives. In the underground organizations, more women than men were engaged in the section dealing with aid to Jews. A number of gentile girls and women were also of great help as contacts or couriers for Jewish underground organizations.[7]

Friedman underscores the "courageous and compassionate women in all the nations of Europe," emphasizing the difficulty in reviewing even a fraction of their exploits.

THE DANES—A TRADITION OF HUMANITARIANISM

In the area of Christian resistance, the Danes were an example of a nation successfully bound together to save the Jewish people. The citizens of Denmark saved nearly 99 percent of their 7,000 Jews. From high officials to fishermen, they actively fought German anti-Semitism, refusing to become Nazified in belief or culture. Harold Flender in *Rescue in Denmark* has suggested many reasons for their success. A primary element, he says, was their tradition of humanitarianism and democracy. The Jewish community was totally assimilated into Danish culture, achieving full emancipation early in the nineteenth century. In 1814 Denmark declared all racial and religious discrimination illegal. This was in stark contrast to Germany, and German citizens who lived in Denmark were sometimes influenced by these attitudes. Georg Duckwitz, a German who had lived in Denmark since 1928, used his position in the German embassy as head of shipping in Copenhagen to gain confidential information about a secret Nazi raid to round up Denmark's Jews in 1943. His advance warning alerted Danes to hide their Jewish friends and neighbors and later transport many of them to neutral Sweden. (In fact, the proximity of Sweden to Denmark was an important reason for their accomplishments. Unlike many areas in Europe, for Danish Jews there was a place to go.) The Danes, considered Aryans by the Germans, were also accorded more freedom in the early stages of Nazi occupation (Denmark was invaded April 9, 1940). The Nazis erroneously believed they could instill anti-Semitism in Denmark via manipulative propaganda.[8]

The leadership of Denmark, including King Christian X and heads of business, medicine, and education, joined forces to resist the Nazis. They provided inspiration for other Danes. Church leaders proved a key influence in fostering Christian resistance and compassionate attitudes. Dean Johannes Nordentoft wrote in a journal for Danish pastors: "Christians will be the first to fight this

7. Philip Friedman, "'Righteous Gentiles' in the Nazi Era" in *Roads to Extinction: Essays on the Holocaust* (New York: The Jewish Publication Society, 1980), p. 414. This essay was written in 1955.
8. Harold Flender, *Rescue in Denmark* (New York: Holocaust Library, 1963), pp. 255–60. Compare Leni Yahil, "The Uniqueness of the Rescue of Danish Jewry," in *Rescue Attempts During the Holocaust*, pp. 617–25.

dirty anti-Semitism." He later declared that those who "remain silent or disapprove by merely shrugging their shoulders" were actually Nazi collaborators. Pastor Ivar Lange of the Frederiksberg Church declared to his Lutheran congregation that he "would rather die with the Jews than live with the Nazis." In fact, on October 3, 1943, Danish Lutheran bishops sent a protest letter to the German officials in Denmark (it was also to be read in every Lutheran church in the country). The letter is indicative of the Danish Christian response to anti-Semitism and racial or religious prejudice. It stated:

> We will never forget that the Lord Jesus Christ was born in Bethlehem of the Virgin Mary, according to God's promise to the Chosen People of Israel.
>
> Persecution of the Jews conflicts with the humanitarian conception of the love of neighbors and the message which Christ's church set out to preach. Christ taught us that every man has a value in the eyes of God.
>
> Persecution conflicts with the judicial conscience existing in the Danish people, inherited through centuries of Danish culture. All Danish citizens according to the fundamental law, have the same right and responsibility under the law of religious freedom. We respect the right to religious freedom and to the performance of divine worship according to the dictates of conscience. Race or religion should never in themselves cause people to be deprived of their rights, freedom or property.
>
> Notwithstanding our separate religious beliefs we will fight to preserve for our Jewish brothers and sisters the same freedom we ourselves value more than life. The leaders of the Danish Church clearly comprehend the duties of law-abiding citizens, but recognize at the same time that they are conscientiously bound to maintain the right and to protest every violation of justice. It is evident that in this case we are obeying God rather than man.[9]

Many Danish Christians put their words (and faith) into action in the fall of 1943 by hiding Jews and then transporting them at great personal danger to Sweden. It was a mass rescue operation stemming from a basic consensus among Danes that Jewish people must be saved.

"THE MOST NATURAL THING IN THE WORLD"

In France collaboration with Nazis was the usual procedure for the Vichy government, and in the early days of occupation many citizens exhibited little compassion for the Jewish people. But pastor Andre Trocme and his French Protestant community in Le Chambon saved approximately three thousand Jewish children and adults. A pacifist Huguenot, Trocme and his people knew persecution; they had strong ethical standards and had a keen sense of the value of human life. From the day Trocme's wife, Magda, found a Jewish refugee on her doorstep and immediately said, "Come in, but come in!" to the time she invited the two policemen who had arrested her husband to stay for dinner, this Chris-

9. Ibid., p. 69.

tian couple was driven by established, daily ethical patterns. When philosopher Philip Hallie went to France to find out why goodness occurred in Le Chambon while the specter of evil surrounded it, he found that the religious leaders (including Trocme's assistant pastor, Edouard Theis) inspired their whole village of three thousand to a higher plane of Christian living. It is interesting that their response to Hallie's praise (Hallie was dejected and disheartened by his study of the Holocaust and the evil involved) was almost identical in the village and surrounding countryside: "How can you call us 'good'? We were doing what had to be done. Who else could help them? And what has all this to do with goodness? Things had to be done, that's all, and we happened to be there to do them. You must understand that it was the *most natural thing in the world* to help these people."[10]

What made the difference between the few Christians who helped the Jewish people and the multitude who did not? As one studies the lives of Christian resisters during the Holocaust, the reoccurring emphasis on established ethical patterns of Christian thought and practice looms large. They strove to be Christlike in their attitudes toward other religions and races, seeking to unlearn the prejudice bolstered and sustained by the community around them. Because prejudice is a learned behavior, they geared their lives to immunize themselves from its infection. Some were transformed by cultivating friendships among despised groups, learning to their joy that Jews (and others) were human beings like themselves. Godly thinking provided personal enhancement and comprehension of the infinite value of a human life and God's love for *every* person. Stirred by the realization of their own human frailty, these resisters established patterns of sacrificial living for others long before the Holocaust milieu tested them. Their sensitivity in the "little" areas of ethical judgment built up, brick by brick, a strong foundation for when the big decisions arose. In fact, the "big" decisions were not major crises because of their daily life-style. They simply did what they knew was right.

These patterns are manifest, for example, in the Ten Boom family. The children had observed in their father the absence of racial and religious prejudice, and so cultivated this Christian spirit within themselves. Their father held true to his daily patterns to the very end of his life. When brought before the Gestapo officer in charge, Ten Boom had the opportunity to be set free by giving his word not to cause any more trouble. The officer could not believe that someone would arrest such an old man in Holland. Ten Boom, however, sensed an ethical shadow his biblical belief could not tolerate. Standing erect he infuriated the Nazi by replying firmly and clearly: "If I go home today, tomorrow I will open my door again to any man in need who knocks."[11] Incarcerated, he died ten days later, a Christian testimony to all who came in contact with him.

10. Philip P. Hallie, *Lest Innocent Blood Be Shed: The Story of the Village of Le Chambon and How Goodness Happened There* (New York: Harper & Row, 1979), pp. 20–21. Italics added.
11. Corrie Ten Boom, *The Hiding Place*, p. 128.

His daughter Corrie, as well as his other children, continued to be a blessing to others and perhaps are a lesson to each one of us raising children. Our offspring observe us closely. They sense our attitudes and prejudices, picking up biases we believe are safely hidden away. Such children can just as easily perceive a parent's nourishing love for fellow human beings and imitate this valid Christlike spirit. But it will only be accomplished if the Christian parent is a daily "resister," unlearning the prejudice that surrounds him.

Moshe Bejski, while chairman of the Yad Vashem Committee for the Designation of the "Righteous Among the Nations," noted that religious conviction often motivated people to help Jews even when their society and church were anti-Semitic or indifferent.[12] This was quite a testimony to him, and it underscores the small but vibrant Christian resistance movement. The documents testify to the humanitarianism and ethical patterns of this remnant. Often unnamed, a higher honor awaits them.

One such individual was briefly recorded in Emmanuel Ringelblum's journal: "A Christian was killed today, the 19th of November [1940], for throwing a sack of bread over the Wall [of the Warsaw Ghetto]."[13] The short note bespeaks a lifetime.

12. Moshe Bejski, "The 'Righteous Among the Nations' and Their Part in the Rescue of the Jews," in *Rescue Attempts During the Holocaust*, p. 635.
13. Emmanuel Ringelblum, *Notes from the Warsaw Ghetto*, ed. and trans. Jacob Sloan (New York: Schocken Books, 1974), p. 89.

14

Jewish Resistance Movements

When the world learned about the extermination of six million Jews, many theories arose attempting to explain how such a heinous catastrophe could occur. Ironically, in many of these theories the victims themselves were condemned. Drawing their information from German sources, scholars such as Raul Hilberg and Hannah Arendt conclude that the Jews went like sheep to the slaughter, rarely raising as much as a finger in protest. Hilberg's otherwise fine study *The Destruction of the European Jews* falls short of the mark in stating: "The reaction pattern of the Jews is characterized by almost complete lack of resistance. In marked contrast to German propaganda, the documentary evidence of Jewish resistance, overt or submerged is very slight." Quoting from Anti-Partisan Chief and Higher SS and Police Leader, Erich von dem Bach Zelewsky, Hilberg dispels the myth of a Jewish world conspiracy along with the fallacy that the Jewish people are friendly to Communism. Unfortunately, in its place he propounds the fallacy of Jewish passivity, emphasizing: "The Jews were not oriented toward resistance. They took up resistance only in a few cases, locally, and at the last moment."[1]

---

1. Raul Hilberg, *The Destruction of the European Jews* (Chicago: Quandrangle Books, 1967), pp. 662–63. Erich von dem Bach Zelewsky remarked about the inability of the Jews to resist: "It gives the lie to the old slogan that the Jews are conspiring to dominate the world and that they are so highly organized. In reality they had no organization of their own at all, not even an information service." Compare Alexander Donat, "Jewish Resistance," in Albert H. Friedlander, *Out of the Whirlwind: A Reader of Holocaust Literature* (New York: Schocken Books, 1976), pp. 50–67 for a critique of Hilberg, Arendt, and others.

Resistance, however, is a multi-dimensional phenomenon. Passive resistance can become a most active opposition under extremely difficult conditions—like those forced upon Jews by the Nazis.

MANY SMALL REVOLTS

Normal standards of resistance become irrelevant in the face of starvation, disease, mental anguish, and the cruelty of the ghetto and the camp. The maintaining of dignity in the midst of systematic dehumanization and keeping the will to live while being crushed in the crucible of death were forms of Jewish resistance and valor. Mothers constantly reminded their children that the Nazis and their cohorts were animals, and encouraged their teenage sons and daughters to hang onto life. Many mothers starved themselves in order that their children might live. Belief and trust in God was fervently sustained by others in a glorious tribute to Jewish heritage and history as a people of the Book. Jewish partisans (underground guerrilla fighters) with limited provisions and under dreadful conditions fought gallantly. In a number of ghettos, revolts occurred; and in at least two notorious death camps, Treblinka and Sobibor, Jews were actually able to terminate the Nazi operation. These were difficult exploits, especially since the general populace was anti-Semitic, eager informants were plentiful, and the Nazis were relentless in their pursuit. And yet, the Jewish tailors in German commissary shops of the Warsaw Ghetto who shipped a transport of military uniforms with trousers sewn together and buttons on backwards are heroes in the annals of Jewish resistance as much as the Jewish partisans fighting in the forests of Lithuania.[2]

Emmanuel Ringelblum, an eyewitness who used his writing as a form of resistance, attested to the role of women and children in the smuggling operations that kept alive a community sentenced to starvation. "The smuggling of goods past the Wall [of the Warsaw Ghetto] continues, resulting every day in the sacrifice of a large number of wounded and dead. Often minors and children are among the victims." In a tribute to these Jewish resisters, he concluded: "There is good reason for the proverb that three things are indomitable: the German Army, the British Isles, and Jewish smuggling."[3] In other excerpts, he related courageous actions of young girls with names like Chajke and Frumke who boldly traveled from the Ghetto with "Aryan papers" and "Aryan faces" to smuggle contraband and serve as agents on the most dangerous of missions. "The historian of the future," noted Ringelblum, "will have to devote a fitting chapter to the role of the Jewish woman during the war. It is thanks to the

---

2. A book that should be read by every student of the Holocaust is Yuri Suhl, ed. and trans., *They Fought Back: The Story of the Jewish Resistance in Nazi Europe* (New York: Schocken Books, 1975).

3. Emmanuel Ringelblum, *Notes from the Warsaw Ghetto*, ed. and trans. Jacob Sloan (New York: Schocken Books, 1974), p. 265.

courage and endurance of our women that thousands of families have been able to endure these bitter times."[4]

THE WARSAW REVOLT

Women and young people were also active in the Warsaw Ghetto Revolt of 1943. Jewish partisan groups began to mobilize in the Ghetto as deportations increased and reports of the extermination camps were verified. The heartstrings of the Ghetto were touched as famed child specialist and educator Janusz Korczak led his young charges in the Ghetto orphanage to the railway station in August 1942. Part of their orderly march was by chance caught by a Nazi taking movies, and observers likened the little children's bobbing yellow stars to a field of buttercups. One might have thought they were on their way to a picnic, but in reality they were being transported to Treblinka to be exterminated (as were hundreds of thousands from Warsaw).[5] Such deportations affected every Ghetto fighter, as friends and family were taken. In January 1943 the Nazis began another deportation but met with armed resistance from fighters who killed a number of Nazis. Sporadic attacks took place throughout the Ghetto.

Able at last to smuggle arms into the Ghetto, the resisters, led by twenty-four-year-old Mordechai Anielewicz, prepared for a Nazi assault on April 19, 1943. Ber Mark in *Uprising in the Warsaw Ghetto* relates what happened:

> As German columns, singing heartily, moved into the intersection of Nalewki, Gesia, and Franciszkanska streets, they were suddenly barraged by Molotov cocktails, grenades, bombs, and bullets. The first shots came from the house at Nalewki 33, followed immediately by all other stations. The Germans were hit so suddenly that they fled in panic, leaving their dead and wounded on the pavement. When soon after they attempted to retrieve their casualties, they could not—so strong was the fire from Jewish positions. Soon, the rebels jumped out of their hiding places and took to shooting at the Nazis with pistols.
>
> Great enthusiasm was aroused in the Jews by Germans fleeing at first confrontation. The lusty song of S.S. men turned into cries of pain from their wounded. Tamar, a fighter, cried out, "This time they've paid!"
>
> Soon the German officers reestablished control in their ranks. Von Sammern's staff was alerted and aid quickly came. The newly arrived soldiers did not dare advance openly, but they began chaotic shooting in the direction of the houses from which shots had earlier originated. Once more the two sides locked in battle. Once more the Jews not only held out, but also forced a second German retreat.
>
> The initial battle on the corner of Nalewki and Gesia lasted two hours, from 6:00

---

4. Ibid., p. 294. The account of Chajke and Frumke is found on pages 273–74.
5. Janusz Korczak's memoirs reveal a man desperate to save his orphans from disease and starvation in the midst of constant oppressive measures by the Third Reich. Korczak was famous enough to have friends willing to smuggle him out of the Warsaw Ghetto, but he refused to leave his young charges. Note *The Warsaw Ghetto Memoirs of Janusz Korczak*, ed. and trans. E. P. Kulawiec (Washington, D.C.: University Press of America, 1979).

to 8:00 A.M. Only the German side suffered. Thanks to their convenient positions the rebels lost not one person.

With the Nazi columns completely emptied out, the rebels came out of their hiding places and threw up their arms and congratulated one another. Then they pulled uniforms, helmets, and arms off the Nazi corpses that lay in the street.[6]

The Nazis later moved in tanks and armored cars with terrified S.S. following behind. The Jewish combatants, however, set them on fire with a bombardment of Molotov cocktails.

Juergen Stroop was transferred from Galicia (where he was an SS anti-partisan expert) to Warsaw to direct the destruction of the Ghetto. His official report alludes to the tenacity of the Jewish resisters and to the relentless commitment of the assault forces of the Third Reich to quell the revolt. Only the total devastation of the Ghetto could defeat the Jewish partisans. Stroop explained:

> The resistance offered by the Jews and bandits could be broken only by the energetic and relentless day and night commitment of our assault units. . . . I therefore decided to embark on the total destruction of the Jewish quarter by burning down every residential block, including the housing blocks belonging to the armament enterprises. One enterprise after another was systematically evacuated and destroyed by fire. In almost every instance, the Jews then emerged from their hiding places and bunkers. It was not unusual for Jews to remain in the burning houses until the heat and their fear of being cremated forced them to jump from the upper floors. They did so after throwing mattresses and other upholstered items into the street. With broken bones, they still tried to crawl across the street into housing blocks that had not yet been set on fire or were only partly in flames.[7]

"During the armed resistance, females belonging to fighting groups were armed just like the men," Stroop reported. "Not infrequently, these females fired pistols from both hands."[8] The report was dated May 16, 1943—the Jewish resisters had held off 5,000 Nazis armed with the best German equipment available for nearly one month! Similar rebellions occurred in many other ghettos (such as Bialystok and Vilna).

DEATH-CAMP REVOLTS

Ringelblum described Treblinka as the "slaughter-house of European Jewry." Second only to Auschwitz in the number of victims killed, at least 800,000 Jews

6. Ber Mark, *Uprising in the Warsaw Ghetto*, trans. Gershon Friedlin (New York: Schocken Books, 1975), pp. 21–22. The latter half of this book contains primary documents concerning the uprising. Compare Reuben Ainsztein, *The Warsaw Ghetto Revolt* (New York: Holocaust Library, 1979).

7. *The Stroop Report: The Jewish Quarter of Warsaw Is No More!* trans. Sybil Milton, with introduction by Andrzej Wirth (New York: Pantheon, 1979), p. 9 of the report.

8. Ibid., p. 8. The report consists of three parts: a descriptive narrative introduction, daily communiques on the progress of the operation, and a series of photographs. Stroop was awarded the Iron Cross First Class for commanding the destruction of the Warsaw Ghetto. Sentenced to death after the war, he was hanged in Poland in 1951.

were exterminated there. Transports of victims arrived from Germany, Austria, Macedonia, Greece, Yugoslavia, Slovakia, Czechoslovakia, occupied Soviet territory (especially Belorussia) and from various cities in Poland. Three hundred thousand Jews from the Warsaw Ghetto were sent to Treblinka in sealed cattle cars between July and September of 1942. Located fifty miles northeast of Warsaw, the camp maintained a number of security precautions to ensure complete secrecy of operation. Treblinka occupied a clearing one mile square and was surrounded by a wooded area. Soldiers from the outside were forbidden access to the camp. An electric siren system warned all planes to change course. The main storehouse was camouflaged with timetables from alleged trains, station clocks, ticket sales, and so forth. Most ironic was the enormous arrow painted with the words: "Change for eastbound trains." These deceptions gave victims the impression that they would be changing trains and going farther east. An average day brought three or four trains of sixty cars each, with 80 to 150 men, women, and children cramped into each car. The stench from the corpses lingered in the air.[9]

Sporadic acts of resistance occurred in Treblinka. For example, a young Jewish man from Warsaw who worked with the "death company" caught a glimpse of his wife and child escorted to the gas chamber. He immediately attacked and killed SS man Max Bill with a knife. Such resistance was a prelude to the great revolt on August 2, 1943. A Jewish locksmith sent to repair the lock on the door to the arsenal had made an imprint of the key. In a well-planned action, arms were removed by a debris removal detail and distributed to Jewish "combat" units in the camp. Instead of disinfectant, stolen gasoline was poured into the disinfection sprinkler and sprayed heavily on certain areas of the camp. At 3:45 P.M. a rifle shot pierced the air as a signal for the revolt to begin, and hand grenades were thrown at the "disinfected" spots. An enormous fire consumed the camp, and the arsenal exploded. Seven hundred workers were on the campgrounds, but only 150–200 succeeded in escaping. All but twelve were caught and murdered by the Nazis, Polish peasants, and Ukrainian fascist groups. A few small transports continued to arrive, but in November the Nazis decided to blow up the remains of the camp. As survivor Samuel Rajzman explained: "We realized our aim fully and in martyrdom. Treblinka was wiped out. A fortress of horrible Nazism was erased from the face of the earth."[10]

In the Sobibor death camp, a camp heavily guarded by SS men and Ukrainian auxiliary police, a revolt on October 14, 1943, forced Himmler to close it. In spite of four rows of barbed wire fence more than ten feet high surrounding the camp, a ravine filled with water, and a mine field, the inmates staged a revolt that freed approximately sixty men and women to join partisan groups in the

9. On Treblinka note Alexander Donat, ed., *The Death Camp Treblinka: A Documentary* (New York: Holocaust Library, 1979). For the extreme precautions the Nazis used to deceive their victims compare Eugen Kogon, *The Theory and Practice of Hell* (New York: Berkley, 1958), especially chapter 4, "The Physical Set-up of the Camps."
10. Samuel Rajzman, "Uprising in Treblinka," in Suhl, *They Fought Back*, p. 134.

countryside. The report of the Order Police in the District Lublin dated October 15, 1943, stated:

> On October 14, 1943, at about 5 P.M., revolt of the Jews in SS-camp Sobibor, 25 miles north of Cholm. They overpowered the guards, seized the armory, and after firefight with camp garrison fled in unknown direction. Nine SS murdered, 1 SS man missing, 2 foreign guards shot to death. Approximately 300 Jews escaped, the remainder were shot to death or are now in camp. Military police and armed forces were notified immediately and took over security of the camp at about 1 A.M. The area south and southwest of Sobibor is now being searched by police and armed forces.[11]

Even in the infamous Auschwitz, Jewish resisters staged a revolt that succeeded in blowing up one of the four crematoriums.[12]

NEARLY IMPOSSIBLE CIRCUMSTANCES

The difficulty in executing a successful resistance movement is clearly evident in the efforts by Jewish partisans in Lithuania and White Russia. While small bands of Jews were spread throughout the forests after the Nazis attacked Russian-occupied territory (including parts of Poland, Lithuania, Latvia, and Estonia), a large Jewish rebellion was forestalled by the German threat of collective responsibility. The escape of one individual or the murder of a Nazi automatically meant death to whole families or groups. The partisan was thus torn between his desire for active resistance and his responsibility toward his community. At a time when few could comprehend that anyone would deliberately attempt to exterminate an entire race or religion, the pressure brought to bear on the partisan by his own community was enormous. Jews naturally felt that the partisan's rebellious ways were hurting the community and thwarting accommodation to Nazi demands.

In addition, Nazi deception was uncanny and relations with non-Jews were difficult. In discussing these factors, Lester Eckman and Chaim Lazar concluded:

> Jewish partisans in Europe lacked all the basic conditions required for warfare and were weighed down with the special difficulties brought on by the Holocaust. In spite of these dilemmas there emerged a Jewish partisan movement of tens of thousands of fighters, with the common purpose of preserving the honor of Israel. Jewish partisans were daring men, imbued from childhood with love for Torah,

---

11. Raul Hilberg, ed., *Documents of Destruction: Germany and Jewry 1933–1945* (Chicago: Quadrangle Books, 1971), p. 223. Compare Alexander Pechersky, "The Revolt in Sobibor," in Albert Nirenstein, ed., *A Tower from the Enemy* (New York: Orion Press, 1959), pp. 303–47; and Miriam Novitch, ed., *Sobibor: Martyrdom and Revolt* (New York: Holocaust Library, 1980).
12. Note Konnilyn G. Feig, *Hitler's Death Camps: The Sanity of Madness* (New York: Holmes and Meier, 1979), pp. 363–64.

Israel, and the dignity of man. Surrounded by beasts, they remembered that they were Jews, who must comport themselves according to Jewish ethics and morality. In eastern Europe, in Russia, and in the western Ukraine there was hardly a single town without some underground nucleus from which sprang a Jewish partisan group. We can also conclude from the ever-growing collection of documents in our archives that in sixteen occupied European countries there was not one with Jews living in it in which there was no Jewish underground and Jewish resistance . . . The following must be remembered: the Jewish partisans fought a war which was without comparison in history, and under the most unfavorable conditions.[13]

From the death camps to the forests; from the covert worship service to the mother hiding with her babe in her arms; the full story of Jewish resistance is a tale yet to be told.

13. Lester Eckman and Chaim Lazar, *The Jewish Resistance: The History of the Jewish Partisans in Lithuania and White Russia during the Nazi Occupation 1940–1945* (New York: Shengold Publishers, 1977), pp. 16–17. Compare Yitzhak Arad, *The Partisan* (New York: Holocaust Library, 1979); and Nahum Kohn and Howard Roiter, *A Voice from the Forest: Memoirs of a Jewish Partisan* (New York: Holocaust Library, 1980).

15

The German Church Struggle

In the past few years there has been a growing fascination among theologians and theological students to create a society under the direct authority of "God's Law." Taking their cue from Calvin's Geneva or the Puritan experiment in the Massachusetts Bay Colony, these postmillennial advocates of Christian reform increasingly speak in terms of "Protestant nations" and "Christian nations" versus "pagan nations." American Christians are told that what the decadent United States needs is more *Christian* law practiced by more *Christian* lawyers to bring in a *Christian* society with *Christian* economics to reach the world and make it *Christian*. The concept has intrigued a number of Christians outside the fold of postmillennialism (a view of the future which insists that the world can be made progressively better and that the Christian church will bring in the Millennium). Even Christians who believe that only the second coming of Jesus Christ will initiate the Millennium have been influenced by this view.

Nevertheless, this seemingly honorable, ethical, and conscientious movement is not supportable scripturally—even with a theocracy and the Shekinah glory of God in their presence, the Hebrews had massive problems with human depravity, which marred their obedience to God. It also has consequences of which the student of history must be aware—consequences to which proponents of such theology are oblivious.

The Bavarian churches also thought they had a head start on a Christian society when a new government, one that fostered "God's Laws" and opposed "godless socialism," came to power. This statement was drawn up to be read on Easter Sunday from Lutheran pulpits:

A state which brings into being again government according to God's Laws should, in doing so, be assured not only of the applause but also of the glad and active co-operation of the Church. With gratitude and joy the Church takes note that the new State bans blasphemy, assails immorality, establishes discipline and order with a strong hand, while at the same time calling upon men to fear God, espousing the sanctity of marriage and Christian training for the young.[1]

Unfortunately the year was 1933, and the new regime was Adolf Hitler and his Nazi party.

Christians who thought they knew God's political, economic, and ethical system actually supported a regime that was godless, hated the church, and would perpetrate some of the greatest atrocities known to mankind. The Nazis appeared as the angels of light and successfully deceived even supposedly knowledgeable Christians into casting their vote of support for darkness.

EVANGELICAL AND FASCIST

As the Nazis consolidated their power in the early months of 1933, German Protestants were active in furthering their own position with the new state. All of the forces of *Volk* and fatherland came to fruition as church representatives undertook the formation of a new national Evangelical church.[2] On April 25, 1933, Hitler named Army District Chaplain Ludwig Mueller as his representative to the Evangelical church with the specific charge to establish a Reich Evangelical church. Mueller was the leader of the Faith Movement of German Christians (referred to as "German Christians") in East Prussia, a movement launched in 1932 to support right-wing politics and economics. It espoused a "positive Christianity" that rejected "Christian cosmopolitanism" and believed that National Socialism and Christianity should complement one another. "Christianity," they held, "should not lose its connection with the folk and national socialism should not become a movement without faith in God." Compromising with Evangelical church leaders at every turn in order to obtain a working constitution for the new national church, Mueller was present when the German Evangelical Church Confederation approved such a constitution on May 27, 1933.

1. Richard Gutteridge, *Open Thy Mouth for the Dumb!: The German Evangelical Church and the Jews, 1879-1950* (Oxford: Basil Blackwell, 1976), p. 72.
2. Since the Reformation, church and state in Germany were not separated. Secular and ecclesiastical governmental officials cooperated in administering the state church (referred to as "Evangelical" because of its Reformation heritage). The state, with control of the purse strings, appointment of higher church officials, and enactment of laws was the dominant power. The German Evangelical Church Conference was formed in 1852 to help unite the local churches in a confederation. After World War I, the Weimar Republic gave new freedom to the churches (the monarchy having abdicated), and the German Evangelical Church Confederation was established to provide a more centralized union, while retaining the essential freedom of the local churches. The complexity of the state church allowed for diverse movements to rise within it. The ascent of the Nazis and the general acceptance of their racial and *Volk* ideas came to fruition in a new national Evangelical church.

On July 12, 1933, Hitler informed President Hindenburg that the drafted document had been signed by representatives of German churches. Article I read: "The inviolable foundation of the German Evangelical church is the gospel of Jesus Christ, as testified to us in the Holy Scriptures and brought to light again in the creeds of the Reformation. The full powers which the church needs for her mission are thereby determined and limited."[3]

Church elections were held on July 23, with thousands who had rarely entered a church voting. The "German Christians" movement swept the offices, and a number of laws were soon enacted. One law discharged those who "on the basis of their previous activity do not guarantee that they will at all times unreservedly support the national State and the German Evangelical Church." Another retired all pastors and officials of "non-Aryan descent" or those "married to a person of non-Aryan descent." Ludwig Mueller was elected Reich bishop at the National Synod held in Wittenberg on September 27, announcing: "The old has passed away. The new has emerged. The Church's political struggle is past. Now begins the struggle for the soul of the people." On December 21, 1933, Mueller incorporated the Evangelical Youth of Germany into the Hitler Youth organization. From this period on, all athletics and all political education of the Evangelical youth groups were in the hands of the Nazis. Mueller informed Christian parents that "the incorporation had been for him a difficult decision to make, over which he had wrestled with God in prayer."[4]

AN INSUFFICIENT PROTEST

A storm of protest ensued as churchmen realized they were losing their freedom. On September 21, 1933, Martin Niemöller, pastor of Berlin's Dahlem Church, wrote to ministers inviting them to join a "Pastors Emergency Alliance." Concerned with the political power of the "German Christians" movement, Niemöller's letter interpreted what had transpired in the preceding few months.

> At a recent meeting of the Prussian General Synod the German-Christian majority forced through a series of laws changing the constitution. The objections of the minority, which were based at least partly on the church's confessional nature, were not met; a thorough preparation or even a discussion of the matter in committee was not permitted.
>
> On the day after the General Synod six General Superintendents were dismissed

---

3. Ernst Christian Helmreich, *The German Churches Under Hitler: Background, Struggle and Epilogue* (Detroit: Wayne State U., 1979), pp. 133–41. Compare Peter Matheson, ed., *The Third Reich and the Christian Churches* (Grand Rapids: Eerdmans, 1981), pp. 24–26, for the other articles in the new constitution. This book is a collection of documents (and partial documents) from the German church struggle and is a helpful guide for the student.

4. Arthur C. Cochrane, *The Church's Confession Under Hitler* (Philadelphia: Westminster, 1962), pp. 111–18.

from office and retired without any sort of explanation. Since this time there has been widespread confusion, perplexity, and deep unrest among the congregations in and around Berlin. This state of affairs is aggravated by stormy goings-on in some congregations. Church organisations, for example, which do not want to lend their wholehearted support to the "Faith Movement of German Christians" are forbidden the use of the rooms in the church house on the instructions of the congregation's church council. In other instances, specific measures have been taken against individual pastors at the behest of the "Faith Movement" in their respective congregations, the goal being "disciplinary removal." Characteristically, the church "leaders" and authorities have capitulated to these endeavors, since the people now demand that the promise given in the election campaign should now be kept.

These events have given rise to a shameful faint-heartedness among many ministerial brethren; although serious-minded men, some have even gone over to the "German Christians" against their own better judgement, knowing that what they did was contrary to their ordination vow and was a violation of their consciences.[5]

Within a week, two thousand pastors responded by attending the Barmen Synod, the first synod of the Confessing Church. The Barmen Confession of May 1934, written under the guidance of Karl Barth, repudiated the false doctrine of the "German Christians" and recalled the German Evangelical church to the central truths of Christianity. It also rejected undivided loyalty to the State and the State's attempt to usurp the role of the church.[6]

Unfortunately, although Niemöller attacked the laws against non-Aryans in the ministry as a violation of the confessional stance of the church of Christ, and although many of these men fought for the rights of their Hebrew Christian pastors, the Confessing Church failed to cry out against the violation of the civil and religious rights of the Jewish people. Dietrich Bonhoeffer, who realized in 1933 that the critical issue was the Nazi treatment of the Jews, was an exception. Niemöller, Barth, and other theologians and churchmen admitted later to fighting improperly for the Jewish cause. Franklin Littell in assessing this history notes:

> If men of such stature, men who have worked tirelessly in the Church Struggle, can look the churches' failure in the eye and confess their own shortcomings, why should others hesitate? The reason seems to be that the same spiritual weakness that makes some men trimmers and quislings in the hour of decision makes them suppress the critical issues later. And—as the real leaders of spiritual resistance have been the first to make Christian confession—the churches did fail; most of the church leaders

5. Matheson, ed., *The Third Reich and the Christian Churches*, pp. 36–37. On Niemoeller note Dietmar Schmidt, *Pastor Niemoeller*, trans. Lawrence Wilson (New York: Doubleday, 1959), pp. 83–100.
6. J. S. Conway, *The Nazi Persecution of the Churches, 1933–45* (New York: Basic Books, 1968), p. 49. Compare Donald D. Wall, "Karl Barth and National Socialism, 1921–1946," *Fides et Historia*, 15 (Spring-Summer 1983): 85, and Eberhard Busch, *Karl Barth: His Life from Letters and Autobiographical Texts* (Philadelphia: Fortress, 1976).

failed, and even the resistance largely failed to understand the signal importance of the rejection of the Jews to the malaise of Christendom.[7]

It was not until May 1936, after the Confessing Church had split (moderates leaving) and the infamous Nuremberg Laws had been decreed, that the remaining "radical" Confessing Christians issued a statement specifically condemning the Nazis' hatred of the Jews.[8]

Using the same skill with which he circumvented the Weimar Constitution, Adolf Hitler outmaneuvered church leaders, even denying the "German Christians" leadership at the proper moment in order to incorporate them, moderate Christians, and the Confessing Church under the administrative umbrella of the Reich Ministry of Church Affairs. Systematically the Nazis reduced the freedom of the German church through financial and legal intimidation. At the same time, they began promoting the Nazi Party as the successor of the church. This propaganda and legal campaign was delicately balanced to retain the allegiance of devoted church members while creating a National Socialist civil religion for a younger generation and Party elite. The large majority of Christians accepted the status quo, supporting the war effort with patriotic fervor.

Protesters were treated like members of any resistance movement. Niemöller was reproached by the Nazi hierarchy and fellow pastors. Arrested on July 1, 1937, he was tried in 1938 and sent to Sachsenhausen concentration camp (and was later transferred to Dachau in 1941). A worldwide effort was launched to free him, but to no avail. Barth was dismissed on June 22, 1935, from his position as professor of theology at the University of Bonn. He spent the rest of his life in Switzerland as professor of theology at the University of Basel. Bonhoeffer joined the German underground. Implicated in a plot to kill Hitler, he was arrested on April 5, 1943, and executed on April 9, 1945—only three weeks before Hitler committed suicide. A number of less celebrated Christians also maintained their integrity in opposing the Nazis.[9]

There were others, however, on the opposite end of the spectrum. Note the following letter dated October 7, 1935, to Julius Streicher, editor of the hate sheet *Der Stürmer*:

> Dear Editor of the *Stürmer*,
>   Just today I received the August number of the *Stürmer*. As a Lutheran Pastor I must thank you for the courageous words with which you replied to the incredible

---

7. Franklin H. Littell, *The Crucifixion of the Jews* (New York: Harper & Row, 1975), pp. 46–47. Compare Peter Hoffman, "Problems of Resistance in National Socialist Germany," in Franklin H. Littell and Hubert G. Locke, eds., *The German Church Struggle and the Holocaust* (Detroit: Wayne State U., 1974), pp. 97–113.

8. Note Cochrane, *The Church's Confession Under Hitler*, pp. 268–79, for the complete text of this statement, which was written on May 28 and handed in on June 4 (the date Cochrane has chosen in his appendix title).

9. Terence Prittie, *Germans Against Hitler* (Boston: Little, Brown, 1964), pp. 94–126. See Matheson, ed., *The Third Reich and the Christian Churches*, for some of the documents pertaining to Nazi limitation of the church.

statements of the Provincial Brethren Council [of the Confessing Church] in Saxony. We stand enthusiastically behind your struggle against the Jewish death watch beetles which are undermining our German nation. So too against those friends of Jewry which are to be found even in the ranks of the Protestant pastorate. We will fight alongside you and we will not give up until the struggle against all Jewry and against the murderers of Our Saviour has been brought to a victorious end, in the spirit of Christ and of Martin Luther.

    In true fellowship, I greet you with Heil Hitler!

                Yours,

                Riechelmann,

                Pastor.[10]

In April 1933 the German church had refused to protest boycotts against Jewish businesses, the removal of Jews from the civil service, and other anti-Semitic abuses lest it provide "fuel for hostile propaganda against the New Germany" and offend the Nazi hierarchy. A decade later, church property was being confiscated, seminaries and religious educational institutions closed, and clergy closely monitored.[11]

ROMAN CATHOLIC COMPROMISE

The Roman Catholic church also compromised with Hitler. Because of its political party and labor union, the German Catholic church was very visible. Consequently, the Nazis prepared for a wholesale attack against priests. As soon as Hitler gained power, Catholic clergymen were mistreated by the SA and arrested. Rectories were ransacked and parish schools intimidated. The laity of the Catholic church, caught up in the spirit of the New Germany, brought enormous pressure on the bishops. The Catholic church believed it had no choice but to negotiate for the best terms possible with Hitler. On July 20, 1933, the church signed an agreement with the German government. Cardinal Eugenio Pacelli was the Vatican representative who formally affixed his signature to the document. In the spring of 1939 he became Pope Pius XII, known as a master of the language of diplomatic ambiguity. Unlike a number of priests and bishops who opposed Hitler and helped Jewish people, he refused to denounce the Nazis throughout the war and restricted his public statements about murdered Jews to mild expressions of sympathy for "the victims of injustice" (declining to say

10. Note Conway, *The Nazi Persecution of the Churches*, p. 377, for the text of this letter. His appendix on pp. 339–98 contains eighteen other documents pertaining to the church struggle.
11. Of particular interest is the letter from Alfred Rosenberg (Hitler's leader of spiritual and ideological education for the National Socialist party) to Martin Bormann (Hitler's deputy and secretary) on Nazi church policy. Some Nazi leaders were suggesting that the entire Protestant church be placed under state tutelage and that Hitler be proclaimed as its supreme head. Rosenberg was opposed to this in the letter, hinting that the Nazis would completely suppress the Christian church after the war. See "Rosenberg to Bormann," 18 June 1940, Nuremberg Document PS 067, National Archives Record Group 238, reproduced in John Mendelsohn, ed., *The Holocaust* (New York: Garland Publishing, 1982), vol. 4, *Propaganda and Aryanization, 1938–1944*, pp. 142–46.

"Jew"). John F. Morley in his study *Vatican Diplomacy and the Jews During the Holocaust* concluded about the lack of spiritual direction from the Vatican:

> Thus, reserve and prudence were the criterion of papal diplomacy, according to both the Pope and his secretary of state. It was a criterion that could not coexist with humanitarian concern. To avoid offending Germany, and to maintain prudent reserve, the Vatican had to act, or neglect to act, in ways that ignored the depth of suffering that was so widespread among both Christians and Jews. . . .
>
> It must be concluded that Vatican diplomacy failed the Jews during the Holocaust by not doing all that it was possible for it to do on their behalf. It also failed itself because in neglecting the needs of the Jews, and pursuing a goal of reserve rather than humanitarian concern, it betrayed the ideals that it had set for itself. The nuncios, the secretary of state, and, most of all, the Pope share the responsibility for this dual failure.[12]

The historic anti-Semitism of the Catholic church was a definite factor in the reluctance of many German Catholics to help their Jewish neighbors. Even the debate during Vatican II in the 1960s and the failure of a strongly-worded first version of a statement on the Jewish people (i.e., to "not teach anything that could give rise to hatred or contempt of the Jews") underscores the ambivalence of a number of Catholic bishops and clergy to this very day.[13]

And yet, with reference to the German church struggle, there were individual Catholics and Protestants who gave sacrificially of themselves (some giving their lives) to help the Jewish people and to stand steadfast against a powerful Nazi regime. Their struggle is a lesson to us, because standing for what is right is not easy. Pressures are brought to bear through our employment, our families, and our friends. Spiritually unhealthy attitudes toward other religions or races blind us to love and decency, while we rationalize that justice is occurring. Propaganda may lull us into compromise and complacency, postures from which we may never return. One of the greatest lessons of all is how wonderful words, even religious and biblical words, can be twisted into rationalizations for genocide—for the brutal murder of men, women, and children. The struggle against all this is not easy. As one of the delegates to the 1950 Synod of the Evangelical Church in Germany, Praeses Kreyssig declared: "In every train which carried Jews to their death-camp in the East, at least one Christian should have been a voluntary passenger."[14]

Martin Niemöller, who stated in 1933 that he did not possess a "warmth of

---

12. John F. Morley, *Vatican Diplomacy and the Jews During the Holocaust, 1939–1943* (New York: Ktav, 1980), pp. 208–9. Compare Saul Friedlander, *Pius XII and the Third Reich: A Documentation* (New York: Octagon Books, 1980).

13. See David A. Rausch and David D. Brodeur, "Catholic and Jew," *Midstream: A Monthly Jewish Review* 29 (January 1983): 14.

14. Gutteridge, *Open Thy Mouth for the Dumb!* p. 303.

feeling" for Jews, emphasized in a sermon in 1945 what might be considered an epilogue on the German church struggle. He declared:

> There were in 1933 and in the following years here in Germany 14,000 Evangelical pastors and nearly as many parishes. . . . If at the beginning of the Jewish persecutions we had seen that it was the Lord Jesus Christ Who was being persecuted, struck down and slain in "the least of these our brethren," if we had been loyal to Him and confessed Him, for all I know God would have stood by us, and then the whole sequence of events would have taken a different course. And if we had been ready to go with Him to death, the number of victims might well have been only some ten thousand.[15]

In a lecture in Switzerland in 1946 he asserted: "Christianity in Germany bears a greater responsibility before God than the National Socialists, the SS and the Gestapo."

15. Ibid., pp. 303–4.

16

"Hitler Kaput!"

Crude paintings of gallows with Jews or blacks hanging from them, surrounded by swastikas, "KKK," and other emblems of racist groups, have been found in many cities of the United States in the past few years. In chapter 1 we noted the appearance of such symbols of hate on synagogues and in letters such as the one received by a black pastor.

Nazis used such defacement and intimidation throughout their rise to power and during Adolf Hitler's government. For example, the mortuary of the Jewish cemetery in Trebnitz was defaced in November 1930 with a picture of a Jew strung from a gallows. In front of the gallows was a swastika and three crosses. Above it was painted the slogan HEIL HITLER Juda Verrecke ("Death to the Jew"). Even tombstones were inscribed with swastikas, the emblem of Nazi hatred. This symbol from 1930, preserved for posterity in a photograph, stands in marked contrast to another photo, which shows a sign painted on a wall in 1945 stating, "HITLER KAPUT." This sign pictured not a Jew but a swastika dangling from the gallows.[1]

GERMAN DEFEAT, JEWISH DESPAIR

The defeat of Germany early in May 1945 brought national humiliation and disgrace. The propaganda machine that had lied to the German people about

1. For photographs of the Trebnitz cemetery and other cemeteries desecrated throughout Europe note Zosa Szajkowski, *An Illustrated Sourcebook on the Holocaust*, 3 vols. (New York: Ktav, 1977–79), 1:130–52. Compare William S. Ruben and Paul Ruben, *Escape from the Holocaust* (New York: Manor Books, 1978), p. 226 for one of the many places in which the "Hitler Kaput" photograph appears. *Verrecke* is only vulgarly used of people—usually it denotes the death of cattle.

Jewish world conspiracy, Jewish financial interests, and Jewish control of the press had also lied about Germany's "secret weapon" to win the war, as well as about German military successes. As assassination plots against the Führer increased, he lashed out in unabashed fury toward the German people, accusing them of not fighting hard enough.

On April 30, 1945, Hitler abandoned his nation by committing suicide. His Minister of Propaganda, Joseph Goebbels, followed him the next day by committing suicide with his wife—after they had their six children poisoned by lethal injection. The insipid propaganda network continued to roll as the Goebbels' bodies burned in the Chancellery garden. Hamburg radio interrupted a symphony to announce: "Our Führer, Adolf Hitler, fighting to the last breath against Bolshevism, fell for Germany this afternoon in his operational headquarters in the Reich Chancellery." Even in his last will and testament Hitler sought to further the propaganda effort by using the same clichés that brought him to power more than twelve years before. He blamed "international Jewry and its helpers" for World War II and the ruin of German towns. In a last desperate plea he called for "hatred" and declared: "Above all, I enjoin the government and the people to uphold the racial laws to the limit and to resist mercilessly the poisoner of all nations, international Jewry." As he faced death and his accounting before God, Adolf Hitler showed no remorse for his deeds, choosing to blame others, including the German army, for not exhibiting "faithful devotion to duty unto death" and for the carnage he had brought to pass. He chose to promote racial and religious contempt with his last breath.[2]

To the Jewish victims who lived through this hatred, life seemed damaged beyond repair. Some committed suicide in the months following their liberation, unwilling to cope with the loneliness and memories. With family and friends murdered, consumed with guilt over being spared, they decided that living was no joy. Others like Mordecai Lichtenstein, who spent eighteen months in the Auschwitz extermination complex, tried to carry on. A wood merchant from Bendszin, Poland, he served as an interpreter for British prisoners-of-war to the Russians who had liberated them. He explained:

> As the British and I had become great friends they suggested that I might go with them to this country [England] though I would have had an opportunity of being sent to Palestine. With the British I was evacuated to this country via Cracow, Odessa, Port Said and Gibraltar.
>
> Before I left Poland I wanted to see Bendzin for a last time. I wish I had not returned to this once flourishing Jewish town which has now become a ghost town. Of 30,000 Jews living there five and a half years ago, only 160 were registered on February 15th, 1945 and I assume that even these figures are too high. For beggars might have gone from one place to another and registered at each of them.

2. See Joachim C. Fest, *The Face of the Third Reich: Portraits of the Nazi Leadership*, trans. Michael Bullock (New York: Pantheon, 1970), pp. 60–63. Compare William L. Shirer, *The Rise and Fall of the Third Reich: A History of Nazi Germany* (Greenwich, Conn.: Fawcett, 1959), pp. 1458–76.

Now I am here [in Britain], I live [in 1945] in the elegant flat of a friend from Bendzin, I am free, but I cannot feel happy. My parents-in-law were gassed, my brother-in-law Moses hanged, and his wife and her friend died from typhus in the women's camp. I lost sight of my second brother and my brother-in-law, Wolf, during the shooting near Laband, and I do not know whether they have survived that assault. Worst of all, however, I do not know anything about my wife's fate. I only know that the women were evacuated from Auschwitz like ourselves and taken across the Oder.

"I am very grateful for the hospitality Britain has offered me," Mordecai said, "but whether a man of my experience will ever be able to enjoy life again, that remains to be seen. At the moment I cannot believe it."[3]

A GLIMPSE OF THE HORROR

For the soldiers who liberated the concentration camps, the sight was unforgettable. As Allied forces squeezed the Nazis in a vise toward Germany, outer camps were abandoned and working prisoners were forced to march long distances to the inner camps. Many died, others arrived too weak to move. This resulted in thousands of corpses piled throughout the camps, rampant disease, a shortage of food, consequent massive starvation, and emaciated men and women barely clinging to life. Tears streamed down the faces of war hardened veterans as they viewed this atrocity. For some, the nightmare would never disappear. One World War II veteran wrote to me, turning down an invitation to relate his experience to the class: "No! Brother Rausch. I cannot tell of the sights, or the smell, or the sleepless nights, or the overpowering bitter, throat-choking hate that can shake you to your very soul. You can feel it, but you never forget it." Of the concentration camp prisoners that haunted his dreams, he noted:

Gaunt hollow eyed apparitions. Their clothing was ragged cast offs, flapping around their bony bodies. As they came down the street, usually alone, heads down, shuffling along with ragged bundles, the townspeople turned their heads as if embarrassed by the sight. The American soldiers stood quiet and watched with dread and revulsion as the almost walking dead came home. The prisoners didn't talk, they did not cry. It was as if the only thing that mattered was being able to take one more step nearer home. That fragile memory that kept them alive all those years. If they finally reached their goal I do not know. But for some the home they came back to was a pile of weed grown rubble. The family bombed out or dead and moved away. How do you put in black and white what hopeless means?

A horrified world viewed films of Bergen-Belsen (a transit camp and not an intentional extermination complex), where a British soldier on a bulldozer was forced to move thousands of corpses like garbage into a mass grave. In like

3. Ruben and Ruben, *Escape from the Holocaust*, pp. 232–33.

manner, the postwar horror of the corpses at Dachau was a key factor in its later reputation as a death factory. Although the Nazis had tried (unsuccessfully) to cover up their barbarities in the East, the emaciated humans, mass starvation, and death clearly visible in these German camps touched for a moment the heartstrings of the world.

WHERE WAS HUMANITY?

The question immediately arose, Where was the world when this was occurring? Where was humanity? It has taken several decades to respond to that question.

As early as 1933, when press reports were reaching England and the United States about Nazi persecution of Jews, the German church insisted to their brethren across the ocean that the accounts were mere propaganda. For example, on March 30, 1933, General Superintendent of the Methodist Church Dr. Otto Dibelius of Berlin wired a statement to England and America which read in part:

> The undersigned leaders of the Methodist Church in Germany enter a strong protest against the public meetings and the press reports in America and England about alleged prosecutions of Jews and atrocities by the National movement in Germany. They see in this the attempt to revive the dreadful atrocity propaganda of the [First] World War from which the psyche of the nations has scarcely freed itself. Under these conditions the endeavours for an understanding between the nations must be most heavily endangered. Apart from few slips by individual and irresponsible persons, against whom the new government has immediately taken the strongest measures, peace and order have never been endangered. Our Church has always been leading in all endeavours to restore true peace among the nations. The German Methodists, who are represented in all provinces of the German Reich, therefore send an urgent appeal to entire world-wide Methodism for reasons of truth and justice to help combat the pernicious activities of this lying propaganda against Germany. . . .
>
> Today, the German Reich is firmly united as never before in our history. In millions of German hearts there is the ardent wish that the German name may again stand pure and spotless before the whole world. Revolutionary times, even if experienced in discipline and ethical eagerness, are hard times. Don't aggravate these hard times for the German people by believing sensational reports!
>
> Have confidence! Again: Have confidence![4]

In a nationalistic optimism that minimized Jewish suffering and Hitler's true nature and maximized the dangers of Communism, Dibelius stated words that would return to haunt Christians in Germany. He concluded: "You will live to

---

4. See J. S. Conway, *The Nazi Persecution of the Churches, 1933–45* (New York: Basic Books, 1968), pp. 342–44. Compare Richard Gutteridge, *Open Thy Mouth for the Dumb!: The German Evangelical Church and the Jews, 1879–1950* (Oxford: Basil Blackwell, 1976), p. 78.

see the time when that which is now happening in Germany will lead to an end for which everybody who loves and honours the German character can be grateful! And that it will not only be in the interest of Germany, but to the advantage of the entire world!"

In his definitive study *The Terrible Secret: Suppression of the Truth About Hitler's "Final Solution"* historian Walter Laqueur suggests "reckless optimism" as one of the central reasons for failure to understand Hitler's program of injustice and brutality. "The ideal time to stop Hitler was not when he was at the height of his strength," Laqueur emphasized. "If the democracies had shown greater foresight, solidarity and resolution, Nazism could have been stopped at the beginning of its campaign of aggression."[5]

Laqueur proves that news of Hitler's Final Solution had been received throughout Europe in 1942. The Nazis had problems keeping silent their own soldiers involved in the death operations, while foreign visitors circulated the reports. In June 1942 the London *Daily Telegraph* reported the slaughter of one million Polish Jews, even describing the gassing vans and mass exterminations. The paper insisted that it was the Nazis' aim "to wipe the race from the European continent." The *New York Times* repeated the story, but placed it in the middle of the paper, the editors evidently not fully convinced of its truth. The governments of the United States, Britain, and the Soviet Union suppressed the reports of mass murder for a variety of reasons: it would hinder the war effort, the public would not believe it, it would hurt the morale of the resistance movement, and so on. Jewish people found themselves on the low end of the scale of Allied interests. Groups such as the Vatican and the International Red Cross also had information, but were paralyzed with fear. They responded by retreating to the safety of their own bureaucracies. The world indulged in wishful thinking as the only antidote to the utter despair of the situation.[6]

A Feeble Effort at Justice

Nevertheless, numerous declarations from such leaders as Roosevelt, Churchill, and Stalin protested the Nazi regime's savagery and promised that after the war the guilty would be punished. When the Waffen SS (SS stationed with regular army units at the Front) shot American prisoners of war in what appeared to be intentional murder, a government division was set up in 1944 to collect evidence of such crimes. After the defeat of Germany, a national and international debate ensued as to whether there should be a war crimes trial, and what the nature of such a trial should be. A United Nations War Crimes Commission was set up on October 26, 1943, to compile lists of war criminals and gather evidence, but little was done. The nations involved in this effort,

---

5. Walter Laqueur, *The Terrible Secret: Suppression of the Truth about Hitler's "Final Solution"* (Boston: Little, Brown, 1980), p. 208.
6. Ibid., pp. 74–75, 196–238.

however, signed a charter on August 7, 1945, establishing an International Military Tribunal to try the Nazi leadership for (1) crimes against peace, (2) war crimes, and (3) crimes against humanity. The master list of major German war criminals was 122. Of these, twenty-one would be tried, including Göring, Hans Frank (Governor General of Occupied Poland), Streicher, and Alfred Rosenberg (Nazi party theoretician and Reich Minister for the Occupied Eastern Territories). The trial was held at the Palace of Justice in the city of Nuremberg, and began on November 20, 1945. The verdict was read on September 30, 1946. "Throughout the trial," wrote Robert E. Conot, "the specter of Hitler had inhabited the courtroom. Hitler was the sun about which his minions had revolved, and once he was gone they wobbled and spun aimlessly, lost in the void."[7]

The Nuremberg Trial provided for the world the opportunity to view the revolting atrocities of the Nazis. Even the defendants were sickened by the films of crematoria, gas chambers, medical experiments, and mounds of corpses. The Jew-hater Streicher, who contested the full figures of the number of Jews killed, admitted that millions of Jews had been murdered. The trial proceeded with a scrupulous regard for due process according to the law, and the defendants were given every opportunity to clear themselves. The documentation of the crimes in numerous, uncontestable documents, however, sealed the fate of the guilty. Ten of the defendants were hanged, seven received prison sentences, and Göring cheated the hangman by committing suicide. The experience affected each participant in the trial, from justice to legal assistant. Morris Abram, an Oxford law student who was assigned the trial record of Göring, emphasized:

> As I observed the defendants in the dock each day in the courtroom, I was struck that these defendants—Goering, Hess, von Ribbentrop, Keitel, Frank—did not look different from other men. Yet they, with Hitler, Himmler, and Goebbels, had planned and perpetrated atrocities on a scale hitherto undreamed of. The evidence lay in written orders no defendant could contest and in films taken by the Nazis themselves. The incongruity of it astounded me. Sophisticated men, some even handsome, none cretins or palpably deranged, had in the twentieth century led one of the most civilized states in the brutal ravage of European society.[8]

"My experience at Nuremberg convinced me . . . that the trials advanced the rule of law," concluded Abram, who was to become an eminent American lawyer himself.

And yet, in spite of Nuremberg and the other trials, justice was far from complete. The damage was too deep, involving too many. Conot questioned, "But what of the others?" He then responded:

7. Robert E. Conot, *Justice at Nuremberg* (New York: Harper & Row, 1983), p.507. This book is one of the most complete on the subject, using the documentary evidence skillfully.
8. Morris B. Abram, *The Day Is Short: An Autobiography* (New York: Harcourt, Brace, Jovanovich, 1982), p. 73.

From the evidence presented, it was clear that beyond the twenty-one men tried, decision makers and perpetrators of major criminal acts ranged into the hundreds, their deputies into the thousands, and the rank and file directly involved into the tens of thousands. Of the concentration camp guards, no more than a couple of hundred were put on trial. Over 2,700 additional war crimes cases, most of them involving multiple defendants, were docketed, and 1,900 were under active investigation. . . . By 1949 the Cold War had undermined any further inclination for prosecution, and the next year the start of the Korean War completed the process of diverting the world's attention.[9]

In spite of the proved complicity of the German industrialists who exploited the slave labor, most received light sentences. "Of the hundreds of German firms that used concentration camp inmates," concluded international law expert, Benjamin B. Ferencz, "the number that paid anything to camp survivors could be counted on the fingers of one hand. . . . German industry showed no sign of remorse."[10]

To Succeeding Generations

By the end of World War II, two-thirds of European Jewry (over one-third of the world's Jewish population) had been murdered, which took its toll on that generation and on succeeding generations. Like so many in the new generation, Catherine Noren, an American photographer, discovered this history (a history her Jewish family had attempted to blot out by silence) while by chance perusing her grandmother's chest of old photographs. She found that for centuries her family had lived in Germany, and that her grandfather had started a factory for weaving and printing fabric in Dachau. After the rise of Adolf Hitler, twenty-six members of the family in Germany were sent to concentration camps—nineteen died. Catherine's parents escaped with their infant to Australia in 1938, nine years later emigrating to the United States. Today, few of her family remain in Germany.[11] In similar fashion, Karen Spiegel Franklin, in a recent quest for her Jewish roots, uncovered eleven generations of the Gerstle family. Approximately fifty were victims of the Holocaust—a whole branch of the family nearly wiped out by genocide.[12] The story is a heartrending and common one, al-

9. Conot, *Justice at Nuremberg*, pp. 516–17.
10. Benjamin B. Ferencz, *Less Than Slaves: Jewish Forced Labor and the Quest for Compensation* (Cambridge, Mass.: Harvard U., 1979), pp. 188, 192. "Even the severe hardship cases of those who had survived work for I. G. Farben at Auschwitz got no more than $1,700 each," Ferencz estimated. "Krupp's Jewish slaves and those who toiled for Siemens had to settle for $825. The AEG/Telefunken slaves each received no more than $500, and the Jews who worked for Rheinmetall received even less" (p. 188).
11. A cassette filmstrip with photographs of Catherine Noren's family, "The Camera of My Family: Four Generations in Germany, 1845–1945," may be rented or purchased from the Anti-Defamation League of B'nai B'rith Center for Studies on the Holocaust.
12. Karen Spiegel Franklin, *Eleven Generations of the Gerstle Family* (Yonkers, N.Y.: privately published, 1982). Note page 9 for a listing of the victims of the Holocaust. The family's life centered in the town of Ichenhausen, Bavaria. One family member returning to visit said, "The only place I felt at home was the cemetery. There I was surrounded by my family" (p. 17).

though the memories of the beloved differ. The lack of aunts, uncles, cousins, grandparents and other close relatives among Jewish families with European backgrounds attests to the enormity of the Nazi crime.

The relatives of those who died at the hands of the Nazis are threatened today by racists and their sympathizers who would complete (in word and deed) the task that Hitler attempted. Willing to pollute any mind or employ any lie, they seek to manipulate the spirit and soul of the unsuspecting. As we have seen, Hitler is not *kaput*—and neither is the swastika hanging from the gallows. The spirit of Adolf Hitler is alive and well, on a quest to devour persons and nations.

17

The Holocaust and the Middle East

Former Anglican Archbishop of Jerusalem George Appleton stated in an interview in March 1983 that during his first year in Jerusalem in 1969 his West Bank Arab friends were talking about "throwing" the Jews of Israel into the Mediterranean Sea. By his last year (1974), he claimed, "nobody was saying that!" He found in a changed attitude more hope for the Middle East situation. He observed an increased recognition of Israel among the Arabs (if not an acceptance, by some, of Israel's right to exist).[1] His statement, coupled with recent events, underscores the complexity of the Middle East situation. Factions (both religious and political) and armies in Middle Eastern countries have persistently doomed the process of peace. Moreover, press coverage has not helped. While the average American would never claim expertise on Central America or Africa, many believe themselves well-informed about the Middle East—a posture that leads to superficial analyses and clichés. Unfortunately, few have a concept of the historical background of the current Middle East impasse and the important events during and immediately after the Holocaust that led to the founding of the State of Israel and gave rise to the complicated rivalries viewed in the Middle East today.

The advent of the nineteenth century found Palestine under the control of the Ottoman Empire, a group of conquering Turks that at one time subdued the entire Middle East and was knocking at the door of Europe. The empire's administration was extremely corrupt, and Palestine was in a state of decline. The country's total population remained under 250,000 during the first three

1. Kol Israel (Jerusalem, short wave), "Face to Face," 15 March 1983.

178

decades of the nineteenth century; hence, only a small portion of the land was utilized for agriculture. Local chieftains fought each other for supremacy in the mountainous rural areas while Bedouin tribes roamed the desert areas to the east and the south. Security was minimal, and entire villages were destroyed by warfare or abandoned. Egypt conquered and controlled the area from 1832 to 1840, but the Ottomans afterwards regained control.

After 1840 both Jewish and Arab immigration increased. Representatives of Christian churches from Europe and America as well as Moslems and Christians from Syria, Lebanon, Egypt, North Africa, and Turkey all came to Palestine. Nevertheless, by 1895 only 10 percent of Palestine was cultivated. Absentee landlords purchased hundreds of thousands of acres from the financially strapped Ottomans and settled Jewish and Arab tenant farmers on some of it (for example, Sursuk, a Greek entrepreneur from Beirut, owned over 60,000 Palestinian acres). By the end of World War I, 144 wealthy landowners owned approximately 750,000 acres in Palestine. Concurrently, Jews owned and had reclaimed from marsh areas and deserts more than 100,000 acres. Urban areas also expanded (in 1909 a group of Jaffa Jews founded Tel Aviv, destined to become the country's largest city).[2]

During the nineteenth century both Jewish nationalist and Arab nationalist movements expanded. Both opposed the Ottomans. When the Ottoman Empire became the ally of the Germans in World War I, the British sought and gained the support of both Arabs and Jews. During World War I the British promised to support the founding of an Arab state in the Middle East. This state was to include areas of present-day Syria (east of Damascus), Iraq, and Saudi Arabia. The British also promised the Jews (in the Balfour Declaration of 1917) a national home in Palestine. It must be remembered that neither the Arabs nor the Jews had a state in this area, and that only hindsight affords us the luxury of viewing the storm clouds forming on the horizon. Nevertheless, moderate Arabs and Jews appeared in good rapport when the Ottomans were defeated in World War I. The French and British moved into the area and carved out "mandates": the French were to control the Syria-Lebanon area, the British the Palestine and Iraq area. When the French kicked out Emir Faisal (moderate leader of the Arab movement who had declared himself King of Syria), the British quickly moved to make him King of Iraq. They also created Trans-Jordan out of the Palestine Mandate area west of the Jordan and made Faisal's brother, Abdullah, king of that territory. The League of Nations approved these actions in 1922.[3]

2. Ruth Kark, "Landownership and Spatial Change in Nineteenth Century Palestine: An Overview," Seminar on Historical Types of Spatial Organization, Warsaw, Poland (April 1983). Compare Roger Owen, *The Middle East in World Economy 1800–1914* (London: Methuen Publishers, 1981), and Abraham Granott, *The Land System in Palestine, History and Structure* (London: Eyre and Spottiswoode, 1952).

3. Sydney Nettleton Fisher, *The Middle East: A History*, 2d ed. (New York: Alfred A. Knopf, 1969), pp. 366–74. A map appears on page 368. Compare Harry N. Howard, *The Partition of Turkey: A Diplomatic History, 1913–1923* (Norman, Okla.: Oklahoma U., 1931); and Leonard Stein, *The Balfour Declaration* (New York: Simon and Schuster, 1961).

In spite of these efforts to appease the Arabs, trouble still simmered in the Middle East. Arab literature insisted that the small Palestine area left was an "integral part of Syria" and that "over 500,000 of the inhabitants of Palestine are Moslems and only about 65,000 are Jews."[4] In "The Case Against Zionism," H. I. Katibah, who had earned his Master of Sacred Theology from Harvard and worked in conjunction with the Arab Palestine National League, published arguments against Zionism from the period—arguments that sound very familiar today. Under "Some Facts About Zionism" he listed:

1. Modern Zionism is a reaction against anti-semitism, and like it is born of resentment, pride and prejudice.
2. Zionism is a stumbling block in the path of liberal internationalism.
3. Zionism is one instance of the persistence of old pre-war politics under the new post-war order.
4. Zionism is in appearance, pseudo-liberal, but in reality it is reactionary.
5. Zionism is a source of trouble and enmity between east and west.
6. Zionism, if allowed to be fostered in Palestine, will make of the Near East a second Balkans.
7. Zionism cannot solve "the Jewish Problem," but instead will add a new chapter to that problem and a new trouble to this weary trouble-ridden world.
8. Palestine is too small to realize the national aspirations of the Jews, too sterile to support a large number of them, too remote from the centers of industry to make it a favorable colonizing center.
9. The Zionist colonies in Palestine could not have succeeded without the charitable assistance from Jewry all over the world. Up to the present they are not self supporting, in spite of immunities enjoyed even under the Turkish regime. Several immigrants who have been recently brought to Palestine by the Zionists organization have awakened to the economic fallacy of Zionism and left the country in disappointment. Contracts for public works have been mostly awarded to Zionists. These contracts are paid for by taxes, 90% of which come from non-Jewish Palestinians.
10. The present government of Palestine presents many anomilies unparalleled in history:
    a. It [the British Mandate] is a government of foreigners, by foreigners, for foreigners.
    b. It is a government based on a religious claim, yet purports to be modern.
    c. It is a mandate in the name of a people scattered in every country under the sun, but not one half of one percent of whom are in the land which is supposed to be their home-land.
    d. The destiny of a whole virile nation is jeopardized, and its development arrested to make possible the realization of a reactionary Jewish doctrine, spurned by all liberal minded Jews.[5]

4. For an attempt to strike a balance on these deep-seated views, see James Parkes, *End of an Exile: Israel, the Jews and the Gentile World*, new ed. (Marblehead, Mass.: Micah Publications, 1982). Chapter 6 treats "The National Home and the Arabs," pp. 36–48.
5. H. I. Katibah, ed., *The Case Against Zionism* (New York: The Syrian-American Press, n.d.), p. 45. This was published under the auspices of The Palestine National League, 85 Washington Street, New York City (this particular edition probably late in 1921).

Such rhetoric was as inflammatory to the British as it was to the Jews. And, though the booklet urged that "we do not hate the Jews, for we have lived with them before the war in perfect harmony," anti-Jewish riots broke out in Jerusalem in April 1920 and harassment by Arabs continued for the next two decades. The British nonetheless continued their policy of appeasement, making at the beginning of their tenure in the Middle East one of the greatest blunders possible. They appointed the right-wing Palestinian Arab nationalist leader responsible for the riots, Hajj Amin al-Husseini, to be Mufti (official expounder of Moslem law) of Jerusalem in 1921 and chairman of the Supreme Muslim Council in 1922. This action later bore dire consequence for moderate Arabs as well as the Jewish people.

Many Middle East history texts are reluctant to address the Mufti, because both Arabs and Jews agree that he was a fascist. It appears to me, however, that the link between the Mufti and the Holocaust is so crucial that we can ill afford its being lost in the complexities of the environment of the Middle East.

In spite of British appeasement at every turn, the Mufti maintained an anti-Jewish and anti-British attitude and policy. He was directly responsible for the horrendous anti-Jewish riots in Palestine in 1929 and 1936, and for leading a full-scale rebellion against the British from 1936 to 1939. For this the British finally dismissed him, forcing him into exile in Damascus and Beirut. From these positions he strengthened ties with Hitler, supported the Nazi cause in the Middle East, traveled to Nazi Germany and lectured SS officers in the 1940s, and defended the Nazi program of extermination of the Jews. He even toured the death camps with Himmler. After meeting with Hitler he was awarded $500,000 and promised the postwar aid of Adolf Eichmann to "solve the Jewish problem in the Middle East." After the war he escaped French imprisonment and traveled to Cairo, where he participated in the 1948 attack by the Arab armies against the fledgling State of Israel.[6]

The British policy of appeasement toward the radical Arabs bears a resemblance to the policy they pursued with Hitler. In both cases the consequences for the Jewish people were disastrous and led to conflict. The British, in neglecting to honor their own Balfour Declaration, attempted to limit Jewish immigration into Palestine. Arab oil supplies and "peace" in the Middle East were important factors, even as they are today. The British realized that the Jews did not represent a powerful force in world politics, but were in fact an unpopular minority. They were dispensable. By 1931 there were 175,000 Jews in Palestine amid a total population of more than one million. By 1947 the Arab population was 1.2 million (more than doubled by immigration and birth rate from the 1917 figure). The British were restricting Jews while simultaneously the persecution of the Nazi regime was growing stronger. In 1939 the British tried to suspend all Jewish immigration and land purchase in Palestine. Jewish underground organizations were appalled. Great Britain was attempting to seal the

---

6. See Jos Schechtman, *The Mufti and the Führer: The Rise and Fall of Haj-min el-Husseini* (New York: Thomas Yoseloff, 1965).

only safety valve the European refugees had.

As the war progressed, the Jews understandably believed that the British were consigning them to death. Although thousands were able to immigrate illegally, many more were stopped. The tragedy of the *Struma*, a very old boat carrying 769 passengers, the cream of middle-class Romanian Jewry, is a case in point. In December 1941 the British ordered port authorities in Istanbul to stop the boat en route to Palestine. Pleas went out to save the more than seventy children on board. In February 1942 the Turks dragged the ship out of the harbor (over the protest of the Bulgarian captain who refused to let his crew depart with it). Whether by mine, torpedo, or faulty conditions on the boat, it sank—killing all but one of the passengers.[7]

World War II set the stage for a confrontation of the varied forces of Middle East politics. Arabs viewed the Nazis as liberators from British imperialism; Jews supported the Allies wholeheartedly, but balked on British immigration policy. In 1944 the French ended their mandate in Syria and Lebanon, both of which became independent. The British found the Middle East too volatile to control and relinquished their mandate to the United Nations in February 1947. Although they had allowed Trans-Jordan to become an independent state in 1946 (called Jordan in 1949), they were in continual conflict with Jewish guerrillas, who were incensed over the mass murder of their people. In addition, the United States opposed what it viewed as a "pro-Arab" British policy, and many in the United Nations believed a compromise was possible.

In 1947 the United Nations Special Committee on Palestine recommended the partition of the remaining Palestine area to solve the Arab/Jewish conflict. During the resolution debate in the United Nations, the newly formed Arab League of Nations (under partial instigation from the Hajj Amin al-Husseini) threatened war. Nevertheless, the United Nations on November 29, 1947, voted in favor of the partition plan, which it believed fairly divided the remaining area along Jewish owned/Arab owned territorial lines. Even the Soviet Union gave its approval. Within a week, over one hundred Jews were killed by Arab guerrilla attacks and terrorist explosions in Palestine. In January 1948 the first detachments of the Arab Liberation Army entered Palestine from Syria and Jordan. In fear, the United Nations Security Council did not put the partition resolution into effect, but at the same time did not rescind the order.[8]

The State of Israel was formed on May 14, 1948. Five Arab armies (Egypt, Syria, Trans-Jordan, Lebanon, and Iraq) immediately invaded Israel, claiming that they would exterminate the Jews and push them into the sea.

One can easily see the historic passions of both groups in the subsequent

7. Note Nora Levin, *The Holocaust: The Destruction of European Jewry, 1933–1945* (New York: Thomas Y. Crowell, 1968), p. 582, for the testimony of the lone survivor on the *Struma*. In addition to the seventy children, 269 women and 429 men drowned.
8. For a discussion of this volatile period and the varied guerrilla groups in Palestine, see Yehuda Bauer, *A History of the Holocaust* (New York: Franklin Watts, 1982), pp. 337–49. Compare Fisher, *The Middle East*, pp. 640–55.

encounter. The new State of Israel had a large percentage of Holocaust survivors. The memory of another threatened extermination that had become a reality was permanently etched in their minds. The Arabs judged the partition plan as unfair. The Jews, they believed, should not have their own state in Palestine. Both groups viewed themselves as legally and historically right.

It was at this juncture that the Palestinian Arab refugee problem, a problem remaining today, began. As with so many enigmas engendered in the Middle East puzzle, Jewish and Arab accounts are far apart. The Arabs maintain that Jewish terrorism drove them out. The Jews maintain that panic at the ensuing battle and urging by the Arab leaders to leave until they "crushed the Jews" created the refugee problem. On many occasions the Arab High Command declared to the Palestinians: "A cannon cannot differentiate between a Jew and an Arab. Leave the country for two weeks and you will come back victorious."[9] For its part, Jewish scholars have amassed hundreds of quotes from British sources, and from Arabs themselves, decrying the fact that the Arab High Command asked Palestinian Arabs to leave and then abandoned them to refugee camps.

On the other hand, Palestinian Arabs have given testimony to their harassment by Jews, and James Parkes has admitted that there was a small Jewish terrorist element that believed "Arabs should be treated in the way in which they had always boasted that they would treat the Jews." But Dr. Carl Hermann Voss, a liberal Christian minister, who traveled in 1951 to Palestinian Arab camps outside Beirut and Amman, emphasizes that the refugees made clear to him that the Arab High Command ordered them out. These people were bitter at being left to their homeless state. Voss emphasizes that from the *Nation* to the *New York Times* current publications were aware what the Arab Liberation Army had created by its pronouncements.

Those Palestinian Arabs who stayed were not only welcomed as citizens of the new Jewish state, but also were able to obtain considerable wealth. Furthermore, Arab nations persecuted, robbed, and expelled *their* Jewish residents. While approximately 600,000 Palestinian Arabs left the Jewish state, at least the same number of Jews from Arab lands were forced to emigrate to the fledgling State of Israel. Thus, the historian has to cope with both a Palestinian Arab refugee problem and a Palestinian Jewish refugee problem![10]

In the fall of 1948 the United Nations Security Council called upon Israel and the Arab League to negotiate armistice agreements. Egypt finally agreed

---

9. In February 1962, Salim Joubran, an Arab citizen of Israel, told American audiences this and quoted the Arab High Command as stating this. Broadcasts, leaflets, and Arab leaders in Palestine were used to relate this to the Arab population at various times.

10. Carl Hermann Voss, interview held during the Second International Scholars Colloquium on America-Holy Land Studies, Washington, D.C., August 1983. Dr. Voss is currently engaged in writing his autobiography and a companion volume on the Middle East that will add great insight into this period. Compare *Myths and Facts 1978: A Concise Record of the Arab-Israeli Conflict* (Washington, D.C.: Near East Research, 1978); "Who Really Created the Middle East Refugee Problems?: Arabs Who Should Know Speak Out," Israel Information Centre, n.d.; and Martin Gilbert, *The Jews of Arab Lands: Their History in Maps* (Oxford: Martin Gilbert, 1976).

when it was clear that Israel was in the Sinai and advancing at a rapid pace. The Armistice Demarcation Lines of 1949 gave the West Bank to Jordan and the Gaza strip to Egypt. The refugees, to the shame of their Arab brethren, were not absorbed into the Arab nations but instead were used as a political football by those who had ordered them to leave Palestine. The armistice was only viewed as an intermission, and these complicated factors have mushroomed into other wars and a Middle East situation that appears insoluble.

Today it is not popular on the religious scene to support Israel. From the *Christian Century* to the World Council of Churches, most liberal Protestants have opposed the State of Israel and its policies. It must be remembered, however, that the founding of Israel had international backing and strong Christian support. In addition to the prophecy-minded evangelical Protestants who had advocated the return of the Jewish people to their "promised land," there was a contingent of liberal theologians who consistently opposed Hitler and supported the new Jewish State. The American Christian Palestine Committee was founded by these individuals and included such eminent liberal theologians and spokesmen as Paul Tillich and Reinhold Niebuhr. The Holocaust and its aftermath played a role in their decision, as well as the belief that the Jewish people *must* have a nation to depend upon in times of trouble. Israel was committed to providing a sanctuary. Most important, these individuals believed that the Arab contentions were simply wrong, and the American Christian Palestine Committee literature sought to prove to others that the Arab arguments were vacuous and erroneous.[11]

Although one may disagree with the State of Israel without being anti-Semitic, it must be noted that present-day racist groups often convey anti-Semitism through anti-Zionist or anti-Israel code words. The student of the Middle East must be very careful to avoid being deceived by such utterances and propaganda.

Furthermore, it must be remembered that the Holocaust has left its mark on the Middle East situation—it has taught lessons not easily dispelled. From the Nazis' false promises to the international community's failure to open its doors; from British intransigence and vacillation to Arab hatred and terrorism, six million Jewish deaths have doubtlessly left an indelible impression on a country that continues to be surrounded by hostile forces. In a way, it is miraculous that the Israelis—Holocaust survivors, children, and friends—are as trusting and benevolent as they are.[12]

---

11. Note *The Arab War Effort: A Documented Account* (New York: American Christian Palestine Committee, 1946); *Truth About Palestine* (New York: American Christian Council on Palestine, 1946); and *The People Speak on Palestine: American Public Opinion on the United States and United Nations* (New York: American Christian Palestine Committee, 1948).
12. It is indeed ironic that a United Nations that once voted almost unanimously for the partition plan and later in 1948 recognized the State of Israel, today evidences a willingness to pass readily any resolution *against* Israel, regardless of its validity.

18

Another Holocaust?

As the United States prepared to enter the 1980s, ominous signs appeared on the horizon. In Michigan's Upper Peninsula racists shot at Chippewa fishermen, smashed their boats, and slashed their tires. Bumper stickers announced: "SAVE A FISH—SPEAR AN INDIAN." In Seadrift, Texas, industrious Vietnamese refugees were accosted by American fishermen, who burned their boats and fire-bombed their homes. The refugees had aroused the ire of the fishermen because they worked long hours for lower wages, underpricing other fishermen. Predictably, racist groups such as the Ku Klux Klan tried to take advantage of the situation, even though they usually claimed that immigrants did not work but always turned to welfare. Sadly, these "boat people" who had recently immigrated to the Promised Land of the United States and worked hard in crab processing plants to save money to purchase the boats, found American resentment in cities across the land comparable to their persecution overseas, exacting a toll that they believed was far worse than the squalor of the resettlement camps.[1]

As we struggle toward the decade of the 1990s, threatening signs menace our society. In June 1983 two Ku Klux Klansmen were arrested for the murder of nineteen-year-old Michael Donald. The F.B.I. charged that they had lured Donald into their car, beat him to death, and left his body hanging from a tree on a Mobile, Alabama, street. The black teenager made the mistake of stopping to help some apparently lost whites find their destination. In Brooklyn thirty-four-

---

1. Note "The Not-So-Promised Land?" *Time*, 10 September 1979, p. 24, and "The Chippewas Want Their Rights," *Time*, 26 November 1979, p. 54.

year-old William Turks had no choice. The hardworking black subway car main-
tenance man was dragged from an automobile by a mob of white youths, who
were shaking it, throwing garbage at it, and breaking its windows. The participant in the mob who tackled Turks as he tried to flee "fit the description of
acting with depraved indifference to human life" (according to prosecutor Andrew Plump). Turks was then beaten to death with clubs and fists.[2]

Even in quiet Idaho, racist terror rages. *People* magazine published a five-page
article on The Aryan Nation, a neo-Nazi stronghold sporting thirty-foot watch-
towers with armed guards and signs that warn "Whites Only." The group's "pastor," Richard Butler, preaches in its chapel on Sundays, praising Adolf Hitler
and spewing forth invective toward blacks and Jews. The twenty children on the
compound receive training in what teacher Cynthia Cutler describes as the "four
R's": reading, 'riting, 'rithmetic, and *race*. Although there are only seventeen
blacks and fifty to one hundred Jews in a population of sixty thousand spread
over thirteen hundred square miles of the Idaho county, incidents of racial harassment have increased 550 percent over previous years. Eight-year-old Lamar
Fort and his seven-year-old sister Neisha have been frightened and harassed by
uniformed men shouting obscenities at the black children from their cars. Their
mother was in shock, stating: "I didn't know anybody talked to a child like that."
Sixty-two-year-old widower Sid Rosen, a Jewish man who owned a steakhouse
restaurant in Hayden Lake, Idaho, for eighteen years, found Nazi swastikas and
"Jew swine" painted in black over his entire building. The only adult Jew in the
entire town, Rosen sold the restaurant. He now lives in fear for his nine-year-
old son, Sam, on his eighty-acre ranch. It is interesting that convicted murderer
Frank Spisak (see chapter 9), once a lieutenant in the Social Nationalist Aryan
People's Party (an Aryan Nation splinter group), admitted that he had tried to
take refuge in Idaho before his arrest.[3]

The KKK—A New Look, an Old Hatred

A refined and more visible Ku Klux Klan (KKK) is experiencing resurgence
throughout the United States. With arguments that the Klan robe and hood
have "never been used for wrongdoing" and serve only to preserve "anonymity
in doing good works," a soft-sell advertising campaign has been underway for a
few years. As we have seen, this campaign includes the cover that the Klan is
working for the "White majority." In July 1983 the Invisible Empire, Knights
of the Ku Klux Klan, revealed its bylaws and oath in an attempt to convince
Americans that its bad reputation is just rumor.

Announcing that its members will no longer be permitted to conceal their
identities by wearing masks in public, the Invisible Empire hoped to move into

2. "Two Arrested in Murder of Black Alabama Youth," *New York Times*, 17 June 1983, and "Trial
of 2d Brooklyn Youth in Racial Death Begins," *New York Times*, 10 July 1983.
3. See Joshua Hammer and Bill Shaw, "The Trail from Three Racial Slayings Leads Back to a Ring
of Neo-Nazi Fanatics in Idaho," *People* 20 (29 August 1983), pp. 44–48. The photographs by
Dale Wittner in this article are quite revealing.

mainstream politics and cope with international issues. As a first step, the Klan asked the United States to send troops to patrol the Mexican border to combat an "invasion of illegal Mexicans and other Latin American allies." Smooth talking, college educated Bill Wilkinson, leader of this fastest growing Klan group, dresses like an executive and has the uncanny ability to draw the worst of racial prejudice out of the most unlikely individuals in brief conversation. Wilkinson's forays into politics are generally attempts to identify the Klan with stands that the public will agree with. In a foreign policy statement released through his state leaders, he asked (among other things) that the Reagan administration tell the Cuban government to stop supporting revolution in Latin America or face U.S. military action. "Kleagle" Van D. Loman of the Ohio Realm emphasized that the Klan would nominate and endorse more candidates for public office, noting: "Whether welcome or not, they're going to get it." Several Klan factions have embraced the "Kingdom Identity" church, a "new" Christian movement theorizing that Adam and Eve were not the first humans, but rather the first white man and white woman (the "colored" races were created before them and are inferior to the white Anglo-Saxon "chosen people of God"). Loman told reporters that blacks and Jews are still barred by the Klan, but that Catholics are now admitted.[4]

It is a chilling thought that although the Klan has fewer than twelve thousand registered members, it commands the sympathy of at least ten times that number. Furthermore, its greatest proselytization effort—and perhaps its greatest success—is among young people. Eighty percent of all KKK members are under thirty years of age, and the Klan Youth Corps has chapters in at least six states for children eight to seventeen. Klan members sometimes hold dual membership in neo-Nazi organizations. For example, the former Grand Dragon of the Texas KKK is now part of the armed guard of The Aryan Nation. The misleading factor about most Klan members is that they appear to be ordinary white citizens—with, perhaps, an unusual preoccupation with race. They love their families, go to church, and talk of violence only in private.[5]

THE GROWTH OF NEO-NAZISM

Neo-Nazis in the United States have been spurring a program of anti-Semitism and racism throughout the world. Martin Mendelsohn, former head of the Spe-

4. "Klan Reveals Secrets, Wants Border Patrol," *The Plain Dealer*, 10 July 1983. See also John Turner, *The Ku Klux Klan: A History of Racism and Violence* (Montgomery, Ala.: The Southern Poverty Law Center, 1982), pp. 44–49 (pages 60–61 have biographical sketches on seven key figures in the KKK), and "The Violent Rebirth of the Klan," *The New York Times Magazine*, 7 December 1980.
5. Note "They Must Be Taught to Hate," *IFCO News* 8 (September-October 1981), p. 6. This entire issue is on the resurgence of racism in the United States. The publication is prepared by the Interreligious Foundation for Community Organization, New York. See Turner, *The Ku Klux Klan*, p. 59, for a photograph of a Nazi and a KKK member in North Carolina jointly celebrating the birthday of Adolf Hitler. Also note "The Klan's New Pitch to Youth," *Newsweek*, 28 June 1982, p. 12.

cial Litigation Unit on Nazi War Criminals for the U.S. Department of Justice, is particularly concerned. In a letter, he detailed secret Nazi cells operating in Germany, fueled with hate literature printed in the United States. Recent anti-Semitic acts in Paris, Vienna, London, Rome, and many other European cities and towns gravely concern him. Nevertheless, the current actions being perpetrated in the United States are to him the most alarming. "Hatred and anti-Semitism are shockingly on the rise here," he insists, "being boldly scrawled across our entire nation, threatening all that we hold dear." Mendelsohn detailed:

> IN CALIFORNIA, Nazis were convicted of fire bombing a Temple City synagogue. In Oroville, the media report that Nazis are luring teenagers into their operation with drugs and alcohol. In other cities, storefronts, Jewish communal facilities—even the Simon Wiesenthal Center in Los Angeles—were defaced with malicious Nazi slogans proclaiming "the Nazi party lives again" and urging "Jews die."
>
> IN NORTH CAROLINA, five Nazis were convicted for conspiring to blow up buildings in Greensboro.
>
> IN ILLINOIS, a Nazi in Chicago murdered an elderly Jewish man by forcing him to inhale cyanide gas. Nazis marched in Jewish neighborhoods. And mass public distribution of hate literature is commonplace.
>
> IN LOUISIANA, Federal agents in New Orleans seized a large supply of weapons last April from neo-Nazis and Klansmen planning to invade and seize the small West Indian island of Dominica.
>
> IN PENNSYLVANIA, a flyer passed out in a Philadelphia blue-collar area proclaimed, "We hate Jews. They are the ones oppressing the White Man. We want fighters, marchers, those willing to give money and their time to the Movement."[6]

"The potential for neo-Nazi growth both here and abroad could be enormous," concluded Mendelsohn.

White Power, "the revolutionary voice of National Socialism," attempts to inspire fear of Jews both here and abroad. During the Carter administration, there was a concerted effort by the Nazis to turn the energy crisis into a propaganda tool. *White Power* warned Americans:

> The reckless pro-Israel stance adopted by the United States government is jeopardizing the continued flow of oil to the U.S. from the Middle East. . . . Unless the U.S. begins to adopt a more even-handed attitude with regard to the ongoing Arab-Israeli hostilities, there is a very real danger that our oil supply from this region will be cut off entirely. . . . Perhaps the American people can learn something from the example of the Iranians. The Iranian people hated their government. They felt it was cruel and oppressive. They felt it did not respond to their needs. They felt a small clique of aristocrats, who sold oil to Israel and received help from the Jews in return, was not representing their best interests. They felt this ruling clique was

6. Martin Mendelsohn, letter from Washington, D.C., July 1983. He was writing on behalf of the Simon Wiesenthal Center in Los Angeles, California, and their current endeavor to maintain files of all anti-Semitic literature and groups in America.

insensitive and corrupt. The Iranian people quietly tolerated this state of affairs for many years—and then they rose up and threw the pro-Jewish clique out. We are faced with an almost identical situation in America today. Like the Iranians, it's time for us to "throw the bums out"![7]

One notes how smoothly these American Nazis make the transition from worries over the energy crisis and the Middle East to "Jewish responsibility" and finally to the overthrow of the government of the United States. A follow-up article is entitled "Carter Regime Infested with Jews." Another article in the same issue ("How the Jews Do It!") attempts to engender hatred at alleged Jewish control of the news media and of the U.S. government. During this time period, the Nazis even used Ayatollah Khomeini (before the U.S. Embassy was taken) as an example to further their aims.

War Criminals Who Survived

Although there is a large body of young people, born after Hitler and unfamiliar with the Holocaust, upon which these groups may feed, it must be remembered that many Nazi war criminals are at large. Over two hundred Nazi war criminals found refuge in the United States in the past three decades, *many employed at one time or another by U.S. intelligence agencies*. The Justice Department admitted that the United States protected Klaus Barbie, aiding in his escape to Bolivia after World War II. The United States apologized formally to France in 1983 for hindering efforts to bring him to trial. Barbie, who was expelled from Bolivia early in 1983, awaits trial for murder as the French Gestapo chief from 1943 to 1944. (He had been nicknamed the "Butcher of Lyon.") Other former Nazis, such as Ukrainian guard John Demjanjuk, have been tried of late. Recent investigation has uncovered the Vatican's protective role and contribution in the escape of numerous high ranking Nazi war criminals (including Barbie). Because of the Cold War with the Soviet Union, several of these criminals were used by various nations for post-war information purposes in the name of national security.[8]

Denying the Holocaust

The Nazis insist that the Holocaust did not occur. Party Commander Matt Koehl led picketing Nazi protesters, dressed in full stormtrooper regalia, against

7. "Pro-Zionist Policies Endanger Oil Supply," *White Power* 89 (January-February 1979), pp. 1, 3. See also "War Threat Seen: Will Carter Send U.S. Troops to Israel?" *White Power* 87 (September-October 1978), pp. 1, 3.
8. Note "Nazis at Large," *Martyrdom and Resistance* (New York), September-October 1979, p. 12. Compare "Nazis Impending Trial in France Is Reopening Anti-Semitic Wounds," *The Wall Street Journal* (European Edition), 16 March 1983; Charles R. Allen, Jr., "The Vatican and the Nazis," *Reform Judaism* 11 (Spring-Summer 1983), pp. 4–5; "Delaying Justice for 33 Years: How 'the Butcher of Lyon' got secret U.S. help and protection," *Time*, 29 August 1983, p. 20; "The Shadow of Barbie," *The Jerusalem Post* (International Edition), 20–26 February 1983; and Jane Kramer, "Letter from Europe," *New Yorker* 59 (16 May 1983), pp. 49–50, 53–55.

WRC-TV in Washington, D.C. in April 1978. They were protesting the showing of the "Holocaust" film series as a collaboration of NBC with the "Israeli
Lobby." Koehl filed a petition with the Federal Communications Commission
against the television station for its "contemptuous abuse of the public interest,
convenience and necessity in its unilateral advocacy of the cause of Israel and
Zionism and its blatant disregard for historical veracity." On the picket line he
held a large sign which read: "HOLOCAUST 6 MILLION LIES."[9]

Probably the most prominent group supporting the Nazi insistence that the
Holocaust did not occur is the Institute for Historical Review, established in
1979 by Willis Carto. The Organization of American Historians unwittingly
gave its mailing list to the group, which mailed OAH members the first issue
of its *Journal of Historical Review*. The periodical appeared as a scholarly journal,
and the accompanying letter began:

> Dear Historian:
> I know you must be exceedingly busy, so I won't take up your valuable time with
> sales talk.
> I will just tell you that we have a special offer to make to you—as an open-minded
> and objective historian—in regard to the JOURNAL OF HISTORICAL RE-
> VIEW. You will find a sample copy of the first issue enclosed. You will see that this
> new journal breaks entirely new ground in *revising* standard history texts in an effort
> to "bring history into accord with the facts" as the late Harry Elmer Barnes once
> put it.[10]

Articles in that first edition sought to disprove the existence of gas chambers, to
describe "some of the ways in which the German nation is maligned through
the use of forged atrocity photographs," and to put the Holocaust "in perspective"—as an event with only 300,000 casualties. Following volumes published
by the Institute declared that Anne Frank's diary was a hoax and attempted to
refute other arguments of "the Exterminationists" (those who believe in the
Holocaust).[11]

Considerable funding has gone into the effort to organize a scholarly-appearing
organization to falsify the Holocaust. Editor Lewis Brandon in the second issue
declared that reaction "to the first issue has been very favorable. More and more
academics are waking up to this; the greatest academic hoax [the Holocaust]

9. Note "Commander Launches Legal Attack Against 'Holocaust' Hoax," *White Power* 87 (Sep-
    tember-October 1978), pp. 7, 11. Compare "Chemical Analysis Proves 'Holocaust' a Hoax,"
    pp.10–11 of the same issue.
10. Lewis Brandon, letter, 17 March 1980.
11. The first issue was Spring 1980 and began with an article by Arthur R. Butz, the controversial
    professor of electrical engineering at Northwestern University and the author of *The Hoax of the
    Twentieth Century*. In the Summer 1980 issue Brandon insisted that by disproving the Holo-
    caust and showing that it was "simply a product of the Zionists'" imaginations, revisionism was
    the key to avoiding Middle East warfare and the United States' support for Israel. See "A Note
    from the Editor," *The Journal of Historical Review* 1 (Summer 1980), p. 101.

since Piltdown Man. These academics are encouraged by the high caliber of research which has so far been published in this field." By the third issue, however, the outcry against his magazine had become so intense that he was whistling a different tune. He declared:

> The reaction startled even the staff here. We thought we had become somewhat desensitized to the behavior of the neurotic reactionaries who pose as historians in our colleges and universities, but the response to this mailing really left one speechless with amazement that our education system had become so sick. A selection of the responses is published here in our "Letters to the Editor" section, but these were just the ones which were printable. . . .
>
> The "massed" media big-guns turned against us. On the same day—13 May 1980—two out of the three major television networks lambasted the Institute, and our newborn JOURNAL. . . . We were referred to as "anti-Semites," "defenders of the Nazi record," "disgusting," "peddlers of filth," and "sewage."[12]

"I called up both stations the next day," Brandon solemnly wrote, "my feelings sorely hurt by this unkindness."

Brandon disliked having his group referred to as anti-Semitic. However, once he ascertained that the Anti-Defamation League had informed the Organization of American Historians about the nature of the group, his reaction was curious and revealing. He concluded:

> Needless to say, the OAH meekly obeyed their spiritual masters, and an apology to the membership and to the ADL and to World Jewry and to the little Jewish man in the dry-cleaners on the corner will be forthcoming in their next newsletter. Such is the power that an illegal organization (it [ADL] flaunts the law by acting as an unregistered agency of a foreign government [Israel]) wields over what is supposed to be an independent, free-thinking, academic group of objectivists.[13]

The Noontide Press now publishes "academic" books under the Institute's logo. A Christian I know read through one of the books, *The Six Million Reconsidered*, which is heavily illustrated with the most distasteful pictures and captions that Noontide has published. She looked up in astonishment and said, "You have to *really* hate Jews to publish something like this."[14]

12. "A Note from the Editor," *The Journal of Historical Review* 1 (Fall 1980), pp. 197–98.
13. Ibid., p. 198. See "Holocaust Revisionism," *ADL Bulletin* 37 (September 1980), pp. 9–10, for ADL's view of the Institute and its "scholars." Compare "Liberty Lobby and the Carto Network of Hate," *ADL Facts* 27 (Winter 1982), p. 11, where the ADL reveals that Lewis Brandon is "actually William David McCalden, a British neo-fascist."
14. Note William N. Grimstad, ed., *The Six Million Reconsidered: Is the "Nazi Holocaust" Story a Zionist Propaganda Ploy?* 2d ed. (Torrance, Calif.: Noontide, 1979). Compare Paul Rassinier, *Debunking the Genocide Myth: A Study of the Nazi Concentration Camps and the Alleged Extermination of European Jewry*, trans. Adam Robbins (Torrance, Calif.: Noontide, 1978).

Robert Conot in *Justice at Nuremberg* had these "revisionists" in mind as he pursued his research. He wrote of them:

> A world-wide cult has arisen claiming that the Holocaust never happened. A hundred books, booklets, and pamphlets have been printed alleging that the slaughter was imaginary or exaggerated, and is but a Jewish invention.
>
> All of this might be dismissed as the frustrated thrashing about of a radical, irrational fringe were it not for the haunting parallels to the pre-Hitler era, and the continuing employment of Nazi propaganda methodology. A leader of the French neo-Nazis, for example, asserts that those Jews who died had merely been victims of the wartime food shortage. The Nazis had, in fact, originally planned to starve the Jews to death, allocating 186 calories per capita daily for their sustenance, but had abandoned the scheme for more direct methods after the ensuing epidemics had decimated not only the Jews but threatened to spread to the relatively well-fed German population.
>
> Similar in nature is the assertion that Zyklon B gas was employed only as a disinfectant at Auschwitz. This had been the case until the fall of 1941, when an enterprising SS officer had concluded that if Zyklon B killed lice it could kill people just as well. Thereafter, the gas had been used, first, to murder thousands of Soviet prisoners of war, and then hundreds of thousands of Jews—nearly all of them women, children, and old people unfit for "extermination through work."[15]

"Hitler's dictum that 'the magnitude of a lie always contains a certain factor of credibility, since the great masses of the people . . . more easily fall a victim to a big lie than to a little one,'" suggested Conot, "has once more come into vogue."

The first issue of *The Journal of Historical Review* referred to The *Spotlight* newspaper and gave readers its address. As we have seen, The *Spotlight* has faithfully publicized the Institute for Historical Review. In "Revisionists Challenge Establishment's View of War History," The *Spotlight* devoted three pages to the conference proceedings of the Institute for Historical Review, insisting: "Evidence showing clearly that the propagandized extermination of millions of Jews by Nazi Germany never happened impressed the 125 courageous listeners."[16]

THE *SPOTLIGHT*

It appears that The *Spotlight* spends an inordinate amount of time on Holocaust revisionism and anti-Israel rhetoric; yet the publication vehemently denies being anti-Semitic. In one issue an advertisement appeared for a Third Reich Battle Flag. The advertiser was none other than the Nazi Party in Lincoln, Nebraska. The *Spotlight*'s advertising policy in the same paper states that it will not publish ads that are "in the sole judgment of the publisher, contrary to THE SPOTLIGHT's interest." Immediately under that statement is an advertisement

15. Robert E. Conot, *Justice at Nuremberg* (New York: Harper & Row, 1983), pp. xii–xiii.
16. Tom Valentine, "Revisionists Challenge Establishment's View of War History," *Spotlight*, 26 September 1983, p. 16.

for Pastor Sheldon Emry's "America's Promise" radio broadcast from his Lord's Covenant Church in Phoenix, Arizona. The ad consists of a map of the United States with a cross on it and the caption "Land of Christ." Below it is a map of Israel with a Star of David next to it. The caption: "Land of Anti-Christ."[17]

In September 1983 The *Spotlight* instructed its readers on how to defend "Liberty." Although it noted that "it's late in the game" and "the major media are under the thumb of the powerful international banking cartel," it suggested:

> Here's how to go about fighting back.
>
> When discussing the greedy wretches who seek to level the world for their own gain, don't lose control and angrily denounce them. Emotional outbursts make you look like a "conspiracy flake," which is one of the stereotypes the opposition has created to make irate citizens less effective.
>
> Rather than rail in anger, it is best to use the soft-sell approach most of the time. Cool logic and verifiable data still have a telling effect.
>
> Simple, direct questions stimulate useful conversation.
>
> The same cool, logical approach, along with efficient brevity, should be used when writing a letter to the editor. A letter a week to local papers or any magazines can do wonders.
>
> Brief, incisive points will generally get printed.
>
> Also, in your reading, whenever a good point is made by a writer, or appears in a news item, use that opportunity to side with the writer. Supportive letters are often more effective than negative comments, if only because so many subjects have been brainwashed to "think positive," and downplay all negativity.
>
> Clip out all appropriate letters to editors in magazines and newspapers and mail them to your senators or representative, or all three, once a month. Include a note with the clippings each time, stressing how you have been chatting about these issues with your neighbors. Then list the names of several of those neighbors.[18]

The *Spotlight* staff proposed the same "positive" and "concise" method on talk shows. "When confronting the greatest pawn in the international game—Zionist Israel," they declared, "use the language carefully to stress the inequities of the issues (there are plenty) and avoid the deadly name tag." The staff told readers to begin with the disarming statement: "I think the 'holocaust' was a terrible thing. People were treated brutally. History is full of brutal inhumanity by various peoples."

For the most part, The *Spotlight* and Liberty Lobby have followed this game

---

17. For the advertising policy and the America's Promise ad, note The *Spotlight*, 4 July 1983, p. 17. The Nazi ad is on page 23. It is interesting that The *Spotlight* published an article by the former grand wizard of the Knights of the Ku Klux Klan (Metarie, La.), David Duke. They neglected to mention his former position, only citing him as "leader of the National Association for the Advancement of White People." Duke used an interview with James Meredith to propose racial separation. Note David Duke, "Black 'Civil Rights' Leader Advocates Race Separation," *Spotlight*, 31 October 1983, p. 18. An advertisement for a book denying that the Holocaust occurred is on the same page.
18. The *Spotlight* Staff, "Learn Techniques to Defend Liberty," *Spotlight*, 26 September 1983, p. 14.

plan. To undermine the teaching of biblical prophecy by people like Jerry Falwell and Pat Robertson, "noted missionary and Biblical scholar" Cornelius Vanderbreggen, Jr., of Gelderland, the Netherlands, was given space in The *Spotlight* for a series of "Scriptural analyses." The *Spotlight* explained that "Vanderbreggen's experience with Establishment theologians has been similar to that of patriots with Establishment scholars and historians." Some readers were elated as the "Christian" *Spotlight* branched out into theology, but others were perturbed at the religious bent. The staff finally explained: "The SPOTLIGHT is not a religious publication, nor do we advocate any specific interpretation of the Bible." They insisted that the "series was merely to present an alternative to Jerry Falwell's and Pat Robertson's use of Scripture to justify Zionist expansionism in the Middle East and to disprove the distorted arguments being used to obtain U.S. tax dollars for Israel."[19]

BRITISH ISRAELITISM AND THE CHURCH

Bible teachers and churches that foster British Israelite theories are also fostering racism across the United States. British Israelites believe that the progeny of the ten lost tribes of Israel migrated to England (and, in turn, to the United States through the Pilgrim Fathers). They insist that many of the Old Testament prophecies have been fulfilled in the British Empire and that the white Anglo-Saxon Western peoples are destined to rebuild God's kingdom. Unlike Herbert W. Armstrong, who advocates a type of British Israelitism and yet is supportive of Israel, these individuals invariably are negative in their attitudes toward Israel and toward Jewish people. With their emphasis on the white Anglo-Saxon race as "Israel," some of the more radical groups claim that Adam and Eve were the parents of the white races only. These "Two-Seeders" believe the other races to be demonic or subhuman in origin. Even those British Israelites who would not agree with these radical "Two-Seeders" (such as Pat Brooks in the next chapter) foster negative images about Jews and Judaism. Sheldon Emry, whose Lord's Covenant Church is spreading across the United States, wrote: "It is obvious to all that the Jews hate Christ and Christianity. The facts above reveal the true origin of that hatred; namely, the Jews today are Edomites, and their allies from Eastern Europe are Gog and Magog!" Emry would insist that he is not anti-Semitic or racist. He would claim to be merely teaching "biblical truth."[20]

---

19. Note Cornelius Vanderbreggen, Jr., "'Bless-and-Curse' Verse from Genesis Has Become All Things to All Men," *Spotlight*, 18 July 1983, p. 17. This was the third in the series. Vanderbreggen's entire series is now published in the book *The Promise of His Coming*, available from Liberty Library. See also "Readers Comment on Series," *Spotlight*, 22 August 1983, p. 23. This includes the quoted *Spotlight* staff statement on the series.

20. "The Origins of the Jews," Lord's Covenant Church, Inc., America's Promise Radio, Phoenix, Arizona, p. 4. Compare Sheldon Emry's pamphlet "We Believe Zion" for a statement of what this group believes. These materials and more may be obtained by writing Lord's Covenant Church, Inc., America's Promise Radio, P.O. Box 5334, Phoenix, AZ 85010.

POLITE RACISM

As one views the panorama of American society today, one is alarmed at the number of neo-Nazi hate groups, their arms caches, and the terror and venom they spew forth. Along the spectrum, one is appalled at groups totally insensitive to racism—groups that often call themselves "Christians" or "patriots." The United States is in a danger zone, in many ways similar to pre-Nazi Germany. *Polite* racism is perhaps the most deadly racism. It is the type of racism that Matt Koehl, commander of the National Socialist White People's Party, intends to use "to win power in this country through peaceful political means."

Contrary to the thinking of many, another holocaust could occur against another racial or religious group or, indeed, the Jewish people themselves. Koehl's public words should alert our hearts and stir our souls (for he inadvertently speaks for many varied groups): "Oh, by the way—*we have no plans to go away!*"

19

The Psychology of
Perpetrators

The attractive paperback book *Hear, O Israel* stuns the unsuspecting. On the front cover is an impressive color reproduction of the Ark of the Covenant from the Mennonite Hebrew Tabernacle model. On the back cover is the *Shema*, Deuteronomy 6:4–7, "Hear, O Israel: The Lord our God is one LORD." A photo of a comely, mature woman standing in front of what appears to be the National Archives building with a large Bible in hand graces another page. She is Pat Brooks, "a fiery Christian patriot" and editor of the New Puritan Library, which published this, her seventh book. She relates that she and her husband "studied at Columbia Bible College in preparation for missionary service," yet her theology consists of what that institution today would certainly repudiate. Brooks divides "Christians who regard the Bible as inerrant, infallible, and authoritative" into three major camps: covenant theology, dispensationalism, and the "Identity Movement." She herself embraces the latter, defining it as a movement regarding "the Western peoples, especially the Anglo-Saxons, as Israel." Sheldon Emry of the Lord's Covenant Church and Howard Rand of Destiny Publishers are in her estimation "primary spokesmen for the Identity Movement."[1]

Although her book is filled with Bible verses, although it asks the reader to put aside prejudice and examine her facts, and although it even mentions the sin of pride (which "could lead to a preoccupation with origins, or a prejudice

1. Pat Brooks, *Hear, O Israel* (Fletcher, N.C.: New Puritan Library, 1981), pp. 39–43. The book is dedicated to the "HOLY ONE OF ISRAEL."

toward Jews or other racial groups"), her writing levels a vicious attack on the Jewish people. Quoting extensively from the notorious *Protocols*, and blaming the Jews for Communism, her arguments are undergirded with books published by the Institute for Historical Review and controversial "experts." She asserts nearly every stereotype against the Jewish people that the decadent Julius Streicher advocated. She informs her readers they can order Arthur Butz's *The Hoax of the Twentieth Century* (a book "ignored by the U.S. Establishment") from Liberty Lobby, and appears to have learned well the "disarming" tactic proposed by The *Spotlight*. She writes:

> Frankly, the whole "holocaust hassle" has long irritated this author. *Any* murdered by others oppressing them are too many, whether six or six million. What amazes us is that we *constantly* hear about the Nazi atrocity, while we hear *nothing* of the 145 million plus who have died and are dying daily under Communism![2]

Since she believes the Jews are not only responsible for Communism but *benefit* from that system by controlling it, the implication is clear. To Brooks, the Jews are the real murderers. She launches into quotations from supposedly Jewish witnesses to show Zionist responsibility for the Holocaust and Jewish atrocities in the twentieth century. Revealing her true feelings, she asserts: "Two carefully contrived myths keep the idea of the Jews as a *persecuted* people before the American public. One is the exaggerated six-million figure for the holocaust; the other is the attempt to present Jews as the prime *targets* of Soviet Communism."[3]

One feels, alternately, rage and pity when reading this woman: is she a *victim*, or a *perpetrator*, or *both*?

NAZI GERMANY

"DECLARATIVE PROPAGANDA"

The Nazi regime's persecution and murder of Jews required resources from the entire German nation. The everyday process of administration and clerical detail could not be performed by a single bureaucratic hierarchy or Nazi ministry. Needed was the cooperation of the German people, the stability of business, manufacturing, and transportation. Civil servants at all levels were given a broad mandate to perform their tasks in a manner they deemed most efficient.

---

2. Ibid., p. 106. Compare pages 195–96. Particularly revolting are the stories she tells, such as one about a North Carolina "Christian Patriot" who baby-sat for a Jewish family. The ten-year-old Jewish girl supposedly told the sitter that the family prays to Lucifer. Brooks uses this to base an attack on the Talmud, on which she assumes "most modern Jewish religion is based" (pp. 111–12).

3. Ibid., p. 108. Even Jewish Defense League acts of violence (which almost all Jews condemn) are used to smear organizations such as the Anti-Defamation League and the entire Jewish community.

In spite of the immense strain incurred by genocide on the national bureaucracy, German technicians performed skillfully. The foundational problem permeating Nazi Germany was a psychological one: How does a society rationalize its active participation and approval of continual barbarity against a racial or religious group?

The answer is partly in what Raul Hilberg calls "declarative propaganda." A relentless effort was made, via leaflets, books, speeches, and conversations, to show that the *Jew is evil*. The receptive mind of the German society came to sincerely believe that *the Jews were persecuted and killed because they were evil*. We have seen this psychological tool applied throughout this history of the Holocaust, and it was an arsenal the Nazis drew upon until the end of the war. Hilberg details the process:

> First of all, the Germans drew a picture of an international Jewry ruling the world and plotting the destruction of Germany and German life. . . . The Jew was now the principal foe, the creator of capitalism and communism, the sinister force behind the entire Allied war effort, the organizer of the "terror raids," and, finally, the all-powerful enemy capable of wiping Germany off the map. . . . The Jews were a security risk . . . the spies, the enemy agents . . . the inciters of revolt. . . . In Himmler's words: "We had the moral right vis-a-vis our people to annihilate this people which wanted to annihilate us."
>
> [Second], the Jews were portrayed not only as a world conspiracy but also as a criminal people. . . . Streicher had to say: "Look at the path which the Jewish people has traversed for millennia: Everywhere murder; everywhere mass murder!" . . . In the culmination of this theory, to be a Jew was punishable offense (*strafbare Handlung*); thus it was the function of the rationalization of criminality to turn the process into a kind of judicial proceeding.
>
> [Third], the conception of the Jew as a lower form of life. *Generalgouverneur* Frank was given to the use of such phrases as "Jews and lice." In a speech delivered on December 19, 1940 he pointed out that relatives of military personnel surely were sympathizing with men stationed in Poland, a country "which is so full of lice and Jews." But the situation was not so bad, he continued, though of course he could not rid the country of lice and Jews in a year.[4]

By emphasizing the importance of following orders, or that the superior had no personal vindictiveness toward the victim, or that *if* a criminal act was being committed the superior was responsible, the average bureaucrat (and, indeed, the German citizen) was pacified, and in his own mind innocent.

HITLER'S HENCHMEN—"NORMAL PERSONALITIES"

Although the bureaucratic foundations of the Third Reich ran the gamut of German society—using clerks, professors, and lawyers alike—a select and dedi-

---

4. Raul Hilberg, "The Nature of the Process," in Joel E. Dimsdale, ed., *Survivors, Victims, and Perpetrators: Essays on the Nazi Holocaust* (New York: Hemisphere, 1980), pp. 25–29. Compare John P. Sabini and Maury Silver, "Destroying the Innocent with a Clear Conscience: A Sociopsychology of the Holocaust," in the same volume, pages 329–58.

cated band of "courageous pure Aryans" rose to the top of the pyramid: the SS. George M. Kren and Leon Rappoport have accurately described both the physical and psychological development of this Nazi elite as a cancer. "Consequently, in tracing the history of this institution," they note, "one is dealing with the growth of an amorphous creature which never remained long in a stable condition. Instead, having once been established in the body of the Nazi state, it grew like a cancer, expanding steadily until at the very moment of national collapse in 1945, the SS had reached its maximum state of development."[5]

One is constantly confronted with the mixture of brutality and civility in these men. They came from a broad assortment of backgrounds and religious persuasion. Involved daily in the practice of murder, they could discuss technical improvements in mass extermination at one time and celebrate a tender Christmas Eve with their families at another. They were able to smash the skull of a Jewish child without a moment's hesitation, and yet arrive home to cuddle their own children. As individuals they seem bizarrely schizophrenic.

As a group, the SS was no less so. The SS operated as an exclusive club, instilling both comradery and fear in its members. It exerted a peer pressure matched only by that of adolescence. Since every member knowledgeable of the death procedures was *forced* to actually participate in such actions, group behavior and devotion to the Führer became the substitute for individual conscience and morality. As a growing organism of barbarism, the SS constantly increased the enormity of its crimes. Members were made to feel both valuable and dehumanized by propaganda, self-interest, group interest, loyalty, duty, and patriotism. Nostalgia toward the group is evidenced by former members of the SS to this day.[6]

In the preceding chapter we viewed groups in America with similar psychological makeup and using identical propaganda. It might well appear that a simple solution to our current problem would be to keep these "lunatics" out of power. Unfortunately, in the past few decades psychologists have reminded us that the Nazis were more or less ordinary men. Molly Harrower in her article "Were Hitler's Henchmen Mad?" had experts evaluate the Rorschach ink-blot test given to the elite of the Nazi war criminals as they awaited the Nuremberg Trial. She mixed the tests in with a spectrum of individuals ranging from mentally disturbed to exceptionally well-adjusted (including clergymen and mental patients). Adolf Eichmann and Hermann Göring were diagnosed as "normal personalities." Baldur von Schirach, Hitler Youth leader responsible for deporting Jews from Vienna to extermination camps, was found a "superior personality." So was Hjalmar Schact, Nazi Minister of Economics, who restricted the

5. George M. Kren and Leon Rappoport, *The Holocaust and the Crisis of Human Behavior* (New York: Holmes & Meier, 1980), p. 41.
6. Note John M. Steiner, "The SS Yesterday and Today: A Socio-psychological View," in Dimsdale, *Survivors, Victims and Perpetrators*, pp. 405–56. See also Richard Grunberger, *Hitler's SS* (London: Weidenfeld and Nicolson, 1970), and Henry Friedlander, "The Manipulation of Language," in Henry Friedlander and Sybil Milton, eds., *The Holocaust: Ideology, Bureaucracy and Genocide* (Millwood, NY: Kraus International Publications, 1980), pp. 103–13.

role of German Jews in business. Rudolf Hess, Hitler's Deputy Führer, was deemed a "less-than-adequate personality," while Albert Speer, chief of the Nazi Party Technical Office, was a "disturbed or impoverished personality." A clergyman was also assigned to each category! Harrower concluded:

> These results do not excuse the acts of the Nazis. Instead they demonstrate that well-adjusted people may get caught up in a tangle of social forces that makes them goose-step their way toward such abominations as the calculated execution of six million Jews and the systematic elimination of the elderly and other unproductive people. It may be comforting to believe that the horrors of World War II were the work of a dozen or so insane men, but it is a dangerous belief, one that may give us a false sense of security. It *can* happen here.[7]

To Harrower, editor of the American Lecture Series in Psychology, the Nazis who went on trial at Nuremberg were as diverse a group psychologically as the local PTA leadership or those in national government.

ANYONE CAN BE A TORTURER

Stanley Milgram, a professor of psychology, performed a series of experiments directly relating to our study. Realizing that thousands of ordinary citizens in the name of obedience participated in the Nazi extermination of European Jewry, Milgram recruited American men and women from diverse backgrounds to be his unwitting guinea pigs in testing obedience to authority. In a supposed study of memory and learning, the experimenter explained to his "teachers" that they were analyzing the effect of punishment on the learning situation. Milgram explained his experiment:

> The real focus of the experiment is the teacher. After watching the learner being strapped into place, he is taken into the main experimental room and seated before an impressive shock generator. Its main feature is a horizontal line of thirty switches ranging from 15 volts to 450 volts, in 15-volt increments. There are also verbal designations which range from SLIGHT SHOCK to DANGER-SEVERE SHOCK. The teacher is told that he is to administer the learning test to the man in the other room. When the learner responds correctly, the teacher moves on to the next item; when the other man gives an incorrect answer, the teacher is to give him an electric

---

7. Molly Harrower, "Were Hitler's Henchmen Mad?" *Psychology Today* (July 1976), p. 80. An interesting insight into a colorless bureaucrat of the Nazi regime is found in Avner W. Less, "Interrogating Eichmann," trans. Joel Agee, *Commentary* 75 (May 1983), pp. 45–51. Less states: "As I watched Eichmann sitting there in this condition, I suddenly had the feeling I was holding a bird in my hand, a creature who felt completely at my mercy. But that impression soon passed. His statements and the documents we examined together revealed the cold sophistication and cunning with which he had planned and carried out the extermination of the Jews. . . . What elicited my sense of outrage more than anything else was that Eichmann quite obviously had no feeling for the monstrousness of his crime, and that he did not show the slightest twinge of remorse" (pp. 45–46).

shock. He is to start at the lowest shock level (15 volts) and to increase the level each time the man makes an error, going through 30 volts, 45 volts, and so on.

The "teacher" is a genuinely naive subject who has come to the laboratory to participate in an experiment. The learner, or victim, is an actor who actually receives no shock at all. The point of the experiment is to see how far a person will proceed in a concrete and measurable situation in which he is ordered to inflict increasing pain on a protesting victim. At what point will subjects refuse to obey the experimenter?[8]

Initially, the "victim" was to use a mild protest, but to Milgram's chagrin these proved inadequate. Even with the strongest protests, many "teachers" administered the harshest punishment. The "teachers" obeyed authority so well that painful groans and cries such as "Experimenter, get me out of here! I won't be in the experiment any more! I refuse to go on!" and "I can't stand the pain!" were ignored.

The results are alarming. Although variations were added, such as moving the victim closer and making the "teacher" force the victim's hand on the shock plate, dismaying levels of shock were administered. A welder impassively administered the 450 volts, turning to the experimenter and asking, "Where do we go from here, Professor?" A social worker could not suppress his giggling and laughter as he administered the shock over the victim's screams of protest. A nurse questioned the experimenter about the high voltage levels, but when assured that the victim could take it, continued dutifully on. Especially interesting was the professor of Old Testament in Experiment 3 (an experiment that moved the victim only a few feet away from him). Milgram noted of the somewhat gaunt, ascetic man:

> In this Proximity condition, he adjusted his seat to look at the learner while administering shocks. While reading the word pairs, he employs exaggerated precision in his pronunciation, and seems curt and officious in saying, "Correct." Whenever the learner makes an error, he appears almost to be chastising his failing. Each time he administers a shock, his lips are drawn back, and he bares his teeth. An excessive fastidiousness characterizes all of his actions.[9]

After working his way up to 150 volts, he finally stopped when the victim cried out that he did not want to be in the experiment anymore. During the grunts of pain at other levels, and during the victim's shout that the shocks were becoming painful at 120 volts, he carried on. Since he appeared to consider the experimenter a mere technician, he asserted that he would take the victim's orders from that point onward. When told the true purpose of the experiment and asked what he believed was "the most effective way of strengthening resistance to inhumane authority," he answered: "If one had as one's ultimate authority

8. Stanley Milgram, *Obedience to Authority* (New York: Harper & Row, 1974), pp. 3–4.
9. Ibid., pp. 47–48.

God, then it trivializes human authority."[10] He never sensed the horror in what he had done.

"We in Germany really have not yet confronted the Holocaust thoroughly," wrote Renate Bethge, the niece of Dietrich Bonhoeffer, in 1979. "Such negligence was possible," she added, "since we have but few Jews any more. One hardly ever meets a victim, and the former concentration camps are located in remote areas. . . . In Germany, one does not dare to come to grips with this chapter of the German past."[11]

She believes that we in the United States have a much better chance at gaining insight from the Holocaust and sharing it with the rest of the world. Certainly, the process of scapegoating (the projection of blame for one's own problems, anxiety, shortcomings, and wickedness) upon the Jews by the Germans is a valuable lesson in the psychology of racism. Even the subsequent denial or rationalization of the event is a helpful guide to the psyche of mankind. Hitler's cry "We mold the child!" and his later assertion that children "belong to their mothers as at the same moment they belong to me" lead us to realize that a whole generation of German youth were victimized—indoctrinated in the Hitler Youth and carrying the scars to this present day. And of women, Joachim Fest has stated:

> The degradation of women under Hitler and National Socialism was never fully appreciated by contemporary public opinion, corrupted as it was with the help of popular measures designed to foster the regime's plans; even today its extent has not been fully recognised. It was surely a reflection of this degradation, intensified by the conditions of private life, that of the six women who were close to Hitler in the course of his life five committed or attempted suicide.[12]

Modern psychology has much to say about the potential of mankind—including good, civilized, educated people—to commit atrocities. That Milgram's experiment was performed in the absence of economic despair or social chaos; that it was performed with an amiable, forty-seven-year-old accountant of Irish-American descent as the victim, underscores the dilemma of man's inhumanity to man. Even when the victim claimed heart trouble, he was still "zapped" by subjects at the command of an experimenter.

At times we have invited to our Holocaust class former members of the Hitler Youth to explain the effects of the psychological tactics inflicted upon them as

10. Ibid., p. 49. Milgram's film *Obedience* is distributed by the New York University Film Library and contains candid footage of his experiment.
11. Renate Bethge, "The Holocaust in America and in Germany," *Foundations* 22 (December 1979), p. 361.
12. Joachim C. Fest, *The Face of the Third Reich: Portraits of the Nazi Leadership*, trans. Michael Bullock (New York: Pantheon, 1970), p. 275. This entire chapter is entitled "German Wife and Mother: The Role of Women in the Third Reich" and deals with children in Nazi Germany as well.

young people in Nazi Germany, in order to understand the peer pressure and "excitement" of the era. One German businessman ended his discussion with the hope that we could put the Holocaust behind us and not study or talk about it. Immediately, a student questioned: "If we do not study the Holocaust and analyze its roots, how do we prevent a similar incident from occurring?" In the silence that followed, it seemed as though millions of Jewish and Gentile victims sighed in relief.

20

A Biblical Perspective on Racism

Pinpointing and understanding evil is necessary for maintaining balance in the Christian life and for making good choices. Evil is dangerously effective when unrecognized. Our study of the Holocaust has, it is hoped, helped to this end and taught us the importance of taking a stand against hatred, prejudice, and injustice. If we do not, we are actually condoning these sins. A Christian cannot simply be passive in the face of racism, for his very passivity is action.

RACISM'S CHALLENGE TO CHRISTIAN FAITH

TWISTING SCRIPTURE

The Bible nowhere advocates racism. In fact, it emphasizes God's detestation of it. Even the "chosen people" concept includes the responsibility to light the way for all the world, serving God *and* mankind. Nevertheless, various passages have been twisted by racists for their own purposes—much as Satan manipulated the biblical text to tempt Jesus, endeavoring to nullify divine love. Some have perverted Scripture to "prove" that blacks are cursed and should be subservient to other races. Theologians and ministers mustered these arguments during the heyday of slavery in the United States, contributing to one of the darkest and most shameful periods of our nation's history. Today the same arguments are enlisted by racial hate groups.

References to the Jews in the book of John have traditionally been used to vilify the Jewish people, disregarding that half of those references say *positive* things about the Jewish people.[1] Jesus' harsh words to religious leaders—leaders whom the Jewish populace despised for their hypocrisy—have been taken out of context and misrepresented to stimulate hatred of all Jews. Christians of all generations have used the word *Pharisee* in the worst connotation because of this. Ironically, many of the Pharisees were sincere and earnest, trying to live the life millions of Christians want to emulate. They were fervent defenders of the worship of the one true God and held firm against pagan practices, idolatry, and polytheism. They defended the doctrine of the resurrection of the dead and earnestly asserted that there was recompense for this life in an afterlife. They attempted to imbue the masses with a spirit of holiness. The gospels and the Book of Acts proclaim the quality of character in Pharisee leaders such as Nicodemus, Gamaliel, Joseph of Arimathea, and the young man Saul (who became the apostle Paul). Jesus, appreciative of the Pharisaic tradition (note Matthew 23:3), realized this and warned religious people of all generations about the pitfalls of pride and hypocrisy. By scapegoating the Pharisees of the first century (and, indeed, the entire Jewish population), Christian leaders for centuries have missed the very important lessons directed straight at their lives and ministries. There is ample reason to believe that Jesus would use the very same words to segments of Christian leadership today if He had entered the twentieth century rather than the first.

THE CHARGE OF DEICIDE

Most horrible of all is the allegation that the Jewish people of all generations are responsible for Jesus' death—that they are "Christ-killers." This warped accusation has caused the Jewish people immense suffering at the hands of Christians to this day. It is ludicrous within Christian theology, a theology that claims every man is responsible for Christ's death because all men are sinful.

To blame generations of Jews for the death of Jesus because a crowd cried out, "His blood be on us and on our children!" (Matthew 27:25), does great injustice to Jewish people as well as to Scripture. Most Jews did not live in Palestine at that time, whereas many who did believed on him. Moreover, there are passages in the Bible that indicate that a father's sin cannot penalize his children (Deuteronomy 24:16; Jeremiah 31:29–30; and Ezekiel 18:20 are ex-

---

1. For example, in John 4:9 Jesus is referred to as a "Jew," and in 4:22 Jesus affirms that "salvation is from the Jews." In 7:12–15 one is faced with a divided population, one group declaring "He is a good man." This is buttressed in verses such as 8:31 and 10:19–21. One must remember that "the Jews" were there to console Mary at the death of Lazarus and were "weeping" (lit. "wailing") with her (11:31, 33). In fact, as Jesus wept for Lazarus, "the Jews" said, "Behold how he loved him!" "Many therefore of the Jews, who had come to Mary and beheld what He had done, believed in Him," declares 11:45 (cf. 12:9–11). When one takes the gospels *as a whole*, it is ludicrous to vilify the Jewish population of Judea (even more all Jews) under the rubric "the Jews." It would be the same as vilifying "the Christians" as "*all* Christians" in any similar era of church history (without reference to differences in leadership, diversity of population, circumstances, etc.).

amples). And, may one suggest that the utterance of that crowd was no more effective than Pilate's proclamation "I am innocent of this Man's blood" recorded in the preceding verse? Pilate agreed to the crucifixion of Jesus, and the Romans crucified Him.

Furthermore, Jesus said:

> For this reason the Father loves Me, because I lay down My life that I may take it again. No one has taken it away from Me, but I lay it down on My own initiative. I have authority to lay it, and I have authority to take it up again. This commandment I received from My Father. (John 10:17–18)

Blaming the Jews for Christ's death is tantamount to denying Christ's sovereignty and love in dying for us.

THE MEANING OF CHRISTIAN FAITH

Christians must understand the awesome ramifications of their history of genocide against the Jewish community. Realizing the pain inflicted upon Jewish people by those who called themselves Christians is a sobering experience. When we consider that church Fathers wrote letters filled with hatred, that Hebrew Christians were forced to persecute the Jewish community to prove their allegiance to Christianity, and that Crusaders marched around a mass of burning Jews in a synagogue and sang "Christ We Adore Thee," the word "Christian" takes on a fearful connotation. When we consider that Martin Luther became impatient with the Jewish community in its persistent unconverted state and in a lapse near the end of his life wrote shocking anti-Semitic statements, Reformation Christianity takes on an intolerant connotation. When we consider that Hitler used the name of Jesus and claimed biblical support in exterminating six million Jews, "biblical" Christianity takes on a horrifying connotation.

Our study of the Holocaust has shown us the capacity of civilized people in a civilized society to do monstrous things. Our study of present-day racism has shown us the many similarities between civilized Germany in the 1920s and 1930s and our civilized United States today.

The Christian must therefore reclaim the title *Christian* for himself, returning to the pure source from which it comes: Jesus Christ Himself. If a person is going to continue using the designation *Christian*, he or she must strive to approach the balance of Jesus' life in the area of prejudice and racism—or be honest and refrain from using the name or claiming to imitate His life. These words appear harsh, but prejudice and bigotry are so antithetical to God's law of love and Jesus' life that no alternative remains.

THE TEACHINGS OF JESUS

Jesus' attitude and daily walk were evident in His early ministry. We cannot lightly esteem His Sermon on the Mount, where statements on love, compassion, and understanding abound. "You have heard that it was said, 'You shall love your neighbor, and hate your enemy,'" He declared, "but I say to you, love your enemies, and pray for those who persecute you in order that you may be sons of your Father who is in heaven" (Matthew 5:43–45). In His response to those who brought the woman caught in adultery, Jesus indicated His clear conception of the failings of mankind, of the evil potential of each human being, and of the danger of hiding one's own sins by vehemently accusing another. Jesus understood scapegoating and projection and responded insightfully, piercing their hearts and consciences with the words "He who is without sin among you, let him be the first to throw a stone at her."

Jesus was a master at illustrating how a proper vertical relationship with God would be evidenced by a loving and compassionate horizontal relationship with man. He often alluded to the fact that this relationship extended beyond the barriers of religion and race. Luke 10:25–29 records:

> And behold, a certain lawyer stood up and put Him to the test, saying, "Teacher, what shall I do to inherit eternal life?"
>
> And He said to him, "What is written in the Law? How does it read to you?"
>
> And he answered and said, "YOU SHALL LOVE THE LORD YOUR GOD WITH ALL YOUR HEART, AND WITH ALL YOUR SOUL, AND WITH ALL YOUR STRENGTH, AND WITH ALL YOUR MIND: AND YOUR NEIGHBOR AS YOURSELF."
>
> And He said to him, "You have answered correctly; DO THIS, AND YOU WILL LIVE."
>
> But wishing to justify himself, he said to Jesus, "And who is my neighbor?"

Jesus replied with the story of the Good Samaritan, a story of a man robbed, stripped, and beaten, half dead on the road from Jerusalem to Jericho. Two important religious leaders passed him by, not stopping to help. However, a religious and racial outcast, a despised Samaritan, came upon the dying man, and "when he saw him, he felt compassion, and came to him, and bandaged up his wounds, pouring oil and wine on them; and he put him on his own beast, and brought him to an inn, and took care of him" (Luke 10:33–34).

"Which of these three do you think proved to be a neighbor to the man who fell into the robbers' hands?" Jesus asked the lawyer who had memorized his Bible so well and constantly dealt with the intricacies of biblical interpretation.

"The one who showed mercy toward him," answered the lawyer.

Jesus' reply, "Go and do the same [as the Samaritan]," is a contrast to His previous answer, "Do this [the law] and you will live" (Luke 10:37, 28). Again, mercy, justice, and compassion are stressed by Jesus, not only to one's own, but also to those our friends, acquaintances, and peer groups despise.

Jesus not only taught against racism; He also practiced His teaching. In John 4 He enters the culturally forbidden religious and racial ghetto of Samaria. As He listens to the Samaritan woman, draws upon her conversation, and ministers to her, we see a sensitivity that is extraordinary—and is to be imitated. The men and women of the city ask Him to stay on, and He stays two days. The same sensitivity is evident in Jesus' total disregard of social class: He loved the rich, and He loved the poor. In fact, His love of the despised "tax-gatherers and sinners" brought Him grumbles and provoked gossip within His own religious tradition (note Luke 5:27–32). In fact, Jesus' choice of disciples illustrates His love of the lowly and keen perception of human beings. For example, He chose Matthew, from the detested tax-gatherers, rather than a well-versed lawyer.

OUR RESPONSIBILITY

Can we imagine Jesus walking with any less spiritual balance and maturity in this century than He did in the first? In Nazi Germany, we know how He would have responded to Jews and gypsies. In the nineteenth century, we know how He would have responded to black slaves. In Turkey, we know how He would have felt toward the Armenians, and during World War II on the West Coast toward Japanese Americans. When confronted with the refugee and outcast, one almost audibly hears His words "Truly I say to you, to the extent that you did it [fed, clothed, visited, comforted] to one of these brothers of Mine, *even* the least *of them*, you did it to Me" (Matthew 25:40, italics added). Many people talk of "love," but Jesus exhibited it. Many claim to "follow Jesus," but few have ordered their lives according to His compassion, understanding, and love. Prejudice turns what could be vibrant lives into spiritual disorder and chaos. A theology against racism must be developed by each individual Christian, for he and she are commissioned by Jesus Christ to be their "neighbor's keeper"—to indeed protect the honor and dignity of men, women, and children of all races. The biblical message is clear; the timing of the command is imperative.

Christians have a responsibility to their children and the younger generation. It is interesting that Jesus in the midst of His popularity, weariness, and "career," had a gentleness and concern for children. Mark 10:13–16 relates:

> And they began bringing children to Him, so that He might touch them; and the disciples rebuked them.
>
> But when Jesus saw this, He was indignant and said to them, "Permit the children to come to Me; do not hinder them; for the kingdom of God belongs to such as these.
>
> Truly I say to you, whoever does not receive the kingdom of God like a child shall not enter it at all."
>
> And He took them in His arms and began blessing them, laying His hands upon them.

Christians have a responsibility to inculcate into all children the preciousness of life—a quality emphasized throughout the Bible. A child is eager to mimic adult attitudes and behavior, not only the prejudices we believe are safely hidden away, but also our values. Without realizing it, we often place "attitudinal stumbling blocks" in the path of our children, or we hang millstones around their necks that they may carry throughout life. Our study has shown how the Nazis spent time with the younger generation, attempting to mold their thinking. In like manner, racist groups today are concentrating on the young. It is not alarmist to assume that the next Holocaust may well be perpetrated by the young. However, the exciting and encouraging reality is that the young may be influenced toward balance, compassion, and good. In fact, they may be spared the racial prejudice that plagued their elders. The key is in their observing the proper vertical and horizontal relationship in their elders.

As the Nazis perfected their reign of terror and murder, the old mass graves were causing numerous problems and drawing much attention. Immediate action was necessary. The already decaying corpses sometimes caused explosions under the ground from the gasses they emitted, and under the summer sun a brownish-red mass could be found oozing through cracks to the surface. Finding deadly bacteria in springs and wells, doctors feared serious epidemics. Fish in nearby ponds were dying from poisoning of the ground water by the cadavers. The Nazis proceeded to dig up the mass graves, corpses were burned, the pits covered over, the ground plowed and reseeded with grass. But the task was too large. They could not eradicate the evidence of their crime.

In like manner, prejudice and racism bubble and brew below the surface of the Christian's life, sometimes exploding like those corpses and oozing to the surface. To cover up, ignore, or fail to deal with the problem only leads to more death and destruction. As the workers involved in the body burning details found, the odor of the fluid and pus from the corpses was never totally removed from their hands (even when washed in Lysol, chlorine, or gasoline). The gagging stench from the pits could be smelled by neighboring towns miles away. Such is the calamity one faces.

Prejudice and hatred are part of our heritage, and discovering their intensity and dangers is the first step in combatting them. The importance of this battle cannot be underestimated, for much that we hold dear lies in the balance. The challenge is before us—the process of change demanding. A legacy of hatred is with us—but it need not be our personal future.

General Index

Moody Press, a ministry of the Moody Bible Institute, is designed for education, evangelization, and edification. If we may assist you in knowing more about Christ and the Christian life, please write us without obligation: Moody Press, c/o MLM, Chicago, Illinois 60610